D1336909

ST HELENA

During Napoleon's Exile

BOOKS BY
JAMES KEMBLE

Idols and Invalids
Hero-Dust
Surgery for Nurses
Napoleon Immortal
St Helena During Napoleon's Exile

RURAL LIBRARY
COUNTY
WEXFORD
SERVICE

ST HELENA

During Napoleon's Exile

GORREQUER'S
DIARY

With Introduction,
Biographies, Notes and
Explanations, and Index
of Pseudonyms

by

James Kemble
Ch.M., F.R.C.S.

HEINEMANN : LONDON

William Heinemann Ltd
LONDON MELBOURNE TORONTO
CAPE TOWN AUCKLAND

First published 1969
Copyright © James Kemble 1969

Printed in Great Britain by
Morrison & Gibb Ltd, London and Edinburgh

Contents

Acknowledgments

Facsimiles, transcripts, and translations of Crown-copyright records in the Public Record Office appear by permission of the Controller of Her Majesty's Stationery Office.

List of Illustrations

Preface

Several problems presented themselves in the preparation of Gorrequer's Diary for publication. From its very nature it seemed desirable that editing should be minimal; yet at the same time, in order to make the record intelligible and the narrative readable, it soon became obvious that some rearrangement was imperative in certain cases.

The first problem arose because some of the entries were no more than disjointed notes or discursive sentences couched in ungrammatical form. In such instances I have therefore thought it appropriate to make slight alterations in the phrasing, while insuring no changes in the meaning.

The second problem was concerned with the chronological sequence of the entries. Some entries bear no definite date, and I have done my best to arrange these undated passages in what appeared from the context to be their correct order. As a result, the pagination in the original manuscript diary as catalogued is not the same as in this chronological diary as published.

The third major problem was related to the identification of the persons concealed behind pseudonyms. I think I have unmasked most of them, but I confess that a few are doubtful or obscure, and the identifications suggested should be regarded only as a matter of opinion. I beg forgiveness should there appear any errors. The task has been a difficult one. But I hope that the publication of this long hidden and long awaited Diary of Gideon Gorrequer will prove a source of assistance as well as of pleasure to the great army of Napoleon's followers who perennially maintain interest in the fortunes—and the misfortunes—of this man of destiny.

I thank the Keepers and members of the staff of the Public Record Office who have so willingly given me help, advice and guidance. I have received assistance and information from many sources, both official and personal, including in particular Mr Gilbert Martineau, for which I wish to express my sincere thanks.

J. K.

Introduction

MAJOR GIDEON GORREQUER was unquestionably the man with the closest contact and the most intimate knowledge of Sir Hudson Lowe during his Governorship at St Helena at the time of the exile of Napoleon Bonaparte. He was of all the Governor's staff the man with the fullest first hand information in respect of the administration, the correspondence and the conversations during the period. He thus had great opportunity for close contact with the various personalities in the island, and for observing their official and their private, their expressed and their clandestine activities.

He was aide-de-camp and acting military secretary to Sir Hudson Lowe throughout the entire period of his Governorship. As soon as Lowe received word of his appointment to St Helena, he invited Gorrequer to go as his aide-de-camp, and together they sailed in the *Phaeton* and arrived at St Helena on 14th April 1816. Three weeks later, on 6th May, Colonel Edward Buckley Wynyard arrived as official military secretary; but he in fact, either by design or by direction, did comparatively little of the work of his office. It was Gorrequer who performed by far the greatest bulk of the duties of military secretary.

Gorrequer was a most assiduous secretary; he recorded for Lowe the correspondence and the 'confabs' as they occurred, both with the Government in England and with the residents locally. Not only did he speak fluently both French and Italian, he also had a sharp eye for happenings, a keen ear for rumour, and a sensitive nose for scandal. He was thirty five years of age and a bachelor. His portraits, I think, show much of the character of the man.

In addition to the careful detailed official memoranda which he wrote up in his capacity as secretary, Gorrequer kept a day-to-day personal private diary; a diary written obviously for his own satisfaction—and I should imagine partly to let off some steam—in order to preserve his own impression of the controversial cross currents of events and the conflicting interplay between the characters of the St Helena scene. Reading the Diary now it would seem that he did not wish any of the persons then resident in the island to set eyes on some of these private impressions of his mind and these secret confessions of his heart. But now for the first time we are able to read his thoughts.

Gorrequer left several chests packed full of notes and records regarding his military career. The major portion of these concerns St Helena. Some of this material is already known to us, being duplicates of records available in the 'Lowe Papers' lodged in safe custody at the British Museum. Some portions contain medical details of much interest, letters, lists of staff, expense and pay accounts, memorandum books regarding the administration in the Island, correspondence with the Colonial Office, reports of the medical attendants upon Napoleon and remarks of the Longwood staff. Other records refer to Gorrequer's military career prior to his posting to St Helena; while there exist also references to Lowe's subsequent proposed action at law against Dr O'Meara. Much of this too is already available to us from other sources. But Gorrequer's personal diary is of course unique, an entirely new font of information.

Gorrequer throughout the five and more years of his appointment carried out his duties with an energy which at times taxed both his physical and his mental resources. He seems to have supported Lowe and his policies, at least in public, with a loyalty which he here confesses he did not always feel in private, and even after his return to England he always rigorously refrained from discussing the events of those contentious years. The image projected by this disciplined decorum redounds very clearly to his personal credit. But the image which he presents of Sir Hudson Lowe in this private diary redounds equally clearly to the discredit of the Governor. However, this is far from the only instance in history where we find public utterance and private opinion at variance in records of people in high places. If we read the diaries of Grand Marshal General Bertrand first published in 1949 or of General Baron Gaspard Gourgaud first published in 1899, we sometimes find similar instances of antagonism between their selfless loyal support of Napoleon in the distressing circumstances of his exile, and their private carefully cyphered observations and even acrimonious criticisms upon their Emperor. For example, Bertrand reports that Napoleon sought his wife as a mistress, and that he referred to his Grand Marshal as a nincompoop. If Gorrequer's diary exposes some of the unreasonableness of Lowe's mentality, then in like manner Bertrand's diary adds a touch of tarnish to La Gloire which Napoleon was building up during these years at St Helena.

Gideon Gorrequer was a British subject of Huguenot stock. He was a professional soldier. Born in 1781 he entered the army at the age of sixteen as an Ensign. A year later he was commissioned Lieutenant, promoted Captain in 1804, and Brevet-Major in 1814 prior to going to St Helena. After his return from St Helena he attained the rank of Lieutenant-Colonel in 1826. He served for thirty years in the 18th or Royal Irish Regiment of Foot and afterwards in the 4th or King's Own Regiment of Foot. He was decorated as a Knight Commander of the Royal Sicilian Order of St Ferdinand and of Merit, Knight Commander of the Royal Sardinian Order of St Maurice and St Lazare, Knight of the Royal Hanoverian Guelphic Order and of the Imperial Ottoman Order of the Crescent.

He first met Sir Hudson Lowe while serving in Sicily and the Ionian Isles. Having accepted Lowe's invitation to appointment as his aide-de-camp and acting military secretary, he sailed with him on 29th January 1816 for St Helena. He served there throughout the period of the exile, and after Napoleon's death he returned to England, leaving St Helena on 25th July 1821.

He lived in The Quadrant, Regent Street, Piccadilly Circus, London, and was a member of the United Service Club in Pall Mall. While walking in Jermyn Street nearby his home, perhaps on his way down to his club, he died suddenly on 18th July 1841. He was sixty years of age. It sounds like a case of coronary thrombosis.

After Gorrequer's death the collection of his papers was not known or not disclosed. But word that such existed was rumoured, and attempts were made to get access. As a consequence steps were later taken in an endeavour to protect them. Among these steps were various legal approaches over the years, and eventually a certain Julius Dolmage, who was said to be Gorrequer's nephew, lodged a petition supported by a series of affidavits. One of these which was sworn on January 18th 1855 gives the substance of the various petitions for some form of injunction. The affidavit reads as follows.

'There came into my possession as executor of Major Gorrequer two manuscript books in the handwriting of the testator, containing entries of the particulars of various communications conversations and occurrences of which the testator was cognisant and in which he had taken part by reason of his office of military secretary at St Helena during the captivity there of Napoleon Bonaparte.

'That the said manuscript books also contain entries in the handwriting of the testator being the particulars of various observations and remarks of the testator upon the before-mentioned communications conversations and occurrences.

'That amongst the persons named referred to or represented as parties in the above-mentioned communications conversations and occurrences are the late Napoleon Bonaparte, the late Sir Hudson Lowe the then Governor of St Helena, the late Lord Bathurst one of the then principal secretaries of state of the United Kingdom, the late Mr Barry O'Meara, and the testator himself, besides many other official persons employed in or about the said Napoleon Bonaparte and Sir Hudson Lowe, and other persons not official.

'That the matter of the said entries are of a secret and confidential character, have reference to the Government of the time, and are of such a nature, personal and political, that in my judgment and belief the disclosure or publication thereof would be a betrayal of confidence prejudical to the memory of the testator and therefore painful to the feelings of myself and other members of the family, and would as I verily believe stir up dissatisfaction and deeply wound the sensibilities of many who by family or otherwise are connected with the persons named or referred to in the same entries.

'That a high military officer who was a well known and confidential friend of the testator stated to me on my taking occasion to mention to him the circumstances of these manuscript books having come to my hands and the nature of their contents, that they should be treated as secret and confidential and on no account ought to be parted with or made known to the public.

'That I verily believe and am convinced in my own mind that the said testator would never have disclosed or made known to the public the matters contained in the entries in the said manuscript books or in the said correspondence, and I am unwilling to part with the possession or to disclose the contents of the said manuscript books or correspondence without the order and protection of this honourable court for my so doing.'

In the light of these and other subsequent statements Vice-Chancellor Bacon eventually made an order on December 9th 1881 in the suit Benn v. Griffith declaring that the Gorrequer documents be deposited in the vaults of the Court of Chancery, and not be dealt with except at the discretion of that Court. There was no specific injunction prohibiting publication. The judge remarked that the papers contained statements of such high political importance that they had better not be disclosed. There they have remained without being claimed until by Act of Parliament in 1958 the papers in the keeping of the Court of Chancery were transferred to the custody of the Public Record Office. Now some 150 years have elapsed since Gorrequer himself wrote the papers, and some 125 years have passed since his death. They are now available to us for the first time.

The Diary is all in Gorrequer's own hand. His handwriting is generally good, and once certain idiosyncrasies of style and lettering have been recognised, they are mostly legible. However some words and some passages remain difficult to read, first because they are written on various odd scraps of paper, secondly because in places he writes in minute scrawls at the ends of pages, and also sometimes he densely superscribes certain passages cross-wise over the original writing.

In order to obscure or disguise the identity of the persons to whom he refers, Gorrequer employs throughout his Diary a variety of pseudonyms. The code or cypher to these pseudonyms can be cracked in most cases by a very careful scanning of the context. In some cases light is shed only by cross references over the diary as a whole. Some pseudonyms are obviously distortions or corruptions of the actual names, while others depict some personal trait or characteristic of the subject in hand. Sometimes the same person is mentioned under several styles. Very occasionally, for reasons one can only conjecture, a man is given his real name as in the case of Baron Gourgaud. A list of pseudonyms used by Gorrequer against the names of the persons intended is set out in the Appendix of this book. It is not claimed that this list is absolute, sometimes the names can only be a matter of opinion. Moreover a few remain obscure.

I have arranged the entries in the correct chronological order to the best of my ability. This has been sometimes difficult as certain of the entries bear no precise dates. Moreover Gorrequer himself sometimes confuses his dates in relation to the events. In these circumstances one can only arrange the chronological sequence as seems best indicated by the context.

The story of the events at St Helena has been written many times, and the diaries of other residents there have already been published. The medical history is given in a recent book *Napoleon Immortal*. But Gorrequer's private diary now sheds a new light upon the whole St Helena scene, not only upon the intriguing actions of the piece, but also, and especially, upon the various actors who played their several parts in the drama of Napoleon's exile.

152 HARLEY STREET   J.K.
W.I.
1968.

Biographical Notes

NAPOLEON

To the shattering dismay of Europe, Elba had proved, all too soon, a wholly unsuitable and insecure place for the exile of Napoleon after his defeat by the allies in 1814. The island was but a few miles sail from the Italian coast, or indeed from Corsica his birthplace. For a year the Emperor had lived in mock imperial splendour there with a small army of his own and in considerable freedom. It was of course a lilliputian court both in influence and in magnificence compared with the grandeur of his former days in France. He was however able to communicate without real difficulty with his supporters in Paris and on 26th February 1815 he escaped from Elba and returned to France.

The allies were still squabbling amongst themselves at the Congress of Vienna over the terms of settlement of their respective claims and their relative frontiers following their overthrow of Napoleon's supremacy. When news of his escape reached Vienna the allies recognised with shattering reality that they were now faced with the task of tackling all over again their exhausting efforts to subjugate the man who had held them in terror for so many years of war.

Within a hundred days from the time of his escape, Napoleon had assembled a new army in France, and stood ready to launch a fresh bid for the domination of Europe, and a bid indeed with good prospects of success.

Instead of success however, there came Waterloo on 18th June, his defeat by Wellington, his disillusionment. Defeated by the allies in battle, rejected by his ministers in Paris, Napoleon fled to Rochefort, planning to sail to America to seek refuge there. When this hope was frustrated by a cordon of the British fleet, he finally surrendered himself to Captain Maitland in H.M.S. *Bellerophon* and was taken to England. He arrived at Torbay on 24th July 1815.

It was now for the British Government, as custodian on behalf of the allied powers, to decide upon the place of exile and the conditions of security for Napoleon. Lord Liverpool as Prime Minister and Lord Bathurst as Secretary of War had given urgent consideration to the matter in consultation with the other allied powers, and it was but a week later that Admiral Lord Keith, Commander-in-Chief, Plymouth, notified Napoleon of the decision that it was to the island of St Helena that he was to go for his exile.

Napoleon was then forty six years of age. St Helena is a rock island in the middle of the South Atlantic, some ten miles long by six miles wide, twelve hundred miles from the nearest African mainland. Jamestown is its only harbour. It promised security from escape by virtue of its very isolation. Napoleon was transferred from the *Bellerophon* to H.M.S. *Northumberland* flying the flag of Rear Admiral Sir George Cockburn, and on 7th August they set sail, from Torbay for St Helena.

Napoleon was permitted to choose from amongst his staff those whom he wished to accompany and serve him in his exile. He chose the following.

Count Bertrand (1773–1844) accompanied by his wife and their three children. With a female servant and her child.
Count Montholon (1783–1853) accompanied by his wife and son. With a female servant, Josephine Brule.
General Gourgaud (1783–1852).
Count Las Cases (1766–1842) with his son, Emmanuel.
Louis Marchand (1792–1876) Premier Valet de chambre.
Saint-Denis, also called Ali (1788–1856) Valet de chambre.
Novarra, Valet de chambre.
Piéron, Butler.
Le Page, Cuisinier.
Achille Archambault, Premier Valet de pied.
Gentilini, Valet de pied.
Bernard, Servant of Count Bertrand.
Francheschi Cipriani, Steward.
Santini, Usher.
Rousseau, Lampiste.
Joseph Archambault, Valet de pied.

In all, twenty-six persons. These are among the people who are mentioned in Gorrequer's Diary.

Dr Louis-Pierre Maingault had come with Napoleon from France as his physician. He was a pupil of Dr Corvisart. On hearing that St Helena was to be their destination, Maingault refused to go. The

senior surgeon in the *Bellerophon* was Mr Barry O'Meara. He had
had several conversations with Napoleon during the voyage from
Rochefort and had made a good impression. When Maingault de-
faulted, Napoleon asked if O'Meara could be seconded to his
service as his personal physician. O'Meara readily agreed and the
appointment being approved by Lord Keith, he transferred to the
Northumberland and accompanied Napoleon. He continued to serve
him during the first three years at St Helena, up to 2nd August
1818, and is frequently referred to in Gorrequer's Diary.

Napoleon arrived at St Helena on 15th October 1815. The
island was at that time held under charter by the East India
Company. It had some two to three thousand inhabitants, including
a large number of negro slaves. It was a trading port used by the
Company for vessels travelling to and from India and the East, so
that numbers of distinguished personnel visited the island from time
to time, some of whom get mention in the Diary. Much of the
terrain inland is very barren and rocky with mountains like Diana's
Peak rising to 2704 feet above sea level. But some areas are lusciously
green and well wooded, with hibiscus, frangipani, and other
flowering trees of subtropical beauty and profusion. Most of the
population lived near the harbour at Jamestown, while the homes of
various dignitaries and officials were dotted along the coast line or
at favoured sites inland. Colonel Mark Wilks was Governor of the
island and lived at the official residence, Plantation House; while
the Lieutenant Governor, Colonel John Skelton, resided at Longwood House. Both houses were some four miles inland from Jamestown, and three or four miles apart from one another.* Admiral
Cockburn was himself now to be responsible for the care and the
custody of Napoleon.

Longwood House was being re-decorated and was to be the residence of Napoleon together with his staff. Until it was got ready he
lived for the first seven weeks in the pavilion in the grounds of The
Briars, the home of William Balcombe, a local agent of the East India
Company, and his wife and family. Balcombe figures also in the
early part of the Diary.

On December 9th Napoleon moved into residence at Longwood.
Colonel Wilks continued as Governor, Admiral Cockburn directly
supervising the Emperor and his staff. Meanwhile the British Government had appointed Sir Hudson Lowe as Governor of St Helena,

---

* For further details of the island, *See* T. H. Brooke 'The History of St Helena' 1808;
E. L. Jackson 'St Helena, the historic island' 1903; The East India Company 'St Helena
Records'. *See also* Map herewith, page 35.

and he was to take over both control of the administration of all the island affairs and the custody of Napoleon. Hudson Lowe arrived in H.M.S. *Phaeton* on 14th April 1816 and with him came Major Gideon Gorrequer as his aide-de-camp and acting military secretary. And what Gorrequer did not record for Lowe in official papers, he decided to record for himself in this private Diary, in secret and in cypher.

Apart from the Grand Marshal, Count Bertrand, who lived in a cottage at Hutt's Gate, Napoleon and all his entourage resided at Longwood, and it was here that Lowe called upon him on the second day after his arrival. Napoleon refused to receive him. He had not made an appointment. However in the course of the first four months Lowe did see Napoleon six times in all. Then for the following five years, although living within a stone's throw of each other in this tiny isolated community, the two men never met again. Five years of increasing rancour, personal antagonisms, angry and often abusive exchanges between them. And to add further heat to the fiery atmosphere in the island caused by this central conflict, there seem to have been constant quarrels and controversies flaring up amongst so many of the inhabitants both local and official. Gorrequer's Diary makes this all too plain. The flames did not subside until the death of Napoleon was announced on 5th May 1821. Do they still smoulder?

J.K.

Biographical Notes

SIR HUDSON LOWE

Sir Hudson Lowe, K.C.B., G.C.M.G., is referred to throughout the Diary by Gorrequer as Mach. Occasionally he is called Mac, Mack, Old Mach or Vecchio, Italian for 'The Old Man'. 'Mach' is seemingly a reference to Machiavelli, whose book *Il Principe* sets out a method of governing by artifice. Hudson Lowe was born in Galway on 28th July 1769, just eighteen days before Napoleon. He entered the army as a young Ensign and his whole career was as a professional soldier. This was spent mostly in the Mediterranean where for twelve years he commanded the Corsican Rangers, first as a Major then as Lieutenant Colonel. From 1813 he was in the European sphere and took part in some of the battles against Napoleon's armies. In 1814 he was on Blücher's staff, and when Napoleon escaped from Elba and returned to Paris, Lowe was on the staff of the Prince of Orange, Commander-in-Chief of the allied armies. When Wellington arrived to take over the command, Major General Lowe was sent on a mission to Genoa in May 1815 and was not present at the Battle of Waterloo. He was at Marseilles when he heard of his appointment as Governor at St Helena, on 1st August 1815. He was given the rank of Lieutenant General. He married the widow of Colonel Johnson on 31st December 1815 and sailed in H.M.S. *Phaeton* on 29th January 1816 for St Helena, where he arrived on 14th April 1816.

In St Helena commences Gorrequer's Diary. And from the accounts here recorded, each one must himself judge the characters of the Governor and his secretary and the other figures in the drama, and the inter-relationship between them.

Sir Hudson Lowe left St Helena on 25th July 1821. He died on 10th January 1844 and was buried in St Mark's Church, North Audley Street, London. Recent investigation as to the whereabouts of his tomb has been interesting though so far unrewarding, for no trace of it could be found at St Mark's Church.

J.K.

Chapter One
1817 The Early Conflicts

3 June 1817

Sir Hudson Lowe[1] came to me at the Cottage.[2] And after having enquired how I was, as I had not gone out that and the preceding day in consequence of a cold, he asked me if Tom had delivered me Lady Lowe's message that I had better remove to a room in the House till I was better; and on my answering yes, he said it would be better for me. He advised me to go and stay at the House [Plantation].[3] After having remained some time conversing with me, on going away he said: 'You had better go up to the House and take possession of one of the rooms and remain there until the wet weather is over or indeed stay there altogether if you like it. I thanked him and replied I would remove the next day and stay until the bad weather was over—which I did.

On the 10th he came to me at the writing table in the library and said he was at a loss how to dispose of the gardener and his wife who had arrived—that he could not take them into the House as she could not be the House Keeper, and even if he did he could not get them into the House Keeper's rooms with the other servants without the risk of them embroiling in quarrels—that he had the intention of making some additional rooms where the barracks stood, and had they been finished he would have had no difficulty about them—that as the case stood there was no other place he could think of but the Cottage which indeed had been originally built for the gardener and asked me whether I had any objection to leave it. I said if he had not set his mind upon it, I would much prefer to return there after the bad weather was over. I had all my things about me there and a place for my servant, and I certainly could not be so comfortable in the House. He said he agreed it would be more comfortable and more independent for me, but that in the meantime whilst he was adding rooms to the barracks, would I let him have the lower part and keep the upper rooms locked, and I might return to it afterwards when he had built an addition to the barracks for them; and that besides, he did not think I wanted to go back, as the family would go again into town; so for probably a month it would make little difference to me. I said I would make no objection but that I requested that I may again have the occupation of the Cottage when the gardener and his wife could be disposed of as he mentioned; for I should feel it a real inconvenience otherwise; to which he assented saying 'Oh certainly'.

11 June 1817

He again came to me this morning when I was at my writing table saying that he felt much at a loss to dispose of the gardener and his wife; that I might recollect the Cottage had been built for the accommodation of the Company's gardener; that this man had been assured, when he was engaged in England, that there was a house on the grounds for him to live in, that he would be expected to be lodged, and it therefore was incumbent upon him to see him properly lodged. Had his wife been like Mrs. Jenning (who lived in the House as House Keeper) he would have taken both in the House also; as it was a different case, and he could not think of bringing them into the house to embroil themselves with the other servants. Besides which the woman was with child which was another objection so that he would even be obliged to move Mrs. Humbolt, his present House Keeper to the Castle, who was also with child. He said it would make but little difference to me living in the House as I had a very good bedroom chosen for me, and in the day time I was at liberty to use any other part of the House. There was the Library where I might write. I replied I would feel being deprived of the Cottage as a very great inconvenience; that there were moments when a person wished to be alone and there I was perfectly so—that I had my servant close to me and also a room to put up my spare things—that it was impossible for me to be comfortable having only a single room—where was I to put all my baggage and trunks, my saddling and other things—I did not want to keep these in my bed room.

He replied that there was a cupboard in the passage opposite my room which he would have put in order, and as it was a deep and large one, it would do to put my spare things in, and asked me to go up and look at it. We went up and having seen it he showed me two rooms in the body of the House (both of which were very superior to the one given me, which indeed was the worst of those

unoccupied in the House) and asked me whether I would like them.
But almost in the same breath and without allowing me to speak
he observed that the first was not so large as mine, the furniture
certainly better, but mine was fitted quite new, and furniture had
arrived for them, all very handsome, and I should have what I
liked, and that I might even take the chest of drawers and wash
hand stand out of the one or the other. But that he thought I should
be much better where I then was. As for the other, it was Sir Thomas
Reade's room, and besides it was the thoroughfare for the female
servants to Lady Lowe's apartments, and they were always passing
backwards and forwards before the door, and it would be very
inconvenient my being there. Miss Vincent was frequently passing
that way. He said that, besides, Lady Lowe[4] did not like any men
servants passing in through the body of the House where she would
be exposed to meeting them—that there were only persons staying
for a few days that slept in that part besides the family, and she did
not mind that—besides one of the rooms was fitting up for Lord
Amherst and the other was in use, and there was no other vacant.
So that in fact he was making an offer and recalling it at the same
time. We then went to the room in which I had been put and
looking about began to praise it and to say it was larger than any
other bedroom in the House except Lady Lowe's and another (I
believe he said)—that it was a better room than that in which
Captain Meynell, R.N.[5] had slept when staying here—that Lady
Lowe had fitted it up under her own direction—that the bed was an
excellent one—the only fault was that it was perhaps too large.
I made him observe the only furniture in the room was an old
ricketty dressing table, exceedingly small, an old broken legged
looking glass and a broken wash hand stand, the case of a press, bed
and a chair; that there was no cupboard and no convenience
whatever to put away my things. He said as to that, 'a cupboard
might be easily made or a partition run across for a clothes press'—
and pointing out the cupboard (opposite the door) in the passage,
observed what a convenient thing it would be for my trunks, so near
at hand. He then took me to look at an adjoining room at the end of
the passage in which were two beds, on entering which, I said this
room would be much more comfortable and pleasant for me being
more out of the way, where I could be to myself if I wished to come
up to write or do anything else in the day time, besides it being so
much lighter than the other. That besides there was a cupboard, a
chest of drawers and what ever else was necessary, and it would be
ready by merely removing one of the beds (a small one for children).

He answered the room had been fitted up by Lady Lowe herself with great care, that she had even worked herself at some of the furniture—that it was intended for any visitors passing from India or on their way home (particularly a family with children)—that the small bed was there for that purpose as they would be out of the way and altogether in this room—in fact that the room was fit to put anybody in of any rank, let their station be ever so elevated— that the furniture was all matched and therefore the small bed could not be put into a room with different pattern of furniture.

It was Lady Lowe's arrangement and my going into it would be a great inconvenience to put it to myself. I said I thought it imported very little to people stopping casually for a night whether the furniture corresponded or not—that there was as much space for a second bed in the room I now had and that room would answer as well for persons merely sleeping a night or two whereas I might have frequent occasions for using mine in the day time. He said that as for altering the arrangement that had been made about the room it was a thing he could not think of. He then went again into the other room where he began praising it to me again, saying I might have anything put into it I liked. I replied that in that case I had then better give a list of what I should require in it to George [Boorman].[6] He abruptly answered: 'But what things do you want in it?' I said why the room wanted many things in the shape of furniture; that what was in it was all broken and not fit to remain. He looked again at the crazy things he had before seen, saying 'Oh when the furniture for these rooms is landed you may have some of it.' He then walked out of the room and going downstairs he told me: 'It is an arrangement that has been made entirely by Lady Lowe and I leave it to you to consider it but I certainly cannot think of proposing any change there.' I returned to the Library and he went up that part of the House where Lady Lowe was, and at the tiffin which I declined partaking of, he came to me and said: 'Oh Gorrequer, Lady Lowe says there is no objection to your having that room.'

July 1817

The day before the Commissaires called at the Castle viz. July 1817.[7]

He looked into a porto folio for a letter from Lord Bathurst[8] with regard to some communication he was to make the next day to the Commissaires, and not finding it after looking through, he asked me repeatedly whether I had seen it, or whether I knew what had become of it. It was very strange, very extraordinary, where could it be? He had shewn it to me one or two days before. Had I returned it to him? He did not recollect it. Was I sure I had not put it somewhere. He did not think he had ever got it back, if he had he must have put it up in the porto folio, but it was not there and he was sure he had not put it away in any of his pockets. It was the most extraordinary thing he ever knew—Damned strange, somebody must have taken it away—Who could it be? I repeatedly assured him I had not had it in my hands, even when he shewed it to me he held it in his own. I never had possession of it.

NOTE.—3 or 4 days after, he again mentioned to me about these letters, [saying] that it was very strange; as if he were suspicious I had taken them.

To satisfy him however [that] it was not in any of the dispatch boxes, I examined all the papers during ½ hour and searched everywhere, as it appeared all his remarks were indirectly levelled at me. He [said] at last 'That fellow Stürmer[9] was here yesterday and damn me if I don't believe it was him that took it away. He was in the room alone for some time.' He kept raving all day about this letter and also the next in the same strain, frequently adding he was sure he never had it back after I had seen it. To which I answered as before, I had not had it in my possession even when he showed it to me.

On the 26th July he said 'Well, I found that letter we were so long looking for, in the very porto folio I was looking in for it, where I had put it in'.

On the 25th he missed 3 letters which he had left lying loose on a table, on private business from tradesmen. When I came in the morning he asked me whether I had seen them, if I was sure I had not put them away, repeating this frequently notwithstanding I [had] told him [that] I had thought I had seen them the day before just before dinner, and that 2 or 3 of the servants [had] proved that they were in the window after I could have had anything to do with them.

NOTE.—The Chinese house servant Wai accused and interrogated, who denied having seen them.

Thursday 10th July 1817

This morning the Governor having sent for me between 8 and 9 o'clock for some work to be done, I went down and found him writing. Having stood for 2 to 3 minutes near him waiting for his directions with some papers in my hand, one of which was the draft of a letter, he turned round and on perceiving it exclaimed: 'Why is that letter not written yet out?' I answered it was not possible for me to write it the preceding evening having received it too late from him. He said 'If you could not write it out last night why did not you do it this morning? If you had told me you could not, I would have got somebody else to do it—and here are the ships going away at 10 o'clock.' I said I did not know about the ships sailing so soon—I was unwell the night before and felt so much so this morning that I was doubtful whether I should get up. He retorted, 'Why did you not say so before—you first say you had not time and then now it comes out you were unwell and you seem not to know the ships were to sail, though it was so generally known.' I said he had not mentioned it to me, that I expected they would sail in the course of the day, but did not know the hour. With regards to my not first saying I was unwell, it was that I wished to do my duty whilst I possibly could, that I had been long unwell but had struggled against it as much as I could, and did not expect to have been able to have continued doing my duty so long—that I was overwhelmed with business and was writing from morning till night. It was impossible I could do more than I did. And hurt at his previous observations, I walked away to another window where I began mending a pen. And after a short pause he began, saying that there was no such thing as speaking to me—that the least thing huffed me—that if anything was proposed by me and it was not immediately adopted, or if I was disappointed in that, I was out of humour; that I remained so perhaps for a couple of days, and then it wore off gradually—that it has been observed by several others—that I was extremely touchy and very subject to losing my temper. I replied I had been extremely ill-judged in those cases he quoted, and if I had ever shown such symptoms which I was aware of, though I might show signs of disappointment, it was at being spoken to in the tone he had used and the asperity of his manners on a great many occasions to me. He answered he had not now (when he referred to me about not having finished the letter) spoken to me in that way. I said I did not mean this instance, but in many former ones since I had been appointed to the staff of this place.

21st July [? 1817]

His rage at receiving Old Cappellano's [old Chaplain Rev. Richard Boys] letter.

23 July [? 1817]

His grognante [growling] manner to me when telling me that the
O.O. [Orderly Officer] had mentioned to me the mistake about
our Neighbour [Napoleon]. 'Did you ask him for the day before
that?' 'No.' 'Why didn't you? I wonder you did not think of that'.
That was the day of the greatest importance . . (this was in the
usual [tone]: all that was omitted was always of the greatest importance). This was when the O.O. had pointedly asserted in
writing that he had seen him.[10]

25th July[1817]

He [Sir Hudson Lowe] vented his spleen against Hastings
because of the letter and large box of prints from Delke. Mr Fraser
[? Fagan] said that the Marquis knew of the prints and his writing
of this letter. 'He had better take care not to make it necessary for
me to write about him'. He said that he did not know whether he
would even allow him to go to Longwood if he came here and
asked permission. And that he had said to Fagan[11] that our Neighbour could not entertain.

26th July 1817

He asked me for my memorandum of conversation between
himself and the Commissaires. I told him I had not seen it since I
delivered it to him. He answered that he had not got it and asked me
whether I had not seen it. Made me look all over the papers, exclaiming all the time that it was very strange, very extraordinary,
what became of it. Who could have taken it? He certainly had not
got it and went on that strain for sometime. I told him at last, he
had put it in his great coat pocket after I gave it to him. He soon
after breakfast went out of the room and returned with it in his
hands.

The head of the table [was given] always to the jeune Chevalier
in St. James. Soon after we got to St James, retiring from table to
go into drawing room, he began with the young Chevalier as the
company was retiring; and as I held back to see him go out with the
young Chevalier, he leaves the room for——. His huskiness when
taking down the questions and answers to O'Meara, and they both
spoke almost together whilst I was putting them down, he saying
with sharpness 'Good God you are mistaking the words'. He sent
me to write in the Lady's new room, observing that Her Ladyship

[Lady Lowe] was entirely shut out of the room above by my writing in there, tho' I wrote in the dining room where nobody sat, and by his own desire—my being thrown out to make room for Lady B . . . [Bingham],[12] and the greater part of the time I was looked on to by the maid. Her Ladyship said I had better take a room in the House and I was offered a passage with a bed without curtains, by the maids, she keeping a very large bedroom large enough for office and all. Of course Her Ladyship had given directions where I was to be put.

A few weeks prior to this when some dispatches were preparing and the Estimates came in at the same time and it was necessary they should be examined immediately being near the 1st of the month (it was in the middle of it), he exclaimed in a very unpleasant manner: 'Why did you not give those Estimates to somebody else to examine? Can't anybody else look over them but you?' I answered they were to a serious amount and it required a great deal of attention, and I did not think I could get anyone to do it that understood it, and it was now necessary they should be passed, being so near the time of payment. He answered: 'No, I don't suppose there is anybody that does understand it, but they are always coming when there are other things in hand.' This he had upon 3 or 4 occasions before said to me, and once or twice made me throw them down.

27 July [? 1817]

Stercoraceous [Thomas Brooke, Secretary to the Council][13] answering him constantly 'Yes, oh yes, ooooh yes, certainly, no doubt; Oh, that's exactly it,' and such fulsome acquiescence before he even allowed Mach to express his meaning. Mach at last tired [of it], said: 'Why do you always say yes. You always answer yes to me, to every thing. I wish you would leave that off'.

16 August 1817

When [defaced] was here, Her Ladyship remarked that the Commissaires had not seen Boney, saying that it was because he had played his cards so well.

He remarked to me on the 15 August that people judge sometime from little things of the feelings of others. Dr O'Meara[14] asked for champagne. 'What, himself?' 'Yes.' 'Dr. O'Meara is taking the liberty of calling for champagne at my house! He was raising his head again, and it was time to pull it down again. He thought the other business had blown away, but he was mistaken.'

About the 3 or 4 September [? 1817]

Mach spoke when W. [Wynyard] was there about that blackguard fellow; and soon afterwards said 'damned blackguard.'

A day or two before then, saying about O'Meara: 'he is that kind of fellow that will do anything.' Alluding to his appearing as if coming now and again, and supposing him ready to begin again the same offices towards him as before.

About the last day or two in November 1817 I had a feeling of rheumatism in my shoulders (caught in consequence of his insisting on having a window open within a couple of feet of my back, besides the passage door directly behind me at a little distance). I took the papers I had in my hand up to my room to work on them and did not go down to tiffin. This produced observations from him and her that I was as susceptible of cold as Bonaparte; and that now I could not bear to have a breath of air upon me, but was always shut up in the room (the library)—quite an unfounded statement as the door was constantly open and almost always one of the windows.

One day when sitting opposite the window in my quarter, all the papers were blown off the table. He became very impatient and said it was very odd how the wind should blow in at the window, and said I had better keep it shut in future. He seemed very surprised there should be so much wind from that quarter, being to leeward. After that for some time when he wrote in that room he always had the windows shut.

8th September [? 1817]

Mach's [Lowe] fury on receiving a polite note from Bear [Balmain][15]; calling him a scoundrel. Vignoble [Wynyard] was present.[16]

His brutal treatment of Stercoraceous. [Thomas Brooke].

9 September [? 1817]

His furious gust of rage against Bear for his observations on Magnesia's [Dr. O'Meara] letter to Admiralty. 'I'll lay that fellow sprawling yet before I have done with him.' Cursing next his friendly manners to him two days before. He said how Ninny [Sir Thomas Reade] kept out of the way all these days to avoid work. He found this day in his cupboard confabs with Magnesia Primo [Dr. O'Meara] after telling me two days before I had taken them up to my room and making me send to Vignoble [Wynyard] to hunt for them after he himself had done so.

[The objection to the letter to] the people at Longwood is because

Medico in Capito's [Dr Baxter][17] name is mentioned in the extract
you gave him.

He flew out at this, saying it was not mentioned in it— that the
extract was not for the book but for the letter to Admiralty. I
replied by pointing out to him immediately the extract with Medico
Primo's [Dr Baxter] name, adding that I did not know, but that
the extract was exactly the same in that letter as in the book, that
Russian Bear [Count Balmain] might have seen the book or heard
of it. He exclaimed 'how can he have seen it, mine being the only
one in the island and who could have told him.' I said I could not
take upon myself to explain Bear's motives or the object he had in
writing in the manner he had done. 'My dear Sir,' said he, in a
sneering way, 'I did not ask you any such thing'. He went on in his
galling irritating way reflecting upon me as if I did not enter with
sufficient interest on the matter or cared nothing about it and
treated it with indifference. I sat down whilst he was goading me
on in his taunting way; then tired of it. I observed: 'I said nothing
which ought to have drawn upon me any anger. I answered you
according to my sentiments honestly and candidly. I take as much
interest at least as any officer of your staff. I enter more into what
concerns or regards you here than any of them. Every act of my life
and daily occupations from morning to night proves it, but you
would not speak to any of them in the way you do to me.' He said he
would to anybody who answered as I had done. I replied 'I beg
your pardon, Sir, you never do right or wrong, it always falls on my
shoulders. I am to stand the brunt of your anger on all occasions.
Whatever the other officers of your staff do is right as a matter of
course, but as quite the reverse I must always be in the wrong and
spoken to in this angry way. You showed me a paragraph in a book
which seemed to me verbatim, the same as that in the letter from
Magnesia and if it was not exactly what you read it was very much
like it. I never read the book—you never offered it to me or gave to
me an opportunity of reading it.'

'My dear Sir, take it, there it is,' putting it forward to me, 'Good
God, take it'. I put it on one side. He continued: 'I left it out. I did
not know but you had read it.'

16 November [? 1817 or 1818]

Ninny's [Reade] charitable observations to Mach that the Capo
of the *Leveret* was forced to come and take leave. He said that he

RURAL LIBRARY
COUNTY
WEXFORD
SERVICE

was a queer fellow, and that he never would have come of his own
accord. He mentioned how he had been running him down to Ego
just before; that he was one of a party always crying down Mach's
proceedings, the head of whom was Padre Wallis; that they used to
meet many of them, 'like a Court of Inquiry' for the purpose of
arranging Mach's proceedings.

At this period Mach's old brutality.

142059

1 December 1817

In enumerating the carpenter's work Her Ladyship [Lady Lowe]
saying she really could [not] conceive what they had been doing for
some time. He mentioned some articles, and then added 'There's
Major Gorrequer, he had a writing desk made', saying this in a
tone of voice and manner conveying something like the idea that it
was very little required, though it had been made upwards of 6 to
8 weeks, and even made by his desire to have to order it in consequence of my having been ill from the constant inclination at the
only table. He soon afterwards observed that another article (which
I had referred to him as absolutely necessary about a week before)
which he called a box and which was a stand with 12 pigeon-holes
only to put on the top of a writing desk in the office, had taken one
man three days in making. (Memo: this he mentioned as to the
length of time at random, for it appeared afterwards he did not know
when it was begun. But I am convinced two days for one man would
have been very slow work indeed).

2 December 1817

Having written out the draft of an answer to the apostille[18]
dictated to me by the Gov., he said 'Don't you think something of
the kind will do the general tone of it. I said yes I thought it would.
He then began dictating a letter to me to Bertrand, and after my
writing a great part of it he took it up to read what had been written
and said: 'Did you sufficiently understand it whilst running through
it, to form any opinion of it—What do you think of it?' And as
I was turning over in my mind some of the passages (one of these
passages was that 'he could not offer himself as an holocaust at the
shrine of his Divinity') which having rapidly written I did not
sufficiently recollect [to enable me] to give an immediate answer,
he said 'Is there anything wrong in it, do you think? Perhaps there
may be something too strongly worded in it'. I replied I thought there
might be some alternative in that respect. He rejoined: 'I don't

know what. There's very little to be gained by any thing of that kind
—it has not done much good yet. He then dictated another paragraph where was mentioned 'Their endeavour to emancipate
themselves from all moral restrictions', and asked me whether I
understood what he meant by it (taking up the paper at the same
time). Not exactly comprehending it so as to give an immediate
answer, he began to explain that he meant it [i.e. moral] in opposition
to physical. And so when he stopped, I replied that I understood
his meaning of the words, but doubted much if French people
applied the same idea to the word 'moral' as he had then employed
it, or as the way he meant to convey in the English language. He
said he thought it was clearly expressed and he was sure they would
perfectly understand it at Longwood, and did not think his meaning
could be conveyed clearer. I said I thought the phrase was rather
abstract. He was all this time sitting on the sopha by me, and began
looking upon the papers I had been writing under his dictation.
At the time it struck me by his looks he was not pleased at my
remarks. I remained revolving this paragraph in my mind for 2 or
3 minutes trying if on further consideration it could make a plainer
impression; but not doing so I took up a book of entry of confidential
memoranda, (in which I was writing notes of an interview with
Count Bertrand) when he desired me to take some papers on which
to put what he dictated.[19] And whilst the Governor was ruminating
over the letter I proceeded with my entry, a similar thing to what
I had done sometime before, after having finished the first sheet of
observations on the apostille, which I thought were all he wished at
the moment, having at his first dictation said 'It's only a thought
that strikes me which will only take a few minutes.' And having
taken up the book of entry I put it down again on his saying that that
was not all. After he had walked about for some time without saying
anything, Sir Thomas Reade[20] came in. I was at this time standing
up. The Governor soon afterwards resumed his dictation to me with
a great deal of rapidity, so that I could only follow with great
difficulty, intermixing it with long quotations from letters and
bulletins of N.B.'s [Napoleon Bonaparte] health which I had not in
most instances had time afforded me sufficient to write half of a
paragraph before he began a fresh one. I found it would be impossible
for me to attempt to follow his dictating so rapidly and that [there
were] several passages I already feared might have been not faith-
fully written. I said 'Really, Sir, I can't write so much at once'.
He immediately said 'Good God don't be angry', in a most disagreeable tone of vexation [?] and ridicule and ran up to me

taking away the papers from before me. He could not at this time judge how I looked as I had my back to him. I merely replied 'I am not angry, Sir, but you have been dictating to me so quick as not to afford me time to follow you, and you have generally begun another sentence before I had finished half of the other, which I found it impossible to keep up with'. He replied that in the last paragraph he had not been dictating in that way. I said, 'Not in that last certainly, but it was so long a one that I could not possibly recollect it.' He said that he had considered me all this time as writing so remarkably quick, had I not spoken with temper or in a proper manner. I answered that I begged his pardon, that I had spoken without warmth, and without anger, but that I had spoken in a perfectly proper manner. Then there was Sir Thomas Reade there to whom I appealed whether I had not done so. But it appeared plainly that with all my labour from morning to night it was impossible for me to do right. He replied that some little time before I had answered him in a very indifferent manner, and that when he asked my opinion on the subject of what he was dictating, I had taken up my book again and begun writing as if it was a matter that did not interest me at all. I again begged his pardon declaring that on the contrary I had given it all the interest and attention I could in the rapid way I was writing it down, and had observed to him that I conceived that the paragraph about which he questioned me was abstruse. He had asked my opinion and I had given it according to my ideas, for it did not appear to me to be clear, and I conceived when my opinion was asked I was to express my own sentiments and not try to shape my answer to the wishes of the person who asked it. But the fact was that he was now displeased with me because I had not answered in the manner he wished. But that I could not do, for the sentence was not clear in my opinion. He answered he did not know but that what I said was the case, that he did not desire people to answer to please him, on the contrary he liked opposition.

I then proceeded with the entry of the notes, and after he had walked about for a short time without speaking, he began saying that what I was then doing and what I bestowed so much time about, he considered as nothing; it was a matter of little consequence all that I did in this way; that what he wanted now was my reflections and consideration; that all the sheets I had written, all that he had written himself since he came here was a mere nothing compared to the apostille;[18] and until that was answered he conceived nothing had been done. It was all trash. I replied I had, upon all occasions where he had asked my opinion, answered with all the consideration

I could. That I was not in the habit of answering without reflection, and it was for that reason I did not give a hasty opinion. When I did however, it was to the best of my judgement. But if I was not to do what he was now judging a fault with me, who would do it for me? Who would write all these notes or considerations which he would not allow me to employ a clerk in doing? I said that a few days back I had been left some 60 pages foolscap of entries of description to make. He replied 'Why don't you get Wynyard to do it? Send them on to him.' I said 'How can I, Sir, send to Colonel Wynyard,[16] who is my superior officer, what I thought proper for him to enter and desire him to do it. And that if I should send over to him the originals and the book to enter them in—which might perhaps take him a fortnight to copy—and that you should probably have cause for frequent references in the meantime, I might be blamed for its being kept so long from you'.

He said he himself would have said it; but that he did not know but what he was doing it, for that he saw he had entered some before. I replied he had seen me working for a long time on it every day, that Colonel Wynyard had never entered more than one, and that was when I had asked his leave to send him the book last year; that Colonel Wynyard did not write here as he well knew;[21] and that he had found fault with the books being sent away to him and desired me not to do it. How was it then to be done if I did not do it. He replied that I appeared to like it, as I had never showed any want of temper or impatience about it, or expressed any dissatisfaction at doing it. [He said] that if I had, he could easily have got some officers to have done it, [such as] Mr. Jackson [Lieut. Basil Jackson][22]; that surely there could be found some officer in the garrison he could trust with it, and that he had desired me to call for assistance when I wanted it. I replied 'If I did not object to it or complain, I thought that was of itself sufficient to induce the more consideration to me, seeing me labouring in such a way. Who am I to call upon; and have I the right of sending for officers to come and work for me here?' I said that he had often spoken of a division of labour and of my having assistance, but it had ended there, for he had never done it, though I had been incessantly employed for the last twenty months; that I worked daily from morning to evening with the assistance of only one clerk; that the day frequently was not sufficient; that very often I had to sacrifice my rest to it at night; that almost all those conversations of which he expected notes from me, had been written at night instead of my going to bed; that I would frequently stay up writing them till 2 o'clock in the morning, and this was the work he now found fault with me for doing. He replied that as to the originals it was a different thing; but he did not see much hurry about entries that ought to be done at leisure afterwards, when I had time; as long as there was any sort of record of it that was all that was required. I said that why I took any opportunity of going on with them when I had nothing more important to do, was that they might not swell in my hands, and put it out of my power at last to enter them at all, they being increased so fast, as he might perceive by those 2 large volumes of diary papers. But that it appeared the more I endeavoured to proceed with my work, the less satisfaction I gave. There was no officer in any department of the service who would have worked with more zeal, perseverance and good will than I had, since I had been on his staff, and I did not believe there was any officer in the service who had been more constantly occupied. There was no relaxation, no recreation for me. It was an arduous task, there was no time sacred for me, Sunday nor any other day, it was all the same. I was expected to be constantly at work. There was not a black man, not a slave on the Island who had not more relaxation than I had. They all had had Sundays at their disposal and frequently part of Saturday. But as for me, I was not allowed any relaxation. Not even had I the power of availing myself of opportunities of recreation, nor to enter in any amusement or to take common exercise, so much was my service filled up. How could it then be expected I should take so much interest about this when my mind was so filled with other matters, that my health had been suffering from it. I had the duty of Military Secretary, Aide-de-Camp, the examination of military accounts, of the accounts of the establishment at Longwood, notwithstanding there was an officer [Wynyard]²³ here who had come out in the ostensible situation of Military Secretary and ADC, who did not perform any of those duties, but was prevented by other duties that he was charged with. They therefore fell on my shoulders. He said he did not think I ought to have anything to do with the books of entries. I ought not to have anything of that kind on my hands. That he could make Colonel Wynyard do it, and when that officer was finished, he could make him come and write here.

3 December 1817

In the evening, whilst playing cards, Lady Lowe made some observations on the slow progress of the large room, and the difficulty of getting work done here, and the idleness of the workmen, and said she did not expect the room would be finished for some months more (I forget how many she said). Dr. Baxter observed it would be lucky if it was finished in the course of next year. Her Ladyship said she would not be at all surprised if that was the case. And again speaking of the idleness of the workmen, said that they always had some excuse. The making of the pigeon-hole stand for my writing desk was mentioned, when I remarked that notwithstanding that was one of the things mentioned as causing a delay in their work, I had not yet got it through. It had been in hand so long. And as for its being a job of three days, as they had told the Gov., I actually did not think it would take much more than one to a good workman.

Thursday, 4 December 1817

A short time previous to the Gov's going to town, he said to me 'the box for your papers is nearly ready'. I replied that I had seen it in the yard drying, and that it had yet to have its first coat of paint. He then with a great deal of asperity, changing his countenance at once, said 'You have been exciting Lady Lowe against the workmen'. I replied 'How exciting Lady Lowe against the workmen? I never excited her against anybody'. As he himself was not present when I mentioned what I did the preceding evening, it must have been repeated by Her Ladyship. He retorted 'Why you told her yesterday your box for your papers did not require more than a day's work, though I assured you it had taken 3 good days and by a good workman too'. He then enumerated the dovetailing, putting on hinges, lock etc. . . . I said that it did not certainly appear to me to require near that time, and that as it had been mentioned before Lady Lowe the evening before that so much time had been spent about it, I had made the observation to her on some remarks she made which I had forgotten, but similar to those she had used the evening before. I said that I made it a point of honour never to have anything to say or do with the work people or servants about the House; that I never employed them about anything for myself; that this box was a thing absolutely necessary for the papers which had been scattered about, papers belonging to his office, not to me; that I wished the box had never been made; that I never had employed them before but for a writing desk, nor would I employ them again. The box however was made, I added, by his orders. I had neither made any complaint against the workmen nor excited Lady Lowe against them. I never meddled with any of them. He immediately came running up to me (seeing how hurt I was at this attack) saying: 'My good fellow, I know you do not; but you know Lady Lowe conceives they are idle and I assure you they are not. They work very well, not perhaps so quick workers as in England, but they are not idle. I am extremely happy the box was made and I know it was necessary to you.'

8 December [1817]

How he flew at Darling [Andrew Darling did repairs at Longwood] about the note to Mr. Taylor[24] at Young Cavalieri's. With what asperity and harshness he spoke.

8th December [1817]

Young Brick and Mortar [Wortham] told me Donna [Lady Lowe] repeated to him what Polisson had said about Pick Axe [Lt. Col. Lyster], and also mentioned to him that Il Grazzioso [also Lt.Col. Lyster] blew his naso [nose] on the rideaux [curtains] of the letto [bed]. Also that she desired Black Cat to watch who it was in the habit of doing this trick, and that the next time Pick Axe [It seems also called Grazzioso, i.e. Lt.-Col. Lyster] came up and slept at the House, it was ascertained that it was him.

11 December 1817

His observation about the chest of drawers for the House, being made by Tom's order, which he said the Chinese had been 7 or 8 days doing. He said it was a toy that required a great deal of work. All this was said in good humour and smiling, though so soon after the business of my pigeon hole box; and entirely by Tom's directions. For neither Susan nor the Lady (as they said) knew anything of it. It appeared also he had before had another made, and he himself said he often went into the carpenter's shop.

La Donna spoke about Lyster's dirty comb, spitting on the bed curtains, and over the bed clothes. She went to look at it herself. It was quite beastly. His picking his nose continually; wearing in December 1817 the same grey trousers he wore on the passage. It was a shame really.

16th December 1817

At the Ball he having engaged Lady Bingham to dance the first set, and having been requested by several to form the dances, which

I could not do as they all excused themselves from standing up till they saw the leading couple standing, I asked Lady Bingham whether she had not better take her place. She answered that she had been wishing it some time but waited for Sir Hudson to lead her out. I went to him upon this and told him Lady Bingham was waiting for him to take her out. He answered in a most surly sharp way that the music was not yet ready, and he would not stand up till it was. That was quite time enough. I told him it was then coming up the stair-case and before the dance was formed they would be ready. He continued in the same ill tempered way, saying it would be time enough then. At this time the greater part of the musicians were at the door of the room waiting to come in.

16 December [1817]

He said he would require what would be a work of considerable time to get through, and would take up as many books to enter as were then on the table, viz. 6 books of four or five quires of paper. That it would require confidential persons to copy them; that there were a number of people that wrote well on the Island but it re-quired persons that might be confided in. He turned round to Reade saying: 'You can copy some'. He answered: 'Yes, he would very willingly take part'. The Chief answered 'Well, you can take O'Meara's letters and correspondence.'

16 December 1817

Nicky brown trousers.

Telling me 22 December 1817 [Sic] he thought Dr. O'Meara had charged himself with some message about the arrangements of Bills to be drawn at Andrew Street, Parker and Co, by Bertrand.

17 December [1817]

He wrote a list of the different heads of matter he wished to have transcribed, a great deal of which was already entered. On my observing that it was merely going over the same work again, he answered that it was not; enumerating two things which would not be wanted, viz. letter to government and a part of the private memoranda. But said that, however, I should have no occasion to write a word of it. He did not care if it was even a twelvemonth provided it was done at all; that would be time enough. I proposed, as Wynyard had nothing in hand, he might begin O'Meara's now, particularly as he had been on the point a few days before of beginning the entry of the conversation. He did not assent to this, but put it off by saying there was no hurry at all about it.

18 December [1817]

His furious gusts of passion. He scarcely had breath to articulate at times. How often he repeated: 'dishonourable, shameful, uncandid conduct'. He afterwards told me that when he ran after Mr. O'Meara in the passage, on his repeating the above expression to him he retorted that if he had [not] behaved in that manner, he would have been better received.

As Dr O'Meara retired from the library, speaking indistinctly, he ran after him in a most extraordinary and furious manner calling out loud enough to be heard in all the house: 'What's that you say, Sir,' and followed him into the passage desiring him in a most injurious manner to quit the house. 'Leave the house, Sir, leave the house, Sir,' and repeated the words 'dishonourable etc.' as above stated. Then having once returned as far as the door of the library from following Mr. O'Meara, as the latter's voice was still heard retiring, he made another sally of the same kind after him. I remained in the library not going beyond the door, shocked at all this.

19 December [1817]

Asked me for a rough draft of a letter he had been preparing 2 or 3 days before, in town about O'Meara. I said I had not got it. He said I must have it, for he gave it to me to put up. I told him he had not, that I had not even read it, or had it in my hands. That I had heard him dictate it to Reade, whilst I was writing; but that he had put it up in his Dispatch box. He said it was very strange he had no recollection of it; he certainly was under the impression he had given it to me.

19 December [1817]

Whilst Sir G.B. [George Bingham] and Wynd. [Colonel Edward Wynyard] were there, he [Sir Hudson Lowe] said what a rascal Brough [Lord Brougham] must be, in putting his name to such a paper (that in which were the observations on his restrictions of

October and December 1816). And said 'what a damned fellow',
alluding to Dr O'Meara.

22 December [1817]

He told me after dinner he did not mean to send O'Meara from
here in a hurry. He would keep him long enough yet. He would
worry him with questions whenever he came to him. He did not
care whether he answered them or not. He would rather he did
not, for then the conclusion would be the equivalent to an acknowledgement on his side. He would consider it in that light whenever
he refused to answer any question he put to him.

Treatment of the clerk in June 1816. On my taking the clerk he
seemed to be displeased at my expressing my satisfaction to have
at last found a man that would be useful. On Mrs. Wynyard saying
she was glad to find I should now have some relief from the clerk,
he followed me a few minutes after out of the room, saying he did
not know whether he would keep that man for a clerk; as he had
somebody else in view. He had some idea of giving the situation to
Mr. Janisch. He had told me of his intending to give him the
emoluments of the clerk's appointment on one or two other occasions.
Dirty customs. How when sneezing, splashing in my face and lips,
picking his nose and rubbing it over with a sullen look.

23 December 1817

She had serious complaint to make again about [undecipherable
scrawl] for being found that morning in the rooms where the two
women slaves worked. I then explained that I had been the cause
of it, having desired him to get a . . . from in there and he was
heard by one of these women a few days before. And I having
enquired first before dinner whether it was done, he answered it was
not, so I desired him to enquire again. She answered 'Oh but Miss V.
[Vincent][25] told me she can scarcely keep him out of it; he is always
there. And little S . . .n had found him there and seen him sitting
on the bed of this little girl and had informed me about ½ hour
before.'

Saturday 28 December 1817

In the course of the morning he was speaking about the French
style diplomacy, that provided the end was attained, it did not
signify by what means it was done. And then repeated something

that he said Las Cases had mentioned to him in conversation, something to the effect that you have been employed on the continent and you know that such things are done, of [?] diplomats saying to you at the same time what were a number of little things said in those conversations, which were not taken down, and this is one of them. (As this was not a question, I was standing with my back to him writing at my desk). I did not reply instantly as I did not recollect what he then mentioned having just said, and as the observation was also used, as it appeared to me, in a style of reproach for not having taken it down. Soon after this he came to me when I was still employed at the desk, with a paper, a rough draft of another he was making out, and reading very rapidly some observations he had made in it about the persons present at the conversation with him and Count Bertrand. He said they were of the same impression as himself of something there said (viz. Napoleon Bonaparte not being so ill as represented) by Bertrand. He asked whether that was not my idea of the matter. I, not understanding at all what he was alluding to, after asking what conversation it was, I began looking on the paper. He, seeing I did not answer in the affirmative immediately, as he expected from the civil way in which he had at first spoken, began asking me with irritation and impatience whether that was not my impression of Bertrand's representation of N.B.'s health. After I was master of the subject alluded to, I said it was. He then asked me if he might not venture to put that down. I replied I thought he could. He then became quite serene again.

Sometime after that he gave Dr. Baxter the notes of O'Meara's last consultation to read, and when he had done, he began to look over it (though he had already looked over it 2 or 3 times and an addition had been made to it at his desire) and pencilled some remarks on it. He after a while came up (as I was looking over the last of the monthly estimates) with the notes in his hands to me at the desk saying: 'Gorrequer, don't you recollect?' and on my turning to him instantly to hear what he had to say, he, in a most sullen ill-tempered manner, broke out with angry exclamations: 'Put those things bye, do put those things bye,' and without giving me time to reply, instantly forced up the top of my writing desk in the rudest manner almost against my face and, in a most inappropriate way, thrust the notes and answers on to the writing desk muttering, and walked away in a gust of ill humour and moroseness. He kept me up writing from 3 o'clock to 6 in the morning and then entering the library expressed his surprise to me that he had not been told Mr. O'M. [O'Meara] was waiting, as it was not his intention he should be thought to have desired Dr. Baxter (which I told him) to desire Mr. O'M. to walk in there to wait for him. The first symptoms of his ill humour this morning were evinced by his having dictated to me a letter to Officer Blakeney officially. And after he looked at it he said he did not intend it should be official but private, ordering Mr. O'M. to P . . . Bay; implying it was, exactly after his dictating, beginning with the word 'Sir'.

December 1817

His frequent insinuation about his having desired the day after the boisterous interview[26] with Mr. O'Meara [that I was] to tell him he was to come to Plantation House for the purpose of meeting Dr. Baxter. Which at last he did not. I told him so but notwithstanding, he was continually recurring to it.

Chapter Two
1818 Four Men take their Leave

In the first days of January 1818.
When looking out some of the conversations, which he was altering
to send home,[1] and several explanations of that of 21st July 1817
where there were several severe things which he said to O'Meara,
he observed: 'I'll tell you what, Gorrequer, Lord Bathurst remarks
very properly to me in one of his letters that I am a person too
generous and open in method towards them by allowing everything
to pass through, which they think proper to say, and by this means
giving it effect to a certain degree, and assisting their views. I don't
see why I should do it to Mr. O'Meara. I am not bound to notice
all that I said to him or he to me. I have done it long enough and I
will not do it any longer'. He then desired me to condense the two
confabs 18th and 20th July which I did. The first however of my
constructions did not go home, but the original went with his
observations after nearly 6 months since they occurred. The last
construction he approved of.

4 January 1818
Donna [Lady Lowe], on looking at a picture of his [Napoleon's]
son and my saying how delighted he'd be to see it, exclaimed that
as for her she would not allow him to have anything that could
afford him pleasure or delight. That (meaning the picture) would
only add to his pride and vanity.[2]

4 January [1818]
Scoundrel, rascal, villain, speaking of Dr. O'Meara having
written him such a letter (at the time he was writing an answer to it).
I wished him 'good night': he never answered you.
Mr. O'Meara saying he pledged his word to Napoleon Bonaparte

not to reveal the conversations that passed between themselves, except they had a tendency to his (Napoleon Bonaparte's) escape last May twelvemonth.

NOTE.—this is the original shown to Mr. O'Meara on the 18th December 1817, which he said was correctly put down.

6th or 7th January 1818

Madame spoke about Ile Maurice [The Governor of Mauritius, Colonel Fitz-Gerald, in January 1818 visited St Helena][3]. Standing close to him and just in front, when he turned round to speak to somebody, she remarked: 'what an ignorant, pompous man he is, so disagreeable' and frequently afterwards said she could not bear him, he was the most disagreeable man she ever saw, and acknowledged when she did quizzio [questioned] the boy about school speaking to annoy the mother, although she said she said it because she was angry.

10 January 1818

When going to Longwood he [Lowe] abused a sentry for being too near the road and the picket for being a good deal exposed on the lower side of the hill at the back. He sneeringly said 'I think Sir George Bingham[4] assured me the sentries were all out of sight and the pickets properly concealed'.

About the Young Cavalier's disapprobation of the old fellow's conduct with regard to the people of Longwood or the account of Bd [? Bertrand] being found at the Castle, and also on his keeping the book, and denying something that O'Meara asserted. In October he told me, when I observed I should be very guarded in cancelling the former repetitions [? refutations], that if I had no better argument to offer, I had better say nothing about it.

19th January 1818

Nothing could show the villainy of that fellow more. The greatest scoundrel, rascal.

20 January 1818

On Mr. O'Meara writing that he has offered to show the letter from his friend about Lord Liverpool, he repeatedly answered that he did not dare a damn[5].

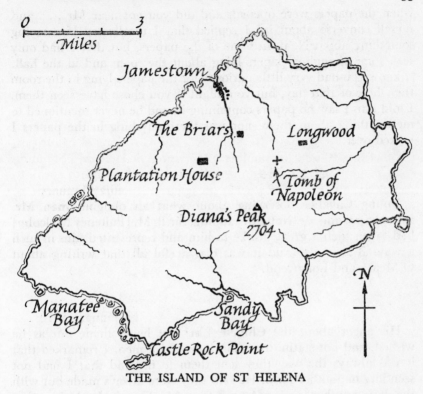

THE ISLAND OF ST HELENA

From November 1817 neither Wynyard nor myself had again private letters given us to copy as before; Old and Young Cavaliers alone copying them.

26 January 1818

Wynyard told me that B. . . had mentioned to Sir H. L. that the magazines and books etc were so suggestive and unpleasant that many even told that he was restored to the throne of France and that it was announced by him. He could not reclaim the information with pleasure if made through him. Some days after he had been a short time with him and he was seemingly very much delighted, saying, well the cat is out of the bag [?] at last. He then asked me: 'Didn't you read their connection with Napoleon Bonaparte's publication in the Times and Morning Chronicle that came by the last packet?' I said: 'No, I did not.' 'Don't you know what it was about?' 'No I never had either of those papers in my hands, nor did I hear what they were about.' 'Why, you were in the room when the papers were opened, and did you not hear Mr . . . and myself converse about it.' I replied that I recollected him saying something about N. B. in some of the papers, but that I had only seen some straggling papers lying about the room and in the hall. 'I know you had very little curiosity for the papers lying in the room the whole of that day, but you might if you chose have seen them. I told him I saw no papers containing it, and he never mentioned to me anything about them, nor was there anything in the papers I looked over.

26/27 January

Young Cavalier observing about what an obliging man Mr. Lusan⁶ was, added: 'Notwithstanding, Sir P. M. [Pulteney Malcolm] had taken such a great dislike to him and represented him in such a way. B . . . also said it was disgraceful all that writing about O'Meara and Longwood.

27 January 1818

His anger about the Chinese List⁷ not being made out as he wished, and not stating the daily number of men. I remarked that it was always the way they sent them to me and that I had not seen any in another form. He said they were always made out with the daily number, such as he got from Mr. Shortis. I told him that Mr. Shortis [Superintendent of Public Works]⁸ was the person I had applied to, who could not furnish me with anyone of them, and was obliged himself to refer to the Purveyor's office for that—where their accounts were kept differently. He said 'Oh that did not signify, and that there must be a proper one got'. I told him that it was met with difficulty. I only got this by frequent applications in 3 days. He then observed 2½ days was too much. He said that he had told me repeatedly before the preceding day and had ordered me to charge this in the Longwood accounts, and that morning again directed me to do the same. They thought that was the charge made by Mr. Shortis for the fine paid in cash by the Purveyor, and thought he had himself said repeatedly it could not be charged less than 1% for the expense of their keep and rations, plus 1% a day for labour. And then he finished by ordering it to be charged. First ordering 12 per day then 25 per day and at last 20 in addition to 5 paid for by the Purveyor. He first ordered me not to put down Darling and Popie's⁹ expense, that he would not have it charged; at one time saying nothing but the House expense, and another time everything even mechanics, then at last nothing but labour. At another time the Purveyor's allowances were not to be included, but the last time [that they] must be included.

27 January 1818

At night after the dispatches had been sent to town, a note from Young Cavalier came saying they had been forwarded, and asking also if young N. [Napoleon] Bertrand was to be allowed to go to Arno's Vale.[10] He put the note in my hand saying: 'what a very extraordinary thing', accompanied by one of those grins. After I had read it and observed that the little B . . . 's [Bertrand] company would not be of much service to him he replied with the same grin: 'Something will soon develop itself in that quarter.

28 January 1818

The fuss he made about a short conversation (which had already been sent in duplicate) with O'Meara at Longwood—the same day as with Cipriani, though he himself had looked over the whole and selected all he thought proper; and that after making that selection I had myself pointed out 3 or 4 others which at my suggestion he added.[11]

He said it was, notwithstanding, his intention that it should go— he meant the whole series—it shewed how necessary it was for him to look over all the papers—it was done in too great a hurry. I simply replied I did nor know he wished to send it. He never showed letters he received from the Government except such as he wanted copies or extracts from—seldom allowing you to copy private letters to ministers, but putting Giovani Cavalieri to do it, but himself retaining the copies.

O'Meara's letter dated 19th Jy 1818 was not sent to him till the 24th.

28th January

At night between 8 and 9 when making up the bag with letters for the bag he said that he had had some time to [consider] the notes of conversations sent with the dispatches made up this day. Don't you [consider] they'll think them very strange, what will they think of them. I said: 'in what way?' 'Why, don't you think they'll think

it damn insolent of O'Meara? Don't you think it damn insolent
yourself; what do you think of O'Meara's conduct? Was it not
very insolent?' (Notwithstanding my alterations, he desired me to
have a duplicate of it prepared). I replied 'On the 21st July do you
mean, Sir?' 'Yes, on the 21st of Jy. Will they not think it very odd I
should not take some steps about it.' I said: 'I don't see why they
should, as you have explained in your letter that you did not take that
notice [which] otherwise you would, out of consideration for N. B.'
[Napoleon Bonaparte] 'How, where?' replied he very sharply and
with anger visible in his frown and countenance. 'In your letter,
Sir,' I replied. After a short pause, perhaps a minute, and buried in
thoughts, he exclaimed 'I did not mention it in my official letter.
What, have you read my private letter to Lord Bathurst?'[12] (This
was one he had given me in the morning to seal with green ribbon,
and which I instantly did without looking at it, and put in under a
blank cover, leaving it for him to direct). I answered that I did not
read it. Colonel Wynyard was present when I stamped it and put
it in an envelope without looking at it. He can say if I did or not.
'Then you must have seen it somewhere else (angrily) for it was not
in the official letter or (and as if recollecting himself) I may perhaps
have mentioned it in conversation'. He then asked me for the
official letters to look over some of them. He said 'Yes, you were right
it was in this letter, I thought it had been in the private one'. 28th—
At breakfast he asked me for the rough sketches of the conversation
to look over, saying he wished he had had more time to look over them
the day before. He took them to the table and looked over them
whilst breakfasting. Then he looked over that of the 21st July
(2/3 of which had been composed by me by his directions and which
he had afterwards asked to examine 3 or 4 times and written notes
upon and said they would do very well).

[5] February 1818

Fitting up Nincumpoop's house [Sir Thomas Reade] with things
come out for our Neighbour [Napoleon]: lamps etc [were] used;
and supplying his house in the country with water and carrying
things, then doubling the rent of the house.

He appointed young J . . n [Janisch][13] to a situation of clerk
when he could not write; and soon after [he was given] a place in
the Gov. Sec's. office in which he did no duty. First £90 but £150
(above Company's pay). How readily he was supplied with a
table, how she espoused his cause, and her coaxing manner to

obtain it, and I was left months with nothing to write on but chest of drawers—writing for £300 a year.

5 February 1818

[He said] that O'Meara was the greatest scoundrel in the world. He never said anything against Bony ever since he came here and [spoke] about Neptune [Admiral Robert Plampin] having told him that O'Meara had said of their being ready to give up if the Battle of Waterloo had been lost. Angry with Neptune in consequence. Also what Baxter had told him was mentioned by O'Meara to him, that Bony would have seen the Neptune had his face not been swelled.[14]

7 February

His anger with Wynyard for having repeated in his note the reference made by Bertrand to the apostille[15]—making an officer of his own personal staff the channel of an insult to him.

10 February

The young Cavalieri [Reade]—how he went out at night. Then he got gloomy when B. [Bingham] said Balcombe [William Balcombe, Purveyor] had purchased the sheep—how we'll do him when we come to that.

11 February

The fuss he made this day and the day before, about a letter from Sir P. [Admiral Sir Pulteney Malcolm.][16], which after all he found in his room upstairs, though insinuating it was very odd—he certainly had not got it. A day or two before this there was O'Meara's letter of 23rd December 1817 which he had mislaid and insisted he had left it on the table of the room where my clerk wrote. Did I think he had taken it? Affirming most positively he was sure he had not got it, he found it upstairs.

He made [a note] and I asked about its not being sufficiently explicit with respect to the restrictions that should be administered through the B. . . . His anger with Reade, and the latter saying afterwards that it was because he had not immediately agreed to his observations on his saying that this was the best thing he ever wrote and that he was never so well pleased with any phrase. On the 26th 8 hours, 25th 9½ hours, 24th and 23rd and many days previous about 7½ hours labour on a report, then giving me a second long letter to copy on the 26th, though I had not finished one of 7 sheets, and though Wynyard had been here 3 days for the purpose of writing and had rarely any of them given him to do.

His promise of allowing me a day or two and the clerk to make out the annual payments of Longwood which he said he was anxious to have by that night, and allowing me no time whatever. He told me he did not want any payments expressed that did not belong to Longwood, and then made a great fuss that I had not included the men working in the garden. Obviously he wished to make it appear as light as he could, as it was to be put before Neighbour [Napoleon].

11 February 1818

Young Polisson—How Donna consoled with him about his cold, advising him what to do when he went to bed, dispensing a number of remedies. Poor T. [Den Taafe] how his eyes were swelled. Some days before, how she interested herself to get him a table to write on, though there were two in his room. [She spoke] about Mr Bowen being a most pleasant man—she always thought him so. Though she repeatedly exclaimed against him, saying what nasty fellows they were all three—the most disagreeable fellows she had ever met with —did not know how to behave themselves. She inveighed frequently against them and both the Baron and Baroness. She thought him capable of doing anything to carry any object he had in mind, even of stabbing a person.

When Old Mac gave Mr O'Meara's private notes to Young Cavalieri to make extracts from, he observed that he had conducted himself very properly till the arrival of Sir P. M. [Admiral Malcolm]. It was that fellow who was the cause of it all.

11 February

He asked me if I had heard a conversation repeated between Sir P. M. [Sir Pulteney Malcolm] and B. [Bonaparte] since he left this [place] which he ought to have told him, and which he might mention (I understood he meant, when he asked me this, to write to him) in a letter.

Two days before my inspection of Gourgaud's papers viz 14 February the governor told me: 'I shall get you to look at Gourgaud's papers, probably tomorrow'.[17] The next day having been employed writing until too late, I did not do it, nor did he ask me. This day however Gourgaud dined at Plantation House and in the course of the dinner told me the governor had informed him I was to look at his papers, and asked when I would see them as it has now become necessary that he should open his trunks to get at his linen. I told him I would speak to the governor about it and hoped it would be the next morning. I accordingly asked the governor the next morning whether I should then go. He said yes, and on my asking him what he wished me to do, he said that General Gourgaud having assured him he was not in possession of any important papers, to tell him that it was more a matter of form that he sent me to look at them. For although he felt fully confident in his assurance, yet it was necessary to examine them and he had asked me to do it. The governor then said 'Jackson will show you where the papers are, and when you return report anything which may strike you.' That was said apparently with a great deal of indifference and as if then placing full confidence in General Gourgaud's assurance, and more than in any examination. When I went down General Gourgaud was not at home, but being told that he was at Bayle House, I sent to say I had come to call on him. On his arrival I told him the purpose of my visit, adding that notwithstanding the confidence the governor placed on his assurance respecting his papers, yet it was a rule to examine the papers of all persons leaving Longwood. This had been the case, as he knew, with Count Las Cases when he had sent me down to look at them. He expressed the greatest readiness to let me see them and said 'mes malles sont en haut si vous voulez bien avoir la complaisance de monter'. At the same time begging Mr. Jackson who had the keys to accompany us. We all then went up into his bedroom where the boxes were opened, Mr. Jackson having, at the time of opening the first, informed me it had been unlocked and some articles taken out for General Gourgaud who was in want of them. Soon after this Mr. Jackson left the room.

13 February 1818
Talking about building the House [New Longwood House].[18] They were but a set of rascals and scoundrels at Longwood. The only way to treat them, and rightly deserved, was to confine them

in dungeons and keep them separate, each in one. However as it appeared to be a very prevailing opinion that B. [Bonaparte] should be kept only in golden or silken chains he must show a deference to it. He however knew that there would be a strong opposition party in England about his removal from Longwood, at the head of which would be Sir George Cockburn. That however he did not care about, as he would show by argument that Rosemary Hall was without comparison a safer place, except indeed Hutt's Gate had been made the boundary, and Longwood was guarded, as had been done for some time, with no access through ravines and valleys.

Feb 14. 1818

General Gourgaud professed to explain to me the contents of every paper which we took up in succession before I looked at them. I notwithstanding ascertained the general subject before I put them aside. If therefore any papers in cypher or shorthand were among the papers they must have been loose ones, and few, slipped in adroitly to escape being seen; perhaps between some of the leaves of the Chapters of the Campaigns of Italy or of the account of Egypt. For I examined all the loose papers I could see or find, and turned over a sufficient number of the leaves of the papers together to ascertain that there was nothing inserted between them to cause any appearance whatever; except scraps which it is possible might have been slipped in here and there, and which, with whatever attention I gave to it, might have escaped all observation. I saw no cypher or shorthand, but algebraical and mathematical calculations.

As for a parcel containing 3 years annotations which must have been of some bulk even in the most contracted cypher, there could have been nothing of the kind among the papers shown to me. In all the papers General Gourgaud declared what he assured me to be their contents before I looked into them; and I did not find him mislead me. He also assured me there were no others in the trunks and took a good many clothes out of them to show me; many of them old and not very good. The papers had not been collected together but were dispersed in different trunks, among his clothes, though appearing to have been laid uppermost. General Gourgaud removed several articles of his wearing apparel to show me there were none left assuring me at the same time those I saw were all in those trunks. I did not examine the pockets of the clothes therefore I cannot take upon myself to say there was nothing concealed in them. I found no difficulty in them.

17 February
After the confab with Magnesia [Dr O'Meara] was over, he
desired me not to take any notes of it.[19]

18 February
After reading the papers found with Gourgaud, [he said] 'What
a villain our neighbour [Napoleon] was'.

23 February
Looking over some of the confabs prepared for duplicate—he
exclaimed he had sent them off in too great a hurry—it was very
careless—there were a number of things that ought not to have been
in them—He then complained that all his expressions were not put
down tho' O'Meara's were—What would ministers think of him
for allowing O'Meara to go on with that kind of campaign. Would
they not blame him for not taking most serious notice of it? He then
said I should put in some expressions of his in answer to the words
regarding them.

They required to be looked over most attentively. I said he had
them in his possession for several months, that they had been given
to him the very day after they were written out, which was immediately after they had taken place, and he had approved them.
He had read them also over again before they were copied out fair,
and known I had made such alterations in them as he thought
necessary. As for putting in anything now it was impossible to recollect what occurred 6 or 7 months ago, and the fact was, sometimes
his language was very sharp, and other times he said little on those
occasions, alluding to where it was said 'he vindicated Lord Bathurst's
statements'.

24 February 1818
The rudeness of manner—the anger of look—rough scolding
voice on asking whether he would allow his seal to be put to
Gourgaud's certificate. 'No, I will not—it is not necessary—it's
never done, nonsense'. Although asked most respectfully and
mildly.

24th again February 1818
About the confabs mainly in the same strain, finishing by saying
he would not send the duplicates of any other but those certain short

ones, which accompanied dispatch 102 about O'Meara's letter and [? Napoleon's] answers; and that in fact in all those conversations nothing more should have been said than 'on such a day Mr. O'Meara said so and so', and the date marked opposite. That it would only perplex and cause trouble to the Ministers, (notwithstanding that I had condensed by his directions some of the longest conversations. And after two days hard work at that, he said the whole must go and he was then satisfied with it. Instead of wishing to make a great many additions, he only would allow the condensed part of one to go; all the others he would have at full length, though I asked him whether he would not allow me to shorten them; which he would not). In consequence of those changes about sending or not sending, sometimes he would, sometimes he would not.

Sheets written out fair did not go, saying they are of no consequence, I shall not want them, the dispatch is the only thing of consequence, it does not signify about the enclosures.

24th February 1818

His anger about the paper blackened at the edge—calling me and speaking in a most ungracious way with a dissatisfied and frowning look, and very angrily—when I said I had sent a great quantity to the town with orders to the printer to have it done immediately, and sent to him again that morning. 'It might have been done in the House'. I merely said that it was not my fault.

24/25 February

When Donna [Lady Lowe] after dinner sent down some Chinese oil paintings for me to look at, after I had asked her at dinner if she would show them to me, she said she would have them down if he assented. They were brought down by Signor Tomaso in a box. He would not assent, but bid him in his usual ungracious gruff way, to take them away again. He did not want to look at them.

26th February 1818

He made the clerk write out a copy of a letter to Count Balmain, and because, as he said, he had begun it in too formal a manner (viz. verbatim as it commenced in the book) he brought it to me to write it over again without the first line or two. When I had done, he said he wanted it on letter paper without margin, that he had

told me so, and that it was the very reason why he wanted it copied
over again, and he made me write it over a second time, making
three copies neither of which were ever used.

26th Feb. 1818

Delight at Old Polyphemes [Admiral Plampin][20] getting that
letter from Balmain. He came in quite pleased soon after he read it,
saying 'Why that fellow is as great a rascal as Bertrand. (to Twilight).
[Captain James Wallis]. Never saw such a letter as he has written
to the Old Neptune. Go into the Library and he'll show it you.'

4th March 1818

Asked me returning at night from Town, if I had observed
Domine leaving the Inn [?]. 'Yes,' I had, 'two or three times'. 'Did
I know why?' 'It was, I understood, in consequence of spasms in his
mouth'. 'And don't you suspect anything else? Don't you know he
is the admirer of B. [Balcombe], him and O'Meara, and that was
the cause.' I observed he was a friend of B's.

5th March 1818

When writing a letter for T. H. B. [Brooke] to hand to B.
[Balcombe] granting leave, [I saw] his disagreeable manners and
looks, because I thought the letter he had dictated would not have
the effect he appeared to wish.[21] His angry remark that I did not
seem to understand the object. What could I think, what was my
view of it? For his part it appeared to him perfectly clear. However,
as it was necessary to guard against being considered by B. in the
light I thought he would see it, he must consider it. At last he
adopted my suggestion after showing much ill humour. He said B's
[Balcombe] application was not his own decision. It had been at
the advice of Domine, Cole[22] and Magnesia [O'Meara], and his
answer would be submitted to the council of O'Meara and Cole
(here not stating Domine) and he therefore must be very careful.
They were trying to set Balcombe above his authority as purveyor
in the same way as O'Meara had said as to his appointment. It was
like the attempt at naval independence. He wished to give Balcombe
as much rope as he could hang himself by. He had got him now
where, if he was allowed to proceed, he would drown and that was
what he wanted.

8th or 9th March

The Vecchio [Lowe] said Arons and Domine (who called this morning to see the Donna) [Lady Lowe] had been sent up on purpose, tho' she [? Mrs. Balcombe] was ill—he had no doubt her illness was owing to her having been charged with some letters from Longwood, or her daughters, and she was afraid of discovery.

March 9 1818

Having again asked, the day before, if I could get a night stand the housekeeper (Mrs. Bad) said there was none to spare, and that I had better get one made by the carpenters of the Establishment. I told my boy to say there was one in a room next to me which was only slept in by casual visitors. He did so and the answer sent over this day was 'it could not be spared.' I inquired if this answer was as from herself. He said she had told him that she mentioned it to Her Ladyship, who gave the above answer but she (the housekeeper) dared not mention Lady Lowe's name.[23]

March 9 1818

Old Cavalieri said after reading B's [Balcombe] letter to me of this date: 'He is now on his high horse'. Giovanni answered 'that he ought to be taken down in that case'. 'Yes I think so'. rejoined the Old One.

He made allowances for anything affecting the Giovani Cavalieri in writing it, he having seen one of the last of them. I heard another person think that he did. But, quoth il Vecchio, that is not the thing. Am I to be told by Montholon that the allowance specified [? for Balcombe] is not to be paid without his being able to reply to him. I told him Mr Janisch had told me that the proper quantity had been stated, and I found him again the note which he had made in the margin.

March 10 1818

He said that when I told him of B's [Balcombe] wishing to go home, I had said he had told me that he would leave Cole [Joseph Cole] in charge. I told him I had not said that, but merely that I said he asked me if he applied for leave of absence if I thought the Gov., if he granted it, would allow him to retain the Purveyorship (and get his allowances) whilst absent. I certainly had not mentioned the other. He said he understood differently, he wished he had understood me better, that he had been better informed of what Balcombe proposed to do about the Purveyorship. He all this time evidently was trying to make me say I had told him about the suggestion about Cole.

11 March 1818

The newspapers were before him in the library when I went in, all piled in a mass, which he was reading except two or three, or more, which were on the table at his side. Which, when he saw me approaching the table, he withdrew, and brought close up to him under his elbow, which he put on the top of them most pointedly that I should read them, and as there were bundles in a file, but all gathered into a heap before him for the obvious purpose that no one should read them. He of course excluded me reading any, and I went up in consequence to my room.

14th March 1818

I mentioned to Jackson that it would be necessary to send back the furniture from Chesmont Grove and said I supposed it would have to go back to Longwood. The rudeness of his manners in asking me for what reason I thought so. What could possibly have put that in my head. He for himself could not conceive what I could mean by it. Now that Gourgaud had left Longwood, for what purpose could it be. I replied that as the Orderly Officer [Fantastico] had those rooms and the other furniture was left in them, I thought naturally enough the bedstead and bedding would be returned there, with the other 2 or 3 things (a sopha and private washstand, I believe were the other things) and not put back with the old furniture, using the new to fill it with Napoleon's (?). (private memo: Las Cases's furniture which he used at Ross Cottage was sent back there).[24]

16th March 1818

His rude impatient manner asking for an explanation of the deficiency of wine which Montholon[25] complained of in his Notes on the list of articles supplied to the Establishment when he returned it to me, though I told him I had ordered the increase as he had directed me on the 24th January, and had repeatedly written to Mr. Janisch to be particularly attentive to send up the [supply].

16 March 1818

My finding out for the first time from him by the Dispatch to the Minister, that Ibbetson [Denzil Ibbetson] was to succeed Balcombe as Purveyor, and the same day on returning from town, desiring me to send him a list of the articles to be supplied.[26]

18 March 1818

At 7 p.m. on my returning from town and having sent back the Dragon (Smythe) in consequence of his not bringing back with him the letter bag, he returned sometime after dinner. When the stewart brought the bag and a letter from the governor in the dining room and on being asked which the bag was, I said that Smythe had thought proper to return from town without asking me if I had anything to bring back, though he was the man that brought the bag down with him in the morning with me. And as there were two, one with another, which he must have seen because one was much longer and that full, projecting above the other, he must have known it. He never enquired if I had anything to send back and had not even thought proper to bring me my horse. He had taken the liberty to bring away with him my great coat which of course would [not] have been the wise thing if it had rained. When I had sat down he looked at me in a most angry way saying in a hasty and unpleasant tone why he followed me up here. After a pause, to give vent to my feeling at his rudeness, I said, 'Smythe had behaved in a most impertinent manner in taking away my great coat; that he was an illiterate fellow, there was scarcely a week he was not complained of, that Mr Pritchard was well aware of what kind of character he was, that he ought to have brought me my horse and also ought to have asked if I had anything to bring back. It was not to be supposed I was to bring back the bag on the pommel of my saddle.

'Oh certainly.' he replied. I observed that I was myself obliged to bring the bag down to the square with me as there was not even one orderly left (except Jones Minto who by accident was in the middle of the square and for whom I was obliged to send a black woman) and I was under the necessity of sending the bag to Sir Thomas Reade, begging he would take care of it. He sent for me this morning a little after 7 o'clock, without any kind of necessity, merely to say he wanted to look at the Plate account[27] and 4000 Napoleon accounts which I had all the preceding day ready for him to look at. When I handed it over to him, he scarcely looked at it, and there was nothing in fact for me to do to them. I had worked until 8 the preceding evening and late every day for some time before.

March 21st 1818

I met Darling [Andrew Darling][28] who told me he was directed by
Sir Thomas Reade (From whom he brought a letter to the governor)
to ask the governor for the furniture that had been sent for the use of
General Gourgaud from Longwood and to let him have it at the
Alarm House. [The residence of Sir Thomas Reade at this time].[29]

He asked about it and remarked how well it would answer for the
Alarm House. He said that if he was going to ask for any, he had
better ask for all at the same time, saying how much he insisted upon
a bidet from among it; which the other said he would get for him
by asking the governor.

21st March 1818

His anger when I showed him Solomon's Bill [Saul Solomon, a
shopkeeper][30] given me by Montholon, and on her Ladyship saying
it was, as I also thought, very high. 'I don't think so—if they choose
to have him buried like a Protestant it was only what was done at
every funeral.'[11] It had been shown to him and he saw nothing high
or improper in it. It was dirty and shabby to make any mistake
about it, and it was a dirty thing also of NB [Napoleon] to give the
poor [man] only £25 and splitting the difference (meaning £50).

22nd March 1818

His anger and fussing when I came down after breakfast about
the journal. He thought I had not examined the papers sufficiently.
And then he discussed the correctness of *on* and *it*, saying he was sure
that the latter was not French, that there was some trick in it. And
though I explained to him I had first written *on* and afterwards *it*
by General Gourgaud's desire, he remarked it was not correct.[31]
When I said it was my full belief General Gourgaud was right, that
the other was an anglicism, he handed it over to Mr. Jackson saying,
'What do you think of it?' On his siding with him, by his look to me
and his observations, [he indicated that] he was sure it was not French,
joking at my knowledge of it with contempt. (I can positively
assert that when I had written out the declaration for General
Gourgaud to sign and his objecting to the *on*, he came up and
asked what's the matter. I explained it to him before I altered it
to *it*, and he said it certainly is all the same). At the same time he
made no comment whatsoever on Mr. Jackson's not having reported
to him General Gourgaud's having said he had such a Journal;

but sought to throw all the blame upon me, which was only prevented by my speaking firmly on the subject. His asperity again the same day about the alteration in the beginning of a letter which he had not desired me to erase. Sending them back again to him after he rode off, for further reports of what [he] had said. It was likely that [he] should not see it. He heard me say the evening before, that I had not [given] them to him to [see]. I gave them back that day.

23 March 1818

His angry, rude, violent manner of speaking when I asked him about the allowance of fish, fruit and vegetable [in order] to inform Mr. Ibbetson. This, notwithstanding the respectful manner in which I addressed him. He [read it] again then he [asked] for a letter to have his confirmation that he had thanked him for it.

24 March 1818

On my writing to Powers [Major Power],[32] about a man to pay, by his dictation, he said the letter must be worded so that he might turn it as he thought proper afterwards.

March 1818

His sulky and angry reply when I asked him whether Fantastico's [an orderly] furniture was not to be sent back to our Neighbour's [Napoleon] house. He asked why. 'To put it back,' I said,' into the room it was taken out of'. 'No, to be sure. Why send back old furniture there; it was to go back into the store in town'. Notwithstanding this, it was nearly all sent to Nincumpoop's [Sir Thomas Reade] and I met Darling shortly after coming up to the House to enquire what was to be done about it, as Nincumpoop had told him to ask leave to send it to his country house. A sopha was kept by Mach, and Young Staff told me Nincumpoop promised to give him one.

Thursday April 2 1818

His irritation and violent way of speaking about the Baron's [Stürmer] note to me of this date, which I showed him—his being continually bothering him.—[He said that he] would not tell him by which ship his dispatches would go—but that I should tell him that he wrote by every ship—[that he] would write today and would write again Saturday.

Soon afterwards he flew out about a letter copied by Wynyard. Then over a paragraph of it that could neither be made head or tail of. It was really a most extraordinary thing that a person in copying a letter where he found either a repetition of words or omission or any other incorrectness in a rough copy, should not rectify them in writing them out fair. It's a thing to be expected only from a Clerk to write word for word without any regard to the propriety of the expressions. That might do for Randal; but no person the least in the habit of composition would copy in that inconsiderate way. It was extremely provoking particularly in an officer of rank. He then brought me the letter and shewed me a phrase in which the word *him* was repeated twice, and asked me if I knew to whom the first of these pronouns was applicable. And when I had answered, which I did without hesitation, 'in the sense of the phrase,' he asked in like manner with regard to the second. Which I as readily answered, proving there was no ambiguity in the phrase, though not of course so clear as it might have been by the introduction of one of the names instead of the pronoun. He then proceeded with much ill humour, peevishness and moroseness saying that if that was to be the way then, in that case, Sir Th. Reade's Clerk or Randal might be the secretary. And going back to his table he kept on growling that he hated to be continuously making alterations and erasures in letters after they were written out fair. It was provoking in an officer of rank. This mistake now rendered it necessary to have the whole of the letter written over again, which would have gone otherwise. (NB. This error might have been easily rectified and did not make it necessary by any means to write it over again.) But I observed, that while he was ascribing the necessity of copying it over again to this trifling repetition, and before he came to that part he had erased with pencil, a great many words and others substituted appeared to me evidently to be the real cause for writing it over again, not the other circumstance. And I have besides seen in almost every letter a quantity of erasures after being written out fair, and whole sentences erased and others, of a totally different meaning, substituted, as if he really never was satisfied except every dispatch contained numerous erasures whether or not necessary. Instead he generally wantonly insisted, for the purpose of giving trouble. Writing them sometimes 5 or 6 times, introducing new terms and then re-establishing the others, then taking them out and putting back the others. Just as he was recommencing his strain of grumbling, Sir George Bingham came in and soon after Wynyard; but he contained himself from saying more. But soon afterwards slipped in another fair copy of a letter by Wynyard which was full of erasures, desiring me to write it over again, though in this there certainly was nothing wrong in the diction, proving the other to have been the effect [of] proneness to encourage every peevish ill humoured sensation and delighting in giving way to his bad temper, and wantonly and purposely wounding the feelings of those who were most assiduous and zealous in an unremitting occupation—and that all this angry petulance was especially aimed at me. I never answered or looked at him the whole time except when [he was] asking me if I could make out the sense of that phrase; but turned away to my work.

4th April

Readiness to allow Ibbetson £200 and Janisch £100 and Killan £85. The latter being, as he observed, a mere drop in the ocean.

The money which is so frequently alluded to as in possession of Las Cases going home, he informed me, was what we observed in his purse when looking at his papers.

He told Cole this day in town, Balcombe had taken him in— that what he said about his desiring him to close his accounts in a particular way, was false. His having before mentioned to Cole that Balcombe had taken him in and then clumsily explaining it by embarking before he closed his accounts.

4th [? April 1818]

If he were [to hear of] anything of importance to let him know.

6th April

Donna refused me a lavandaja [laundress] or to have my bianchesia done at the wash house, but preferred me to have lavandaje in the neighbourhood.

Beginning April 1818

Nincumpoop's [Reade] remark about Cairns's thickness with the Balcombes.[33]

Old Commander (Mac) and his observations that notwithstanding the rain, as soon as Balcombe had received his letter, Magnesia had come down immediately of course to be consulted about the answer. His asking the Giovanni Cavalieri if Cairns did not go in the same ship with Jones to Ascension (The *Melville*). Yes. He then spoke and looked very significantly, smiling as much as to say he had imbibed some ideas which made him cool at Plantation House and to Nincumpoop, and thick with the Balcombes and patronised by the late Polyphemes [Admirals].

Donna: perhaps it was that which made him look so grave the other day at dinner here.

Young Cavalieri: the sickness of the [men of the] *Conqueror* [?] was owing to their being too much worked. They went up in the morning to Hutt's Gate and worked all day, walking back in the evening. Donna enquired whether the Adm. was building there. No. It was for Balcombe they were employed there, enclosing grounds. Old Mac [Lowe] saying he was anxious to know what Gourgaud would say about Balcombe going home. He would get Jackson to find out as it was him gave him the hint about him getting cash at Longwood.

8 April [? 1818]

He said to me at the session when I showed him notes of the Council that they were very satisfactory. And in the evening, on my reporting this day's confab, he said that he thought they were something which would draw out some remarks from them, viz. my having observed that Mr. Ibbetson was fixed at Hutt's Gate. He said 'better to supply them for he was not there for that particular purpose, but for his other duties'. At one time [he showed] great delight to have the papers I brought from Longwood this day, and at other times he did not like the papers: because, once accepted, they would make that the ground for what they expected him to do. Just before that he expressed himself pleased I had brought it, but soon seemed ready to be displeased at my receiving it.

9 April [? 1818]

His violence about me saying I thought there was no salad oil in store, and his replying; 'There was everything there that could be wanted'. His fuss at the olives, on looking over the Schedules, and comparing the appearance of what was expended in addition monthly, saying there was not enough. On it being pointed out that there were pickles put down, he said: 'olives are not pickles, there were plenty rotting in the stores which had been got from England on purpose; instead of wrenching their guts with sour cider, because it was spoiling'. All this time speaking with violence. His telling me afterwards he was sorry I had taken the memoire from Count Bertrand the preceding day, as he must now take notice of it. The night before he repeatedly said 'I am very glad I have got those papers. They are very curious papers. I am very glad I have got them in my possession'. His answer about Cairns when I said he was waiting at the door. 'I told you to tell him I was in the office'. I replied that he had not desired to walk in, and conceived he was busy, and thought it would be intruding. He replied in a most violent manner: 'Do I ever go out to visitors, did you ever know me do otherwise, why did not he come in. Tell him I told you to inform him I was in the office. (All this was said in the most angry tone, with face inflamed). I did not know he was there'. He must have known it however, for Janisch had come in two or three minutes before to the office, and speaking in quite a loud voice said: 'Captain Cairns is outside and wishes to speak to you.'

The fuss he made about a bundle of newspapers, and all the servants running about for them; he said what a damned extraordinary thing, he never knew so strange a thing before; he had sent them up this very morning and left them on the table (pointing to his writing table). Who could possibly have taken them; had I seen them; twice he asked me, though both times I answered I had not.

12th April, 1818

When returning from the Alarm House his saying to me that of course what I said was for the best, and I answered for the idea of the moment. But it was a pity I had mentioned that if Bertrand had anything to say about O'Meara he had better speak or write to him. It was certainly the easiest way to settle the business. This however was one of the instructions he gave me before going to Longwood, desiring me to say these very words if Bertrand began on the subject of O'Meara.

Donna mentioned to me after dinner how odd it was that Grape [Wynyard] and Spouse visited there after Bertrand had behaved so ill to the former. Also Swell [Bingham] and his set [?] were of the party.

12th April 1818

On my mentioning that Young Cavalieri supposed Domine was going to dine with the Coles [Thomas Cole, one of the Town

Majors], he said that he supposed it was a party made on purpose for Magnesia [Dr O'Meara] to meet him and talk over the subject.

Monday 13th [? April 1818]

Any letter you may receive from Bertrand or O'Meara, from what I can judge of their conduct, must be infractious [?]. They are in my opinion two of the most determined scoundrels I ever heard of, and I am very indifferent about Bertrand knowing my sentiments respecting them. Wallis is staying at Mr. Cole's and I understand will be at the races with them.

14th April 1818

His[34] saying to me nothing could be better, more proper, better judged than my proceedings with Bertrand. It was exactly as it ought to have been.

16th April 1818

What a complete scoundrel and villain Magnesia was. There never was such a damned rascal. These expressions repeated three times and even worse. His upbraiding about my ordering the Dragoon by the Alarm House to call on Twilight [Captain Wallis] and his saying he would not wish to have Cole [Joseph Cole] see his private letters and that he hoped the Town Major [Thomas Cole] had seen the mail aboard. Tho' I told him what the latter said to me, adding I did not think the Post Master [Joseph Cole] a man of that description. His questions [about] how I had folded up the dispatch. Evincing the strongest suspicion of Cole's [?] seeing it.

17th April 1818

Same abuse of Magnesia. 'What a rascal, damned scoundrel,' repeatedly. Baxter told me Twilight [Wallis] was not at the races at all.

18th April 1818

Asked Twilight when the Dragoon met him. His answering, just at my gate as I was returning. What a damn wet day it was. How it rained.

Old Mac [Lowe] said what a fool, what an ass Magnesia was to

H.N.E.—3

write his letter about the restrictions, tendering his resignation. But he would not get so easily out of his hands. He was not aware of all the forms he would have to go through before he could get away from him. Spoke about seeing his papers repeatedly.

20th [? April 1818]

Mach's dirty way about it.

About 21st or 22nd [April 1818]

A few days previous when I shewed him the conversation dated 16th or 19th July, the moment he read where he made, as I noted, this answer 'Your shuffling answers' (when speaking to Mr. O'Meara), he immediately denied having said so, and made some qualifying observations in the margin to smooth it down. I replied the words were correctly put down.

23rd April 1818

What a damn fool O'Meara was in giving the snuff box; he had never had hold of him before.

What a scoundrel and rascal, as usual.

This day answers sent to Bertrand and O'Meara. 10 days answering.

When the duplicates were prepared to send home of O'Meara's conversations, his anger at having sent home the originals, as he said, in so hurried a way. He ought to have considered the matter more seriously. He was wrong in sending them at full length, he ought to have only sent such parts as it was necessary for the Government to know. He was not bound to send all Mr. O'Meara thought proper to say. A good deal of what he said might have also been left out.

The dressing glass in my room was taken away because it was a good one and an old one put in. Every room in the house was fitted up and nothing put into mine and anything I asked for was refused. A second mattress was put in and then taken away. Broken bottom chairs for 6 months.

25th [April 1818]

He sent for me in the morning at 8½, mentioning to me in an angry way about the Russian Brig[35] and exclaiming: 'what business

has she here.' I said she was not the first vessel on voyages of discovery that had touched here. I asked should Count Balmain be
allowed to go on board of a man-of-war's boat with an officer.

No, he'd be damned if he should, and he would not mind stating
to the Count that it was refused on account of his frequent interviews
with the people at Longwood without his authorising. At last he
said he would permit a letter to be sent to him by the Commander
and an answer given to it.

Soon after breakfast how glad he was to have received Bertrand's
letter. What a damned ass, what a fool he was to have written it. It
was exactly what he wanted, he had been puzzling his brain
yesterday how he could introduce a hit at him about calling
Bonaparte 'Emperor', and now he had given him the opportunity,
exactly what he wanted. Again he said soon after 'what rascals,
what scoundrels they were—O'Meara was the greatest rascal that
ever existed.'

He explained to Cole that what he mentioned to him about settling
the accounts with Bertrand, who had that day sent for him, were
observations with regard to Bertrand and not with regard to him,
and therefore not to take them to himself.

25th [? April 1818]

His mislaying some of the rough drafts of the dispatches about
O'Meara, saying he was sure he had given them to me; that I
had not returned them; though after making some research he
found it where he had put it.

29th April 1818

Donna [Lady Lowe] signifying through camerina [the maid]
I should not again have the former lavandaja [laundress]. Frequent
exclamations again, 'what a rascal, what a villain,' applying the
epithets both to our Neighbour [Napoleon] and Magnesia [Dr.
O'Meara].

30th April 1818

When I begged of him to give instructions to Ibbetson, about
what he was to say respecting the expenditures mensuelles, the
angry ill tempered answer he gave and would not decide. He said
'Let Bertrand apply, I'll be damned if I sign or approve.'

NAPOLEON
As he was at the commencement of his exile

[? April 1818]

[Speaking] ill to them; was seen to be taken by the hand and well received by them. Their house was open to all such; there were Young Brick and Mortar [Wortham] who had behaved in the most impertinent way to them and Young Polisson who had behaved in so contemptible and dishonourable a manner. They were welcome guests there and they were constantly with them, accusing her [Lady Lowe] of being a cold blooded woman who had not a particle of feeling for anybody. Said she must [be]. If what Mach had stated of the former charms of V [Wynyard], how much he had changed. It must have been wrought by him. It was she in that case that had spoiled him before he came here, for he had treated her [Lady Lowe] with the greatest rudeness such as she never had experienced from any body else. Now and then he would be remarkably civil to her;

then all at once treat her with the greatest indignity and would not even notice her or speak to her; this he did even while staying here immediately after their arrival. He [Wynyard] would sit there (pointing to the head of the table) and though I was sitting next to him he would not condescend to offer me of any dish near him or help me to wine or ask me to drink some with him; she said that she had done more to be on good terms with him than she had ever done to anybody else. Several times repeating that had it not been for his connexion with Mach she would have left off all intercourse with them. Then she spoke of Madame Vignoble's [Madame Wynyard] rudeness in objecting to taking her figlias [daughters] with her to her marooning parties, notwithstanding her primogenita (La Carlotta) [Charlotte, Lady Lowe's elder daughter] had been so delighted with the one she was at, and had said she had never enjoyed herself so much before; excusing herself because of the responsibilities. He said what would be said of her if any accident happened to them. She reproached Mach with taking no notice of these things and of allowing her to be thus treated. Then he immediately answered [?], No, he did not. She [Lady Lowe] then launched out on the rudeness of Madame Vignoble [Wynyard] to Lady Swell [Lady Bingham]. She said she treated her as she would a servant. If she wanted a chair, or the window curtain to be pulled out, or the bell, she made her order her to do so, which the other then submitted to. Then began a panegyric of Lady Swell, whom a very short time before I heard abused as rude and impertinent to her at the house, carrying on winks and hints with Madame Vignoble (and their friends Fehrzen and Mansel).[36] What an excellent good temper and friendly disposition. She always behaved so civilly to her. If she wanted anything in the room or wished to ring the bell, she would jump up from a chair and do it. The furious look of her eyes, her forehead furrowed with wrinkles. Her expressions and gestures, all on fire. Scarcely able to breathe with anger.

1 May [? 1818]

Great Gun Magnesia [Dr. Verling] told Ego that Nincumpoop [Reade] had assured him he had been recommended for a step [promotion] by Mach [Lowe], and that Ego and Nincumpoop were the only two persons in the Island, besides Mach, that knew anything about it. This Nincumpoop denied to me afterwards, and told me Chirurgo Primo [Baxter] had recommended Great Gun Magnesia for the step of Physician,[37] altho' Primo Chirurgo had launched out to me much against it, saying it would be the greatest injustice against the Chirurgo Secondo of 66th [Dr. Henry] and if it was the case, he ought to memorial strongly against so marked an injustice.

1st May 1818

After his dictating to me a letter to O'Meara, he began saying what a rascal and scoundrel he was, and, working himself up into a fit of extreme passion, he declared he never would notice or again invite any person to his house who associated, visited, or had any intercourse with him. Such a rascal and villain that fellow is. After a little consideration, at last he added 'anyone who does it after knowing the circumstances of his conduct.' Proceeding with a repetition of this, turning round upon me in a gesture of rage, he said 'I prohibit you, as an officer of my staff, from ever speaking or taking notice of him, whatsoever'. I replied with very little warmth. 'This is a very extraordinary attack upon me when you know I am not in the habit of seeing Mr. O'Meara and of my having scarcely ever seen him but in your presence. I do not suppose I have ever seen him more than 4 or 5 times except when you were there. When I have spoken to him there was always, I believe, some one present or it has been when you sent for him here. There has been no officer on your staff who has seen so little of the people of Longwood as I have. I have never been there except with you or when sent on duty. I have even gone so far as not to visit once any of the Commissaires in order that I might avoid seeing anybody it might not be agreeable to you for me to see. The fact is you have taken some extraordinary exception against me which I cannot comprehend. You seem to have formed a very erroneous idea of my character. The persons who associate with Mr. O'Meara you should prohibit, not me, who never see him'.

He then began, smoothing up the asperity of his language and saying that when he spoke to me he had expressed himself in a passion which he ought not to have done. It was caused by that letter of the 19th from that fellow. He did not like it. It was a very disagreeable one to him. He must be excused or ought to be excused. He went on: 'See what that letter of mine of the 19th, before the answer to his first letter was sent, has brought upon me. What did these two paragraphs 6 and 7 mean.' There's Captain W. [?Wallis], I am sure that he would think it so and take the part of O'Meara. That fellow is capable of saying anything, even that I proposed to poison him. When he mentions his refusal to comply with what would have dishonoured him, and about my insinuations, how would that be construed by the public in general; what inferences might not be drawn from it.

After having dictated a letter to me to Blakeney, he said perhaps he will be taking it into his head too that I want to employ him as a spy on O'Meara. 'Do you think there is anything in it his delicacy might take amiss?' I said I did not think that in Capt. B's [Blakeney's] situation, there was anything in it which would have that effect, and that I never knew he had evinced any feeling of that kind. He said 'I don't know. When Capt. Wallis came here he would think it so and take the part of O'Meara.' The whole Navy do it. Look at the Admiral the other day; he attempted to condemn the conduct of O'Meara, but did he pass any remark on these matters after reading the correspondence? It was all owing to that scoundrel and damn Polyphemes [Admiral] visiting and bowing at B. [Bonaparte] instead of making [stating] in a proper manner the feelings he ought to have had after that conversation. And now how he boasted of having abused me before him. And I was not told what Captain Jones said in Solomon's shop. 'I am not to know what passes because it is considered as the act of a spy'. But the fact is there is a feeling for Bonaparte throughout, that ought not to be. But he gets the better of them all. Even the old Neptune [Admiral] is not far from it. Mr. O'Meara has been too much considered. There is an instant interest felt for him. I said, as for me I thought it is not my manner or custom to break out into rash expressions against anybody or to add to the irritation; and because I don't do it, I suppose you conceive I don't feel the thing. But I never can do it; it is much more my manner to appease when I can.

He answered that with regard to what he said to me, he certainly did not wish to impose any prohibition upon me about speaking, or not, to whom I thought proper. What he had said was not personal, it did not proceed from any feeling against me. Had Wynyard or Reade been present instead of me he would have said the same thing to them. He had observed I never went near any of the Commissaires and did not mean to say I associated with O'Meara. But persons about him, who knew how he had been treated, ought to feel with him. Before he had shown the papers to Sir George Bingham he, of course, could not expect he would enter into it in the way he ought to do, now that he had read all of them. It was wrong of Baxter to have Magnesia [O'Meara] to dine with him. It was a thing he ought not to have done. Wynyard used to visit those people at Longwood too often and he did not approve of it. However he had spoken to him about it and he had promised to give it up. Every time during this conversation I began to speak on my behalf and meant to pursue the subject by drawing his attention to his harsh mode of treatment to me, he began to talk me down (preventing my speaking by his own) by smoothing what he had said.

5th [May 1818]

Mach in conversation with Balmain. Bony's followers finding the Commissaires always ready to listen to them. 'Rencontrant et jasant avec les commissaires'.

7th May 1818

He sent for me just before dinner. After much conversation in a proper way he lashed out and said 'but I'll be damned if any of the people here could ever put me in mind of anything I could think of myself.'

8 May 1818

Putting Vignoble at the head of his table.

9 May 1818

He asked me what I thought would be the opinion about O'Meara's business at home, and I observed it would depend a great deal on the representation from here, and people's discretion in writing to friends on the subject. He said: 'Oh I care little about this; there scarcely is any body here who can form any proper judgement about ti. The Commissaires are the only ones'.

12 May 1818

His rude attack about the extract of letters saying he did not desire any of them to be copied through. I asked him twice whether I could do it or not, and both times he told me I was to, and his desiring it. Writing out Proclamation.[38] He was determined about a thing which he afterwards altered a dozen times; did not care a damn whether our neighbour [Napoleon] died or not. Donna on hearing about Commissaires going to Egg Island[39] with Domine said the latter wanted to form a Party and be at the head of it.

What cringing. Old Mack inveighing against him also. Hints about Polyphemes (on the 13th) having been led into a view of his preceedings towards Magnesia being personal. Of course Domine told him so.

12 May 1818

Donna was loud about Mrs. Vignoble's quizzing Domine and 'the coarseness and rudeness of his expressions.' One was really ashamed of her.

13th May 1818

Dr. Baxter had never come but when invited to dinner; never called.

His calling Giovani Cavalieri head of his staff. His name will be handed down to posterity together with that of our Neighbour in consequence of the apostille being written on some letter he wrote to O'Meara.

My being obliged to Giovani Cavalieri [about my laundry]—afraid to be allowed to have it done in Co's [East India Company] wash house though all was paid for by the Company and a bad washing given in lieu of a good one. After two years allowed use of the wash house. The immense time in making out Proclamation and answering Magnesia's plichi [O'Meara's letters].

15th May 1818

How he went on, [about what a] villain, rascal, Magnesia was. He had no doubt Stürmer had told Shrug [Bertrand] about his having got a copy of the Piovano's Plico [Rev. Boys, priest's letter] and Magnesia quoting 'des lettres', and he was certain Domine had told the Commissaires that it was a trifling matter, a mere trifling present to the Piovano [Napoleon gave a snuff-box to Rev. Richard Boys] as a return for his attention. The asperity of his manners to Stürmer.

Just after Vignoble [Col. Wynyard] went away in the evening Donna [Lady Lowe] related before Domine and the captain of *Eurydice*, of Dash spoiling all the beds and sophas by sleeping on them; and when it was complained of, how Vignoble had taken the blankets off and made him a bed of them on the floor.

H.N.E.—3*

15th May 1818

Yesterday Donna [Lady Lowe] told the Baron [Stürmer] it was some present for services rendered. Something of no importance and that this was the cause of the Baron's observations.

16th [May 1818]

Mack gave Domine a bout concerning the Commissaires going to Egg Island. On taking one of the first printed Proclamations off the table, he said he should not be at all surprised if Baron Stürmer had got hold of it. He was very likely to employ his servants to come here and bribe the house sentry to get at his papers.

20 May 1818

How he flew out at me when I proposed to change the word *one* of the French persons to *some* of the French persons. It was because of his enquiring why, that I said 'in order to leave nothing to cavil at, if they should assert it was in conjunction between Bertrand and Montholon that the present had been made'. He could not conceive what I meant, what had got into my head. He was quite in a rage, though a few minutes afterwards he admitted it might be the case, and would be safer, though he did not however adopt it. Not allowed to write a note upon ever so trivial a matter without his dictation, or show what you received. Otherwise [he was] always to growl and find faults with you for so doing. Whether you did or did not write, you must be in the wrong if you did not take it to him immediately.

24th May 1818

Nincumpoop [Sir Thomas Reade] had a series of Extracts and letters given to him to show to everybody about Magnesia [O'Meara]. His innuendos about Balcombe being so frightened at [sailing] and wishing to come back. About Gourgaud being such a favourite on board. His abuse of the officers of the *Conqueror*, their shabby conduct to Lamb, though it turned out afterwards he had taken them in as well as staff. His evident apparent dissatisfaction at my stating at bottom of confab with Shrug [Bertrand], his mildness on 9th October. The same about Old Polyphemes [lest he] would send home that part representing [him as]conciliating and mild. Calling the Giovanni Cavalieri [Reade] the first officer of his staff. The heat of the discussion with the Marquis [Montchenu][40] his striking the table with his knuckles, eyes starting out of their sockets. Lamb [George Lamb] and Vignoble's Goose both remarked it at the high table.

25th May 1818

His moroseness because I had received the paper from Shrug [Bertrand]. There was no necessity for my taking it. As for my pencilling the calculations, (seemingly) that was not requested. He would now be obliged to take official notice of it in consequence of my having received it. It would involve [going] into discussions and lay him open to further attacks. It was admitting on his side the truth of their assertions 'l'insuffisance des vivres' and of course from that it would appear that he had granted the amount they asked in consequence of his admitting that there really was a want. They had their points and had got every thing they wanted. It was exactly what they wanted, that I should take the paper. 'See how that fellow O'Meara had taken advantage of it and how it was brought forward in his letter.' He would have now to enter into a long explanation about it, which was exactly what he wanted to avoid. And all that, he said (and a good deal more in the same strain) after he had expressed himself highly pleased and satisfied with me, the evening I brought it in, and at my having done it so rapidly; saying 'I am devilish glad I have got hold of that paper. That is exactly what I wanted. What an ass that Shrug is. I am very happy I have got the paper in my possession.'

30 May 1818

He said that the Commissaires deserved to be kicked out of his house when they came to him after having had interviews with the followers of N. B. . . . [Napoleon]. They knew it was against his wish, some were of 2 or 3 hours duration. This was on my observing how all the Commissaires seemed hurt at his manners towards them. He said he would have nothing more to do with them in future, except the Marquis. He was the only man he could make anything of. He would be able to get something out of him. He would however be cautious. What a rascal the Baron was for saying that he had heard of the O'Meara business only from the Commissaires as mentioned in conversation of 4th May.

There was constant irritation given by the Donna about the

Commissaires, also about the present Polyphemes [Admiral Plampin] and Domine.

His innuendos that he wished he had brought out a literary man, or lawyer or a collegian, in the habit of composition.

30 May 1818

His look and angry appearance when he came and found my bedroom door bolted when I was writing confabs. 'What, you keep your door locked?' 'Sir', I answered. He said nothing, standing at the door, then that he had come to remind me of something that had been said by Baron Stürmer. I said I recollected it and he went away. Afterwards his telling me he had great a mind to kick the Baron out during the blow up.

31 May 1818

He told me of the Baron coming the preceding evening and was all civility and humble. What a damned shuffling rascal. In the letter of Balmain he introduced a sentence that he might, as said, have it always as a loop hole, and to turn as he might find necessary, according as things might turn up in consequence of the letter.

Old Mack [Lowe] showed the letter to Lord Liverpool to Bello Tomaso [Reade] before either to me or Vignoble [Wynyard].

Beginning of June 1818

He asked me to show him the written memos he had given me referring to Confabs with Shrug [Bertrand], as if distrusting my written notes, and he grumbled at my receiving the written memo from aforesaid. Also when in company mentioning about Quinto the Colo, and saying I had refused him to Coles. He broke out that I had not his authority.

9 June 1818

He said he would tell Baron Stürmer that it was owing to themselves they had not seen N. B. [Napoleon]. Had they supported his measures they would have seen him long since and that really was the case. How does that accord with his saying last year he'd be damned if ever they saw him, if he could help it.

10th June 1818

Donna [Lady Lowe] pitying the situation of B. [Bonaparte] and saying he really was to be pitied, contrasting his former situation with his present, and Sir H. [Lowe] saying he deserved more contempt than pity which gave a rise to a lengthened reasoning between them. Both looked at me alternatively, as they spoke, and as if engaging me in conversation. I observed that something must be allowed for the personal feelings of a man who (as he said, trusting to the generosity of the British nation and expecting a refuge in England) had delivered himself into the hands of the English and instead of an abode in England, had found himself fixed at St. Helena.

After having long since told me that the correspondence about the Las Roccas [La Roche][41] was not in his possession but in mine, and that he had given it back to me, he found it about 9th January all packed up together and docketed by himself on the 10th.

He suspiciously asked me about the Chronicles of September 1818 [?], saying he had put it in the office and now he could not find it.[42] It was very extraordinary he wondered who could have taken it away, very odd, what could have become of it.

19/20 June 1818

What a villain Baron Stürmer was, alluding to his selling his effects, said Donna.

22 June 1818

Donna remarked at Dinner she had seen the pigeon holes in the office. She said 'You are always doing something or other. I suppose after you have done every thing else I may expect to have something done for myself'. Mack answered that it might have been done some months ago and was very much wanted, but added in an under tone 'it is for Major Gorrequer'.

Except he had some private instructions given him to force the Commissaires away by such kind of treatment, it cannot be otherwise accounted for.

His persisting in writing to Sir P. M. [Admiral Malcolm] after his quitting the Island, though nevertheless he detained his letter advising him not to agree to it. Further sending however a duplicate with some alterations from the original to [him] in the subsequent 12 months after the first was sent.

28 June 1818

Raving as Donna said [to have] told him Rous stayed for pranzo [dinner] without invitazione.

28th June 1818

His anger because I advised sending the letter that day to the Polar Bear [Balmain]. Why so? It was the most important thing he considered that he had ever written in his life.

29th June 1818

What a villain Magnesia was for carrying forward immediately.

30 June 1818

Vignoble had been humbugged about the Cisterns. They had humbugged him about the damp.[43]

14th July 1818

His rudeness when I was repeating to him (though at his desire) to look over (so as to send them off immediately to Longwood), some parts of letters from Las Cases to Bertrand. He interrupted me and in an impatient tone said: 'Oh don't you be reading that to me now. I am looking after something of a more interesting nature to me'. This interesting matter was skimming lightly over the surface of some newspapers just arrived which he was going to send off to Longwood. Immediately after which he exclaimed 'Think of that fellow Sir N. Watson going to make a damn fool of himself by setting up for Southwark'. And that instant he gave up looking over the paper, and went out of the room for a few minutes. After he came back he asked me for the same letters, which after reading in a surly malicious tone and manners he said 'Look, did you ever see such damn sickening stuff, ridiculous fulsome trash as this is. The damn fool telling of les membres de la famille impériale. Such a blackguard rascally set as they all are. Damn me if it does not make me sick in the stomach to read such damn trash as that.' This was an exclamation at reading the effusion of Las Cases's feelings for the exile and his family. His misrepresentation of the business of La Roche whom he certainly discharged, and allowed to remain in the house till there was an opportunity for a passage—giving the whole thing a different tone in his letter to Buggiardo. His telling Donna about what Buggiardo said of what the Commissaires had mentioned about La Roche, but concealing at the same time what he had said of La Roche himself having told him he was out of place 4 days and confirmed what the others had said.

His not sending Madame Bertrand Lady Holland's letter because there was so much feeling expressed for her and her family, and offering to receive her children at her house if they were sent to school in England. He did 2 or 3 weeks afterwards however, most probably because of 'his beautiful wife'.[44]

On receiving Buggiardo's letter[45] about the cook, he said that now they could not bear that he should have anything to do with what concerned them, but he would take care to have to do with everything in future, more than ever he had.

The ill humour at there not being a duplicate of a dispatch ready, tho' he had most precisely told me the day before it was not necessary and notwithstanding I told him so. 'Oh but then I meant otherwise, it was the most essential of all'; though it practically was for no other real reason than causing more trouble.

He had an objection for a long time to Randal writing any document or references to accompany dispatches, because he said he wrote a clerk's hand (which was not the case), and frequently after having written several he would ask me or Vignoble [Col. Wynyard] to write them over again. Tho' sometimes he would allow the German [Janisch], who wrote ten times more like a clerk and not the 20th part so well.

Would not send Miss Clowton's [?] letter to Shrug's [Bertrand] wife however.

17th [? July 1818]

Several of O.Nk's notes missing which he declared he had not [got]; but that I must have, though I assured him I had not and which he found immediately on going upstairs, in his pocket.

20 July 1818

I mentioned that I conceived probable that what Donna had said about Commissaires not being invited again had reached their ears; and it was in consequence of it that Old Frog's [Montchenu] refusal and that of Bear [Balmain] came. 'Ah, I dare say, Domine heard it and told him.' Laying [the blame for] everything that could reach the Commissaires' ears to Domine's repetition.

Before coming out, when in London, he refused my taking out a Sicilian servant though he himself was taking out 4 foreign ones with him. No doubt Nincumpoop's [Reade] doing, as I had mentioned it to him. Strutting about, knocking about his aiguillettes against chairs and walls by his strut—full of affectation when dictating —his contempt of men generally held clever—never answering, or seldom, to 'good night' or 'good morning'. Stercoraceous [Sir Thomas Brooke, secretary to the Council] said the evident designs of [his] attentions to the Neptunes were merely [in order] that he should have a kind of party to support him against that of No 1 Polyphemes [Admiral Malcolm]. His frequent condemnation of the first of all Polyphemes' measures, when they come to be quoted in opposition to his. His frequent hints at Mme. Shrug [Bertrand] and the blame thrown upon her, and conveyed to Ministers, of her being employed in communications. When the order was sent for the removal of Magnesia [O'Meara] and the row about Il Grazzioso [Col. Lyster] took place, he exclaimed how very fortunate it was that he had little Polyphemes [Admiral Plampin] here at the juncture—what trouble he might have had if such a fellow as x x x (the predecessor of Little Polyphemes) had been here now. In the dispatch preceding this, he began buttering Little Polyphemes to Big Wigs[46] about his cardinal assistance, and the union between them on all points, though up to that moment he had been in the habit of continually saying he derived no assistance, never could get an opinion from him and condemning him loudly on several occasions for being so neutral.

23 July 1818

After his receiving Grazzioso's letter reporting that Magnesia [O'Meara] had refused to tell him about our Neighbour [Napoleon] and answering that he was not his keeper, and after declaiming against the rascal and repeatedly expressing the impossibility of keeping him here any longer, and after venting himself out in that way for some time at length, he calmed and dictated me a note to Magnesia to report whenever asked by Grazzioso.[47] He however soon again became violent and the note, though ready to be written out fair, did not go. For a long time after he cursed over the orders received from home to pack him off. He sometimes determined to to it, at others seemed undecided. No decision took place for 1½ to 2 hours. All this time he detained Vignoble. He at last went out of the room and joined the latter who was in the hall or the library and, after remaining in conversation for 15 to 20 minutes walking about (I believe in the Library or little room adjoining as I heard him walking and talking), he returned to me (followed 2 or 3 minutes after by Vignobles). He said to me 'Well I have come to a decision about what to do with the man. I am determined to act upon Lord Bathurst's instructions and to send him away. I have been speaking to Vignoble (who at this moment entered) on the subject and I have made up my mind. It is of no use to attempt going on any longer in this way as long as that fellow is here, and there will be no end to this kind of work. It is necessary I should do something after this letter and I can do nothing less than sending him away. Don't you think I shall be right in doing so?' I asked if he was determined to carry it through whatever clamour they might make at Longwood about it, for he must make up his mind against a fierce attack from that quarter if he sent him off. He replied that that would not prevent him, he knew he must expect it and he was prepared against it. I then said there appeared to me no medium between sending him away from the Island and submitting quietly to all he chose to do, and disobedience of his orders in every instance he thought proper. He had such positive directions to do so that I thought if he did not do it in the present instance the Government would disapprove of it. It appeared to me of very little consequence whether it took place now or some months later as to the effect it would have at Longwood—that they would be as violent then as now and perhaps more so. The longer he stayed the worse; for no doubt he would persevere in the same line of proceedings. This additional cause of dissatisfaction by the contempt he showed towards him by his conduct to the O. Officer [Col. Lyster was orderly officer at this time], was a good motive for sending him away. He said he thought so too. He could no longer put up with such conduct.

I observed that if the Foreign medical person [Dr. Antommarchi arrived on September 18, 1819] might not be here for many months or if they perhaps could not procure [him] at all, in that case he would have all the time to put up with whatever Magnesia might think proper to do and have his feelings galled every day.

24th July 1818

On Vignoble making some remarks about there being no necessity to justify his measures to them (meaning our Neighbour). After making some sharp reply to Vignoble he exclaimed: 'I have this

day signed a death warrant (man of 66th going to be hanged) and
my signing this letter (acquainting them of the removal of Magnesia)
may be the signing of another. I know nothing more likely to happen
in consequence of my signing it, and it therefore required to be well
considered, and is not a thing to be done in a hurry'.

24th July 1818

On his receipt of Bear's [Count Balmain] note, how he abused
him, saying that after that he was a complete blackguard. What
a mean, dirty fellow he must be to write to him in that manner,
but he would settle him for it.[48]

He asserted in a dispatch (when speaking of the reported dampness
of our neighbour's room) that there was no fire place in any of the
bedrooms in P.H. [Plantation House], after I had assured him
there was one in my room and one in the adjoining room.

He gave me in town a list of questions which he wished to have
put to Magnesia [Dr O'Meara].

25th July 1818

Whilst dictating to me in answer to the concluding paragraph
of Bertrand's letter, he said, 'Now the most difficult point is the
restrictions,[49] what do you think I ought to say to that?' I answered
'which restrictions?' On which he came up to my desk and struck
violently with his hand, poking out his finger across the lines saying:
'MY GOD, THERE, THERE. That part there. Don't you see
there, that restriction . .' Soon afterwards he said to me 'I have two
ways of settling it, one by allowing O'Meara to go about his business
as usual and giving out the Proclamation referring to him, and the
other by allowing him again his freedom receiving at the same time
a guarantee from him. What do you think is the best?' I replied that
his rescinding the orders would be considered at Longwood as the
result of the impression made upon him by the letter lately written
to him. 'Yes, I think that will be the case certainly'. After walking
about a little longer, he sat down and then soon after exclaimed
that there was not a person about him, not a person in the Island
whose opinion or advice he could consult on a matter of this kind.
None from whom he could get the assistance he wanted, whose
mind could seize the subject, in fact none who considered the matter
but himself—Baron Stürmer was the only one to whom he could
look for a sound opinion. I replied that it was not the fault of those

about him if they had not the capacity. I believed there was not one
of them who did not give their opinion, when asked for it, to the best
of their judgement and for the best, and who spoke as they thought—
that for my part I had been the whole of this week working with him
either under his dictation or writing in answer to those letters of
Bertrand and O'Meara from morning till night—that having been
frequently asked my opinion, I had given it to the best of my
capacity and that many alterations had been made in consequence
of my remarks. He said 'Oh certainly, of course whatever opinion
is given is for the best', and admitted that I had been the cause of
some alterations for the best in his last letters. But he had taken my
opinion about not sending an extract of Lord Bathurst's letter to
O'Meara from the ground the other day (meaning the race course).
I replied 'the ground? I don't understand.' He then explained with
the letter which was afterwards written over again. I then recollected
what he meant and said I only observed that the Extract would be
better sent with his regular answer (which he, however, had not
done). 'Yes,' said he, 'but if I had sent it then, he never would have
dared to send me the answer he did.' I merely added that as he had
verbally told him before what was contained in that Extract I did
not think it would have made any difference. 'Oh yes it would. He
would not have dared to write what he did in the face of the Extract'.

I said I was not in the habit of intruding my opinion or advice on
anyone but when asked I gave it in sincerity.

He then proposed assembling the company and consulting them
about this business, or speaking to the Baron alone about it. I
observed that it was a measure very different from any he had ever
had recourse to before, consulting upon points which he never had
been in the habit of before. It came strange to him to thus complain.
Of his two plans I said that the best, I thought, was if he again gave
Mr. O'Meara his former liberty. To put it on the footing of his
having accepted and sent home his resignation and giving it in the
meantime under guarantee. 'Oh then, that's coming to what I was
saying'. Of the two I said that I conceived the last. He said that the
Baron was the only man who could give him a sound advice and
ready opinion on the business. He wanted the advice of a man more
versed in the business of the world. He was of the same opinion with
Bertrand and O'Meara that if he submitted to the restrictions it was
enough he had done already to assist, and that he could not do so
if what he wanted to do himself did not please them. As for giving
an opinion, for my part I was too confused from being so busy at the
same, and as I was at that writing desk from morning to night, it

could not be wondered if I had not the power of giving any at all. Both my health and mind were suffering. I was getting worse every day. The day before I had left the desk with a most severe pain in the breast, so much so that I found a swelling in the pit of my stomach. In fact I was quite knocked up. It would be impossible for me to stand it. It was an unceasing labour. He said he would send for Baron S. to see what he said about the letter.

At 5.½ o'clock, when, supposing I might retire I had left the office with the intention of not returning to it that evening, he sent for me to write out the fair letter for Bertrand. I said 'Now Sir?' He said 'Yes.' He meant to send it off; he wished they should have it before they had time to work out any more impertinent letters, for he dared say he would get something of that kind from O'Meara. When I had written out half of it he said he would get someone to assist me; for instance Jackson or some other who could come up here. I said that if a division of labour had taken place Colonel Wynyard would have willingly attended any day and written in the office, which would have been a great relief. I said that he had mentioned that to me himself and wished it. 'Then why didn't he stay today instead of going away as he did?' I said because he does not know when he is wanted, he can't tell when there is anything for him to do. I said I had been for the last two years, without any kind of relaxation, at it. Had not more than an hour on average daily for relaxation since I had been here. That it was impossible that I could stand it any longer. I had had a very unpleasant business thrown on my hands in the inspection of the Purveyor's [Balcombe] accounts for the last 2 years, for which, however, I had never asked remuneration though Mr. Glover [secretary to Admiral Cockburn] had been allowed it for the time he did it.[50] He said he was not himself idle, that if he did not work, his writing was at least enough. Afterwards he again spoke on the same subject beginning by requesting that I might be relieved entirely from my concern with the Longwood accounts. He said 'Oh certainly, I don't think you ought to have anything to say to that now that Ibbetson has the purveyorship'. But I had never asked to be relieved from that duty. If I had he might have appointed R. who was on the spot and indeed could have done it better for being so much at hand. I said my business was with the accounts, and that for the first 18 months I was with him I had as much business as any three officers on the Staff, and that I could take neither recreation nor exercise. That it had taken up so much of my time, that I considered myself as much entitled to remuneration as any officer in the island who received

addtional pay for extra duty. That I could prove the government had
been saved upwards of £2000 a year at my suggestion, since I had
had the inspection of the accounts. That I certainly had had much
more trouble with the business than ever Mr. Glover had, and that
as there was a precedent I thought myself entitled to the allowance
which, if I had got it, was my intention to propose should have been
divided between Mr. Glover and me as we had divided what he
received for some months for doing extra duty. He said 'Oh, as for
Glover it was only for a very short time he acted, and it was not
worth refusing him.' I thought he said something however to that
effect. I said that besides I had also been made to do what no
Military Secretary did in other places; the examination of the building accounts. It was always done by a clerk of accounts. He did not
make up any answer to this last, but seemed to consider my claim
as not deserving either his attention or recommendation. Asked me
to postpone finishing the letter (which only wanted the signature)
till about dinner time. Asked whether Wynyard or me should sign
it, I replied it was quite indifferent to me if I did.

Then I clearly said it had been the intention at first to send it,
though I had been kept till then 6½ hours at it. As I thought it was
written over and over the next day and after all signed by Twilight.

25th July 1818

How lightly he took the business of Young R. Staff's writing
to Shrug [Bertrand] about the break of regulations, as strong as
anything Magnesia had ever done. Never even spoke to him about
it. Did not remove him as he had declared at first he would, but
seemed rather inclined to support him by admiring his note.

26th July 1818

His observations to Nincumpoop [Reade] speaking of Magnesia
[O'Meara] running in to our Neighbour [Napoleon]. 'That's the
consequence of trusting such a matter to Vignoble [Wynyard] and
Blakeney'.

30th July 1818

Lamenting the unfortunate circumstances of Magnesia's robbery[51]
and reverting to the manner of removing him, his saying how much

better Nincumpoop would have done it than Vignoble. He would
have done the thing in a different way, he would have done it so
much better. Vignoble [Wynyard] ought to have been present when
Blakeney delivered the order to Magnesia. It was altogether very
badly managed. Blaming Vignoble throughout the business in
every part.

31 July 1818

Cole's nasty way in refusing to answer when he asked him: 'Well
what do you think of Count Bertrand, now?—What do you think
of him, Sir? Would you not think me a shabby fellow if I treated a
servant of mine so?'

The way of representing the circumstances to the Marquis
[Montchenu], but not telling him afterwards it had been settled. This
was much like the Gourgaud business of the bill. Much ado about
nothing. The squall between Ostrich [Stürmer] and Old Mack when
the latter answered 'je ne réponds pas à cette question'. 'C'est parce
que vous ne pouvez pas dire que je les ai [dit]'. 'Si vous le
disiez ce ne serait pas vrai et je serais homme à vous en faire rendre
raison, c'est au Baron Stürmer que vous auriez à faire'. 'Je n'ai pas
peur de vous, je ne vous crains pas', repeating this frequently
walking up to him and looking him in the face with a menacing
air. When the other was hesitating about the above question,
'Répondez donc, ne voulez-vous pas répondre?' 'J'en rendrai compte
à ma Cour. Je dirai que je vous ai demandé plusieurs fois et que
vous n'avez pas pu, ou n'avez pas voulu, me répondre. Quand je
suis venu dans cette pièce il y a plusieurs jours vous parler, que vous
n'avez pas daigné faire attention à moi ou même ne répondre
pendant quelque temps, vous vous teniez avec les bras croisés, la
tête courbée (at the same time imitating his look and posture his
arms across), les yeux étincelants de colère. Ah Dieu si j'avais pu
envoyer votre portrait à votre Gouvernement.'

'Vous m'avez traité comme un chien. Le jour que vous m'avez
rappelé quand j'étais déjà monté à cheval. Mais quelle scène vous
a mis en fureur. Mais enfin je ne vous ai jamais parlé d'affaires que
vous ne vous soyiez monté. Vous vous emportez dès le premier
moment. On ne peut pas entrer en discussion avec vous. Ce n'est
pas avec des gens indépendants de vous qu'il faut vous conduire
ainsi, pour avoir de vous il faut vous être dépendant. Je désirai
vous dire ce que je pensais sur ce point et je vous parle franche-
ment quoique vous ayiez dit que je suis diplomate'.

31st July 1818

Nincumpoop said to me in town how badly Vignoble must have managed the business to have allowed Magnesia to have had a peep at Neighbour before he left the place. Also finds faults about the removal of the straps by which the loss occurred. Before I went down to town I was writing and enclosing my 3 confabs with Shrug of 6, 7, 8 April. He again attacked me about receiving the paper from Shrug, saying it was the most unguarded thing I had done since I came here, to receive it. I replied that it was not the way in which he spoke of it for the first few days after it occurred; that on the contrary he particularly approved my receiving it (though I told him at the time there was no necessity for him to receive it, as it was not delivered to me officially but merely to enable me to put down my calculations). He repeatedly told me he was very glad I had brought it, it was very fortunate I had done so. (He never objected to it till about a fortnight or three weeks or more afterwards). He answered he did not recollect that. I repeated positively his having said so, and I observed that there was scarcely anything in that paper that had not been mentioned either in the aperçu given or in any notes or confabs. That it was a paper which signified nothing, and he was not even bound to know I had brought it with me.

NB—upon a former occasion when grumbling about that paper, he asked me whether I had still the notes of observations he had given me for those confabs, as if doubting I had not said what he desired me. I told him I had.

His abuse of 'l'Autrichien' [Baron Stürmer], and notwithstanding writing him on 1st August the kindest letter, full of professions of the feelings he felt for him.

31st July 1818

In writing when taking his depositions and on receiving them, I asked whether they were to be put. 'Why, you are to see Stercoraceous and consult together about it, and you'll see.' Evidently to throw it on my shoulders if any thing had gone wrong.

31st July 1818

At dinner time Vignoble [Wynyard] brought the depositions, a most voluminous packet. After reading it he said there must be two

copies of it done tomorrow, one for Government and one for the
Admiral. I observed it would be impossible to have them got ready
here. He replied 'I don't mean this at all. I don't intend a single
word of it shall be written here. It shall be done in B's [Thomas
Brooke's] office. We'll send it down to him tomorrow'. After dinner
when standing in the library he said: 'These depositions must be
put in hand tomorrow morning very early. What has Randal to do?
He can begin at them very early tomorrow morning.' I replied that
I thought from what he said just before, they were to be done in B's
office, that it was impossible to have them ready here with all the
other business, and that in B's office there were so many clerks
already employed and so little to do, I thought it the proper place,
particularly as it was a business belonging to B's department. I said
that in there (the clerk's office), there was as much done in one hour
as in 3 hours among all of them in the other. He said 'As to that, it
might be'. I asked him if I could then write to B. to send two of his
people over next day to assist. He said he could not spare two and
that I might ask for one and the German [Janisch] would be assisting.
He then began to say I was mistaken as to the number employed in
B's office and by his authority only. He said afterwards he made out
three, and he said that they had besides a great deal to do. He said
that I was mistaken on the subject (though he had repeatedly
declared before that there was as much done in one hour by either
myself or Randal as would be done in a whole day nay a week
sometime by the whole of the others).

Next morning when B. came up, on its being mentioned to him by
the Chief that he wanted 2 copies of the deposition made up, he
answered that he would get it done with the greatest care, he would
get 4 of his young men about it. He immediately enumerated 5
persons, his assistants or clerks. Some of them he mentioned were
not even wanted in the office that day, and would not be there, but
at home in the country. The umbrage he took at acting-captain
Podargus (no doubt by the intriguing of Nincumpoop) on his
return from the Cape, when he called to pay his respects. He asked
me what he had said about Magnesia and when I answered that he
had not even mentioned his name, and that he was no crony of his,
he answered sharply 'Oh but he is though, and this I know'.

1 August 1818

Giovanni Sbirro [Young Police] told me about the Donna [Lady
Lowe]. One bottle of brandy now served only 2 or 3 days—lately, in

consequence of B's observation that she drank a whole one of sherry daily, she had made a rule to make one last 2 days; but then, says Young Sbirro, she had one of cagnini every 2 or 3 days instead of every 5 as before, and besides she won't give even a glass to Nurse out of her sherry, but sends her down to us below. Drinks grog every night and liqueurs, and remarked to me that Old Mach [Lowe] frequently called for the latter himself without offering us any.

2nd August

His suspicious question if I had written anything more to Baron [Stürmer] or answered his last note, though he, of course, knew I had not. My answer 'Nothing since informing him *Griffon* had sailed'.[52]

3rd August

Nincumpoop [Reade] told me, on my mentioning that Polyphemes Primo [Admiral Pulteney Malcolm] would be expected by Magnesia [O'Meara] to support him, 'There I can tell you he will not, that you may be sure of, I'll be damned if he does,' meaning by this that he had written to him, which I knew before from Old Mach [Lowe].

3 August 1818

Orderly Officer (on receiving the report all was well) liable to be hanged for making such a report without being certain of his [Napoleon's] presence.

His extraordinary remarks, as if meant to be a hit at someone (and it could have been no other than me as there were but Nincumpoop [Reade] and Primo Fisico [Dr. Baxter]), that if Magnesia published or made any noise at home on the subject of his ways here, it would not be him he would attack, but those who supported him. Anyone who took his part or spoke in his favour, those would be the people he would pursue. He would ferret them out, he would find some means of ascertaining who they were; it would be them that would suffer. He would bring them to their bearings. All this spoken in a sort of threatening manner.

Nincumpoop said to him in my presence in the office (when Mach said he thought Blakeney more to blame than Vignoble—the idea of a great hulking grenadier like him not stopping Magnesia) 'I don't know that it appeared to me to be the fault of the latter much more than that of the former.' Vignoble should have been present when it was delivered but it appeared he wished to throw the responsibility off his own shoulders on to the other. What business had he to be going after Young R. Staff; could he not have sent an adjutant after him. It was an excuse. Old Mach inveighing on the proceedings altogether saying how badly the whole business had been managed. Fisico [? Dr. Verling] expressed the same thing to me afterwards, showing they must have been conversing together about it, and adding that when he heard of Vignoble going, he concluded it would be badly managed.

Nincumpoop [Reade] said at breakfast that our Neighbour would most probably now change his mode altogether, after Magnesia was gone off, as he would no longer have all the tittle tattle brought up to him as usual by Magnesia. How much this proceeding is the marking feature of Nincumpoop.

Fisico [? Dr. Verling] came up this morning with some anecdotes of Mrs Shrug's [Bertrand] jeremiads, as he termed them, to Old Frog [Montchenu] (who had mentioned it to him) when she said our Neighbour was much worse; and this little anecdote told, he asked for increase of pay which was immediately granted.

Fisico told me once he had just had a conversation with Mach in which he had mentioned to him the great military income of Vignoble, and that Mach had agreed it was very great indeed. Mach refusing to double the extra pay for Fisico of 53rd, above 10 years, and not fully doubling that of ditto 66th, above 2 years, and instantly doubling that of Primo [Dr. Baxter].

He set Young R. Staff [one of Lowe's staff] on a footing with Dragoon [? Cornet J. W. Hoath] upon no principle but that he ought to be upon the same footing, and giving him 7/- a day besides as an assessor of works. Addition to Br. Major Rt. [Captain Charles Harrison], acting without any grounds to put it upon. Nincumpoop [Reade] observed that Bear [Balmain] had said he hoped the skipper of Autrichien's [Stürmer] ship was not of such a fiery temper as it was reported.[53] For the latter was equally so and he feared the skipper, in that case, might throw him overboard. After some witty remarks upon it by Ninny [Reade], Old Mach [Lowe] observed that he believed Autrichien was very easily put down. In those cases however he might talk, when it came to the push ... (This however was not proved by the sangfroid of Autrichien in that discussion against Mach's now breaking way).

His rage at not having better paper with water mark, though I had assured him before [that] I had made every enquiry, that there was none in any of the shops or stores, nor in fact any to be had except what was there, being not prepared [?]. Paucity of tip. Much of caution.

Nincumpoop [Reade] being furnished with everything which could be got up against Magnesia [O'Meara], and showing the papers about, with great activity, to people.

7 August 1818

Young Polisson showed me a letter sent to him by Donna, directed to Old Mach, in an envelope to the Polisson, and on the back of which letter was written 'if I do not claim this letter, enclosed, again deliver it to Mach.' He showed it to me as I was passing his door going to bed, saying he had peeped in the inside and saw that there were others within, addressed to Donna. On the address of the one to Mach it was written 'if I do not claim this again, act upon it'.

Fisico Primo [Dr. Baxter] read the confab between Mach and Magnesia of 25th November. It was shown to him by the former, after I had written it out, and he even added a short remark in his own handwriting of a few words I had omitted, tho' not forgotten, as they were still in a rough memo, but had been omitted by me. He told me afterwards that there was a passage which Mach disputed then, which I had put down correctly, in fact corrected to alter it according to his own fancy and wish to alter; but that he had immediately confirmed all that I had put down, saying he was positive of its being perfectly correct throughout, and told me he was surprised I could have recollected a confab of such a length so well as to have put it down correctly.

10th August

I mentioned what Bear had said to me about going to Rio, when I repeated 'il n'y a plus rien d'intéressant'. He said 'What could he mean? What do you suppose?' firing up, knitting his brows, apparently suspecting me. I did not repeat this until after he had asked me 'What did he say, did he make any allusion to Longwood or Magnesia?'

Young Police telling me Donna [Lady Lowe] was in the habit lately, in all the letters she wrote to him, to say: 'letters before I am taken ill; do this ditto,' as if apprehensive of her couche.

Would not be surprised if Roman Candlestick [Lieut. Charles McCarthy] was to lose his parchment in consequence of writing that letter to Magnesia.

Imperial behaved to him like a Blackguard for receiving the snuff box.

His fury at missing the rough of a letter intended for Bear [Balmain], fixing his eyes on me full of suspicion: 'Had I seen it, a most extraordinary thing, that d . . . him, but it was a most extra-ordinary thing.' He did not know what to think of it. On my saying it must be among some of the papers. 'No.' He had looked over them. But immediately after that turning 2 or 3 of the first laying on the table, there it was. On which he said 'I'm always afraid that fellow Bear may bribe the servants to show him some of the papers'. I immediately contested the idea saying he never would venture on such a step with anyone he could not trust. 'I beg your pardon' says he, 'such a Blackguard as that, is capable of doing anything.'

13 August 1818

Nincumpoop [Reade] told me that he had at last found out what was said in the confab at mess of Deadwood, soon after the first quarrel between Mach and Magnesia, and that he never had been able to come at it till now. But yesterday (I think he said, or the day before) he had said to Pagatore [The Paymaster], speaking about Magnesia, 'By the bye that was a very improper confab held at your mess once by him. It was mentioned to me, but I can't make out what is the true account, as I have heard it repeated several ways'. 'Oh,' said the other, 'I was present at it and will repeat it to you'. This was a trap, Nincumpoop told me, to fish it out of the other, and that he said he had heard it repeated different ways that he might think so, and have no hesitation in repeating it to him. He then told him that Magnesia had said that, since so little delicacy was observed towards him, he would freely express his sentiments; that the restrictions were unnecessary, unjust and arbitrary, that if he went out to meet people he was only allowed to say to this, 'How are you Jack', to that, 'How do you do', 'Good morning to you'. What school boy would submit to such a kind of treatment? It was a shame to treat so great a man in such a way, in which sentiments it appears he succeeded in inducing all the officers present to join. Nincumpoop observed what a fool Pagatore was for telling it. (Old Mach saying that Mr. Catholic [Lieut. McCarthy] would very likely lose his commission for signing that letter).

Speaking of the subject of the mess, he must take some steps about it, damn him; but he would not let Old Yorkshire alone. He thought the best way was to have them all assembled and read all the papers to them—prove Magnesia a liar. He was resolved to damn him, at all events in the eyes of the officers of [66] th.

August Sunday 16 1818

He had a letter written to him ever since the 11th or 12th June about the claim for staff pay ordered to be refunded by me, which I had not asked him to forward in consequence of the press of business in the departure of the vessels since then. Seeing according to all appearances that little was to be done by the approaching opportunity, I said to him I had prepared this letter some time back (holding it in my hand) addressed to him on the subject of the staff pay I was called upon to refund and I begged he would allow me to request the favour of making another application through him to the Treasury about it. He, immediately that I began speaking on the subject, from the appearance of good humour, suddenly began knitting his brows and frowning. He took the letter to read it, saying after a hurried glance through the contents 'that all this argument was not a thing to be issued from me to him, but from himself to the Treasury'. He then proceeded to cavil and dispute my argument, not as to the facts, which he had admitted, but to my stating that his leaving Genoa under charge of a Colonel did not at all prove that his command was an independent one; and to my saying as another proof that it was his having ordered the force to re-embark for Elba without referring the matter to any superior authority was no proof at all. Although he was not obliged to refer to a superior authority to do anything he thought proper with that force, still that was no argument of its being an independent command. Not however, he added, that I mean to say it was not an independent one, for, on the contrary, it certainly was, he had no doubt about himself. Besides, it was unnecessary to enter into all this argument. If they had taken it into their heads it was not a distinct one. All that he could say about it would not make them alter their minds. I said that what I had written was, I was well aware, not an argument to be used in any part, but that what was stated was all facts. I intended it more as suggestions and the grounds to build my claim upon, for his own consideration. He asked me to let him look at the letter he wrote, the preceding year, about it, which, having read he said: 'why really I can say nothing

more than what I did here, it is of no use to repeat this.' I observed
there were in my opinion additional arguments in my letter which
I thought likely to cause, upon reference, a different decision. He
said there was something more in Mr. Harrison's letter than mere
words conveyed. They had taken some objection to something
which made them take up in that way, which depended upon it
(as if insinuating there was something wrong on my part, which
he was not acquainted with, but known to them). I told him I
could not tell what it was, that I conceived it was a great piece of
injustice towards me, and that I was very ill-treated. He said it
was a pity I had received 2 month's pay in advance, at Marseilles[54],
as he was sure that was the cause of it. I explained to him how this
was, that both Reade and I received the same, and that it was only
9 months after our arrival here I heard from Govt. [?] it had been
issued in England, and that it was not known from what time it
was to be paid there. I, of course, had no business to say anything of
what I had received in advance at Marseilles; besides, I answered,
this was not to count, nor did I ever hear it considered in that
light; but however that was settled, they had sent an order to the
Treasury or the Regiment agents for it. He expressed himself of
the opinion that I certainly was ill-treated, and that withholding it
from me was certainly an injustice. But he did not know what more
he could do than what he had already done. He then began calculating from what time the pay was to be refunded to make it agree
with the £86.18.6 (I had not been able to make it out myself,
though I had tried it in various ways). He said 'Oh I'll soon find it
out.' After trying however for a good while, he could make nothing
of it. Then turning to me in the most unkind, unfeeling way and in
a rough, harsh tone, his face firing up, he said 'I don't know what
your circumstances may be, but I can tell you one thing, that there
has never been a period of my life that I would have thought of
making a second application upon a matter of such little consequence.'
I answered he might have been placed in very different circumstances
from mine, but as for my part a sum of £86.18.6. was a consideration
to me, though it might not have been to him, and that were it even
much smaller, so long as I conceived I had a just claim to it, I
conceived myself perfectly in the right to insist.

I said that the Treasury would not consider me a bit the more
for giving it up. He said he only meant to say that if the two month's
pay I had refunded formed part of it (of which he had no doubt) the
thing was not worth persisting in. However if it was exclusive of the
2 month's pay that I was called on to repay (that £86.18.6) he

thought I should be right in persevering. I told him it was impossible for me to say, and that from the way in which it was expressed in the letter from the Treasury, it appeared to be exclusive, and that I would never have disputed the matter had I been called upon only to refund from the date of arrival of Earl Bathurst's letter or that of Sir McN's. He said for his part he did not know what else he could do or what he could say. I observed that the claim might at least be reiterated, that they could not but pay attention to the representation of a person whose opinion in fact ought to decide. 'Very well,' he said, 'I will do it'. He then began to consider whether, had I actually left the Staff altogether at the period of his arrival or that of his departure, I should have received pay for the time I was employed with him. Having looked over the letter I had addressed to him, he said it might afford him arguments to use himself, but he thought I had better confine myself to one of the grounds. According to his suggestion I immediately wrote out another, which having showed him next morning, he said 'It would do perfectly well, it was very clear.'

18th August 1818

His angry way of speaking on coming up to me and desiring me to write a letter to Agents of the Cape—for taking up a piece of paper with the intention of taking it down as he was giving his directions, which was a practice he almost invariably insisted upon being followed. 'Why, surely, now there is no necessity for me dictating it to you. Surely you can do so trifling a thing without me. There is no necessity that I should dictate the very words.' All this said in a tone and manner most revolting.

20th August

There appearing nothing now to do than what was already in hand, I said 'May I beg of you to allow my application to the Treasury to go by this opportunity.' Flushing up with anger he replied 'It's impossible, I cannot neglect thousands of pounds. This time I have much to do, I have got six letters of the greatest importance to write and I cannot do it; but I will next time, fully and effectually.' I said I had merely asked, conceiving there was not much business to do by this opportunity. He said there was a great deal to do, more than he probably would be able to. I repeated what I had first said that I had merely put the question once and had not pressed it upon him. He left the room and in 2 or 3 minutes returned with a slip of paper with some memoranda and showing it to me, and in the same passionate way, said 'There, look at these, they are the letters I have to dispatch today in town, and see whether I have time to write about your business which requires a long letter.' He however returned from town at 3 o'clock, or rather less, and kept walking about the house for full an hour, which afforded leisure enough to do it.

21st August 1818

About Young Police, he said in the evening, coming down all in a hurry: 'Is x x x gone upstairs?' 'Yes, just gone.' 'Oh then I just missed him. I ran down the back stairs from xxx's room whilst he was coming up the front ones.'

22 August 1818

He told me of his intention to appoint another ADC and expressed his objections to one not having his family here, as he would in that case expect to live in the House[55].

His sudden change about Bear merely because he told him about Shrug's recalling our Neighbour's 'sa gloire' after Buggiardo had been arguing with him. No more objection to forwarding his dispatches. He now saw things in their proper light, and had entirely changed his opinion. Quite a favourite all at once.

25th August

Fisico Primo [Dr. Baxter] told me about Polisson having shown him the letters of Donna [Lady Lowe] in case of not claiming them again, and his saying he had looked into the inside and on his asking him what he thought they might be about, the other answering perhaps it was some complaint. He said that she had told him some time before that it was she who was the cause of Incumbent's being retained, but she would also be the cause of his being sent away. Also his boasting to him of receiving letters from her, telling him the white lad was his, and repeatedly speaking to him about her D . . . k . . g [?drinking] so much; and his curtailing all the allowances to the menials, allowing Mrs. Abigail only one glass after dinner, and none to Old Mother B—— after she recovered, cutting it off from the amount of people's bills. His

Napoleon on board H.M.S. *Bellerophon* in 1815 with members of his staff,
L. to R., Planat, Montholon, Dr Maingault, Las Cases, Savary, Lallemand,
Bertrand, and young Emmanuel Las Cases.

St Helena. Jamestown and the Harbour.

The Governor, Sir Hudson Lowe.

Napoleon as Emperor.

deduction about necessity [?] for refusing wine to Old Abigail whilst she was so ill before she went home, and eggs which were really necessary, which she was obliged herself to buy.

27th August

Fisico observed upon the rude blackguard treatment he experienced from Mach.

On his not answering him when he wished him Good Morning, and observing also how Nincumpoop on that day after dinner about [how] B——— had wounded [?] Admiral Plampin.

28th August

Polisson [mentioned] about Donna's relenting and ordering 3 fiaschi [bottles] to Abigail's stanza [room] and next evening repeating that before Fisico [Baxter] and Grazzioso [Lyster], and saying she had appropriated it all to herself.

29th August

Fisico: Donna's occhi [Lady Lowe's eyes] those of a tigress. Mach's [Lowe] remaining in her camera [room] when he was asking about her piscio orduro [muddy urine] and shifting gocci sanguinosi [drops of blood]. Observing to Nincumpoop [Reade] how damned dangerous. His encouraging Mach to persevere in sending felucca [the ship] to Ethiopia in the present state of its crew, and the consequence notwithstanding his advice of the contrary. But even the lives of men were of no consequence to him, Nincumpoop, as long as he could only carry his point and show his influence over Mach. That fellow did not care a damn about men's lives to attain his object. His telling such downright lies the preceding evening about Major B——— being at Baltimore when [he was] left at Washington; and his insisting upon it.

30th August

Old Mach's readiness to receive portion of the Estimates, saying he would not mind appointing an extra clerk for that purpose; and his reluctance in relieving me, though the former got a handsome allowance.

Young Polisson said that Donna, for something sent her up charged at 6, sent back word she would only give 4.

H.N.E.—4

1st September 1818

Mach came to me when writing, and enquired of me in a most suspicious and earnest way whether I had not seen the book in French recently [?] written on himself. He repeatedly put the question to me. And also of the one written from the Cape, evidently suspecting I had them in my possession.

4 September 1818

He positively asserted that he had given me the confab of Chemay [?] with Shrug, that he recollected the circumstances of giving it me, and that it must be away in my papers, though I assured him I had not seen or known of one between those two. He however persisted and after searching among all his papers he said perhaps he might have it, and next day he brought it down to me.

6 September 1818

Polisson told me Donna [Lady Lowe] had sent for him to say that if he wished to see her she would be glad if he would go now. Then she told him: 'Well I have at last got x x x x to send away Yam Stock [Den Taafe][56] he was of no use.' And she told him of the intended successor and piccinina's day to Batezzare. [Battezzare—to baptise.]

7 September 1818

Mach again spoke to me about the new adjutant, hinting about my taking charge of piquets. He did not wish to have another man in the house, speaking again of Mr. John in lieu of Dn Taff.

7 September 1818

Donna ridiculed in the most indecent way the appearance of Mrs. Vignoble [Mrs. Wynyard] the preceding day which was the first time of her appearance out to dinner since she had parturita [given birth to boy.] She mentioned her dress, her looks, the manner in which her clothes and the flowers on her head were huddled upon her as if thrown at her, and as if she really had been endeavouring to make herself look as ridiculous as she possibly could. She wondered how she could make herself so absurd and appealed to me if I had observed her. I answered I never could recollect the dress but that I thought she looked very well. 'I wonder how you can think so. For my part I never saw anything so strange as her appearance altogether, and I am sure I never saw her look worse.'

12 September 1818

He told me he meant to give MD [? Verling] the difference to make up his pay to £1 per day, as Magnesia [O'Meara] had no more. Then the next day all at once he desired to pay him £1 besides the pay.

13 September [1818]

When the storeship had arrived and the bag had not come up yet, Donna said that's because Nincumpoop is not in town. His being in town makes all the difference in the world.

16th September 1818

The Marquis [Montchenu] mentioned that Malcolm thought the Baron [Stürmer] knew of the circumstances of the handkerchief and things brought by Welle.[57] He observed to me afterwards 'What a damned busy fellow that was.'

18 September 1818

Yesterday he desired me to send for Vignoble to copy the letter to be written by him about the refunding, which he had shown me and done, unasked for this time, and all in good humour. He asked me this morning to let him look at it, saying 'do you think it is clear, will they understand it in this manner?' Upon which I pointed out that the alteration to 'the last of the above periods' would make it, I thought, more so. He began knitting his brows and working himself into a gust of passion, saying if it was not clear to them at the Treasury that he, himself, did not understand it, and would not therefore send any letter about it. What business had he to say anything about a sum of £86.18.6. He then began calculating the sum, to see how far back I was to repay, and finished by saying he had no doubt it was meant from as far back as Lord W. B's having the command. I said I could not think that was intended. It never could have been the intention to treat me so unjustly as to deprive me of pay for the time I was acting at Genoa, the right of the appointment of Ms there never could be disputed, as it was agreeable to P.R.'s warrant. For it would be treating me cruelly to carry back the retrospect so far. He again began calculating saying that he could

not, nor was he bound to endeavour to, get me more than 18 days
from the 18th June to the 5th July, that the rest was my own battle
and it was my business to fight. He then became furious, foaming
at the mouth and spluttering, exclaiming that my observation of the
injustice (the words I had a short time before used) was a reflection
upon him. It was a reproach to him. This I immediately denied,
saying it was a mere remark of mine that it would be an injustice
from the Treasury if I was called upon to refund so far back. He
said it was a reflection cast upon him by me, as if he was bound to
see my claim satisfied in spite of the Treasury, and that it was said
with a great deal of ill temper from me. He would not suffer it, and
desired it should not happen again. He had neglected his own business with the Treasury to attend to mine, mentioning repeatedly
that he had taken the greatest interest in this matter, neglecting his
own concerns to attend to mine. I told him it was now 4 months
since I ought to have answered the Treasury's letter, but that I had
deferred it so as not to trespass upon his time; that I would not have
even troubled him about it had not the letter come addressed to him,
that this was the first occasion upon which I ever had put him to the
trouble of writing about me, that I never occupied his time before
about anything respecting myself, nor did I ever wish to do it in the
most trifling degree. He said what business had he to be bothered
about it. It was a matter that I ought to apply about to Lord Wm.
and General H. L. He walked out and returned three times in the
most furious way, repeating that what I had said was a reflection
upon him, that the Treasury letter was a swipe at him which he did
not like, that it was blaming him for appointing me, and making
him responsible for Colonel Burrows, that I had no business to get
pay beyond the 5th July. He made the same unfeeling observation
again as when I first spoke to him, that the sum was not worth
writing so much about, that he never would have thought that for
£20 so much would have been said as had already been done about
it, though he himself thought just before it was £86.18.6. besides
what I had already refunded. However he would try and get me the
allowance up to the 5th July; that he was prepared to do, but that
was all I had any right to expect from him.

18th [? September 1818]

He found Earl B's [Lord Bathurst] warrant, for custody of
Napoleon Bonaparte, which he had some months before declared
he had given me to put up; and he said he had never seen it before.

He found it then in so cunning a place, that he had himself forgotten it. He would not allow Nincumpoop's commis [clerk] to assist in copying the Warrant, nor O.O. Nk. [Orderly Officer Captain George Nicholls], which I asked for, because he would not, he said, let him so much into the secret; although two days before he said: 'Employ him in copying communications to N.B. [Napoleon Bonaparte)'. And this was of no importance whatsoever.

19th September 1818

Vignoble mentioned to me Mach having refused him Francis. 'The Beast'.

September 1818

Donna spoke to me on my remarking (when she spoke of the man Francis having mislaid so many things) that I doubted he must have had a hand in stealing the number of penknives out of the office. Why, she told me, it was your John; and said that she always found him in the morning about the office or library, reading and looking over things. However she added 'now he is found out of course. It's evident'. He only wanted to get suspicion off himself.

24th or 25th September 1818

Grazzioso observed to him on the discovery about Magnesia, 'What a pity it was he had that last interview with our Neighbour.' He replied 'Oh it was a thousand pities that business of yours happening, for had it not happened I would not have entrusted the business to Vignoble. It was Young Staff I intended to charge with it. He was the person fixed upon at all events. It should have been somebody else than Vignoble.'

24th September 1818

Donna inveighed against Racer for his demonstration of anger at not winning the game.

25 September [1818]

Donna's lamentation about the tiresome afternoon she had spent in consequence of Mrs. Vignoble's calling upon her, and her asking to see the fanciulla's [child's] clothes. She was taking her off and mocking her way of asking her, imitating her voice etc. . . . and this before Racer, Grazzioso, Eurydice and others and inveighing against her ancella [maid-servant] and balia [nurse] always running into the room with Signora Vignoble or her bambini.

26th September 1818

Nincumpoop said to me Providatore [Balcombe] was a great scoundrel, as great a rogue as Magnesia.[21]

26th September 1818

Vignoble told me that Platonian had asked Domine to part friends with Nincumpoop, but that he replied he should have always the same opinion of him, he was a damn buggiardo and he might tell him so.

27 September [1818]

The way he came up to my room when I sent word for Croad [Lieutenant Frederick Croad of the 66th Foot Regiment] to return, under the impression Old Nick [Nicholls] had not received the letter for Mrs. Shrug [Bertrand]. The rude way he went on and his lamentation that, of all things in the world, it should have failed to have been delivered (though after it had been dispatched he wanted to have it back again, and if the orderly had not been too long gone he would have sent off after him). He said that he had so clearly explained to me how it was to be sent, under an open envelope, and that if Old Nick was not there he was to take it out of it and deliver it himself. I told him that that was my proposition, but he had not assented to it. He talked of sending it under cover to the Officer of the Guard. But when I observed it was an officer of the 20th and a stranger, he gave up that idea and left the room saying, what I understood to be, 'Send it to Mr. C . . . d.' His name was certainly the last word mentioned. He railed all the time about it, and repeated that he had particularly explained it as he had before said; which was not the case, for there was no possibility of making head or tail of it, except as I took it. He went away and immediately said that the letter had been regularly delivered as the Orderly met Old Nick on the road who took it from under the envelope and delivered it.

27th September 1818

Speaking of Paradox's note to me calling him a scoundrel. 'Don't you see by this he is a scoundrel.'

28th September 1818

His readiness to give Fisico Primo [Dr. Baxter] double increase though Medico 53rd only the ordinary increase. His arguing in the instance of the two letters that it was never intended their increases should be doubled tho' he did it for lieutenants of 7 years and Brevet captains. These were in consideration of long service and to make up for want of promotion, and they deserved it. Besides he was left to act to fix the pay as he thought proper. However if Medico 66th claimed the difference he would give it to him when he came back.

Mach tried on several occasions when he wished to say offensive things to make me write the letters without saying 'by his desire, direction or order', by that manner shaking off all responsibility and bringing the odium upon me if reported. One to Providatore [Balcombe] and one to Magnesia [O'Meara] were sent in this way and others written out but afterwards not sent which I meant to object to. One I did, the long one to Magnesia, which it was first intended I should sign and to which, in consequence of what I said, 'by his direction' was added. He never tried this with Nincumpoop or Vignobles. Mr. Thornton to Mach calling on [torn fragment of page] . . . his 'amiable and valued correspondence'.

29th September 1818

He said 'now you might begin copying this letter as some of the sheets are ready to copy.' On my answering, 'very well I should begin immediately' and on my making a move to rise, he called out 'Oh I would prefer having it written by Nincumpoop.' He added to his dispatch from me, note about Providatore taking no commission, though he had no recollection of the precise words, making it quite a different account, introducing something about his wife which I told him was not the case, and some other part about solemn assurances, and quite different from mine, and from which he was all this time copying.

29th September 1818

Donna told Mach at the Dinner of the horrid looks he gave at the preceding dinner. For her part she could not bear to see him look in that way.

The Office compared by Donna to cause the feeling experienced on entering a church's vault for its dampness, and notwithstanding only one day of fire in it during the whole winter and the wettest season known here. After this hint and my observing the state of the angle and recess where I work being covered with a green mould

one inch thick, fires were lighted (as it was in the breakfast and
ordinary day's dinner room) after this, and after I had suffered most
severely from rheumatism for 2 months. A few days previous
to this observation of Donna, on my making him observe the damp
state of the walls where I was obliged to write daily, he answered
'Oh, of course that's because there has been no fire lighted in that
room all this year and this is the most exposed room of the House to
the weather.' This notwithstanding he had heard me complain of
rheumatism.

Donna's innuendo and jealousy when the recess was made for my
writing. 'Ah you can find plenty of spare time for making all these
sort of things, but not to make chests of drawers for the rooms that
want them.' I believe nearly all the rooms were supplied with these,
but at all events it was a thing scarcely ever made use of, except in
their own room, the others being only slept in by strangers a night
or so at a time.

3rd October

Donna's ridicule of Mrs. Vignoble's appearance and dress at the
dance, the day before.

3rd October

Mach, when anxious to ascertain our Neighbour's presence, said
he would have a hole bored through the ceiling, if he would not
show himself, and set people there to peep through and watch him.
He proposed to O.O. [Orderly Officer] to sneak about the windows
in the evening and put his ears and peep in at the crevices of the
shutters, and afterwards told me how odd it was that people seemed
to conceive these things as such matters of delicacy, people that
ought to have no means contemned.

6 October 1818

Vignoble remarked that Donna's [behaviour] must have been from
drink, she so behaved talking bawdy before his wife. I replied that
[on] the 3rd she talked in a kind of stammer as if really in that state.

8 October 1818

Mach's rage with Veritas [Montholon] when, in the confab, he
first mentioned Magnesia having told them he wanted him to be
una spia [a spy] and afterwards telling me he'd be damned if he

would not denounce Shrug [Bertrand] by this occasion of *Racoon* [a ship] if any proposition was made about Henrico il Medico [Dr. Henry].

8 October 1818

Nincumpoop [Reade] at his country house observed how extraordinary it was Fisico Henrico [Dr. Henry] should have been called by Shrug's wife [Bertrand's], and immediately after having told Fisico Primo [Dr. Baxter] he did not wish to go to the Cape, though the night previous he had shown himself so desirous to go there, and settled it all with Fisico Primo. 'It looks very odd; there must be something in it, depend upon it; it's damn strange.' 'I'll be damned,' said Mach, pacing the room with animation and full of anger, red in the face, 'if there is not an intrigue. You are right, Nincumpoop; that fellow [Dr. Henry] is intriguing to be appointed medico to our Neighbour [Napoleon] and Shrug [Bertrand] is doing it for him, it's evident. I am sure of it or why should he have withdrawn from the arrangements made with Fisico Primo.' After [he had been] going on in this way sometime, I had been recollecting the matter and being certain, I said the arrangement was only made after his being called in and proved; adding, and therefore that could not have been the cause of it. I attempted to justify Henrico saying that he was asked for. I should conceive it proceeded from the Shrug's having frequently met him and being well acquainted. Some days afterwards when he was saying again "Damn me, but Nincumpoop was right about it. It is an intrigue, depend upon it', I said I conceived it was a premature decision, and to suspend his opinion until he had some grounds to go upon, which he had not then.

9 October 1818

Fisico Primo's [Dr. Baxter] tirade in speaking to Mach against Rt. [Regimental] Engineer's having stated it would require 3 years to complete the Chateau [New Longwood House[58]]. He might as well have said at once it could not be done at all. Mach, on this, firing up, declaimed against much ridiculous talks and said he had better at once say he could not do it, and he would himself be bound to finish it in as many months as he mentioned years. Then he talked about Hobhouse's work 'Last reign of our Neighbour', condemning his praise of him and saying it was poor stuff. Fisico observed he had not himself read it, and from what he heard Regt.

H.N.E.—4*

Engineer saying, he thought it had been a good thing, but Emmett was very fond of such writings; it was exactly in his way. Asked if he had seen it. No, he had not.

Mach praised the construction, exclaiming with affectation and self importance what a damned lucky fellow our Neighbour was to have so good a one, to be so well lodged as he would be. What kind of one did he inhabit?

Mach never once bowing or returning any of Veritas's [Montholon] civilities when he escorted us to the door, except merely on leaving the first room, and in an ungracious way and at times not at all. Always looked surly and irritated when he went out, tho' himself extremely observant of this and very rigid if they failed in etiquette towards himself. His angry looks and peevish choleric way of speaking when Shrug was the topic of Veritas.

He insisted frequently and asserted positively that Veritas had repeated several times that the matter was settled with regard to Medico then in attendance, tho' I said I never understood it in that light, and that he had not spoken so decidedly.[59] He even made me alter something in my mode of putting it down tho' not to the extent he wanted me [to do]. Though at the confab of 23rd October Veritas put out of doubt my being right. Now he altered that batch of confabs as not correct.

N.B.—He insisted in a very sulky way, at the first confab with Jesuit, that something I had put down had not been said, though I was quite positive of it; and also something that Magnesia said to me after one of the first actions with him and which he would not allow to remain appearing, saying 'Ah, but that was said to you but not to me. That's nothing to me'; tho' I was reporting to him.

October 9

His anger because I had returned Cairns the journals, but without first asking him. Day of *Racoon's* sailing. Vignoble spoke of repeated grievances and the probability of his going before his 5 years were over, and particularly now as he might get something in the household of some of the newly married royalty merely to get quit of that beast at once.

21 October [? 1817 or 1818]

Donna talked about who made good mariti [husbands]. She certainly did not think Vignoble a good tempered one; but thought

he however made a good husband. Very small party. Frog [Mont-
chenu] and Grazzioso [Colonel Lyster] present.

Nincumpoop and the caricature about Old Frog [Montchenu]
and Long Gut which I brought down to show to the Autrichien
[Stürmer]. He snapped it up immediately afterwards, but denied it
afterwards when Donna asked him about it in his presence. I said
he had it. Later at Castle which he was using I saw it a minute
before he left off writing, at his elbow. The moment he was gone I
searched for it, and the sergeant that day and the next, and when I
asked him a few days later [illegible]. . . .

26 or 27 October 1818

Mach said how completely foiled Magnesia had been in all his
plans. He expected he would have mentioned him by name in
aviso [advice], in order that he might be able to say 'altho' he had
named me and has this against me, he notwithstanding can't do
without me, he can't send me off'. By not using his name had
completely defeated all his plans and by taking measures, notwithstanding the name did not appear, to ruin his character on the
Island, he had succeeded in producing the same effect as if his name
had really appeared on it. Mach had often said to me in confabs
'You seem to have put down anything they said, or everything that
is favourable to them, but not all things I said'. Altho' himself
constantly changing things, tho' knowing, and afterwards having
acknowledged, them correct, many days after having been put
down. Sometimes he would have nearly all expressions in French,
at others all in English.

He proposed to alter the letter to Swell [Sir George Bingham]
altho' he had had it read to the Corps. He curtailed it, saying it was
only a verbal communication and he could therefore alter it as he
chose before he sent a copy of it home. But on my saying it was
better not, he gave up the idea.

Mach wrote to Old Frog [Montchenu] that even captain of
English ships [at Citta ? Malta] in the company's service were
never permitted to communicate from on land—though it is
notorious many did (witness mileastro [?] and whalers).

At one time not permitting clerk to write anything that went
with dispatch. Alone a whole week composing an aviso, and in
preparing an abstract of Regulations which were never completed
for Commissaires. Henry Goldridge [Henry Goulburn][60] said that
the 2nd Polyphemes [Malcolm][61] had appeared in Journals as to

be appointed one of the chiefs of his service, but His Lordship did not know whether accidently inserted or designed, and that His Lordship had however enquired of the head of the chiefs, who had assured him it had never been in contemplation and desired Mach to give the most peremptory denial to it.

Nothing can be more decisive of their approbation of my activity, said Mach, and of their disapproving of the other. He is now a marked character. He had done for himself and he never will be employed again.

Also authority to restrict commissaires, and though not precisely admitting all his suspicions yet evidently giving him their concurrence [?] in it.

About King Coly Coly [Cole], he had a great mind to deprive him of his situation for speaking favourably of Providatore's innocence and pretending not to know the contents of catched [? cached] epistles.

October [1818]

Observation. How long did not Mach inveigh against the present habitation of our Neighbour as not being a good one; but on the contrary frequently saying it was one of the worst that could have been selected both for comfort and security. And all at once changing his tune and saying to Veritas [Montholon] and to me, it was the best on the Island under every point of view and he was so glad it was being built there at last. His extraordinary change and his vacillation, determined on giving in to Veritas to say he agreed [?] about the letter [undecipherable]. Soon after he said could it not go in when he [? agreed]; and then became as obstinately bent against it. My advice now was simply to give him an answer for that moment— and his contrary opinion.

2 November 1818

On looking over the newspaper and seeing the paper given me by Shrug he said 'Ah here is the paper you were sent from Bertrand; I told you at the time you ought not to have received it'. I remarked: 'I beg your pardon, Sir, at the time you expressed yourself pleased I had done so. It was only some time afterwards you disapproved of it.' He answered in his usual style of asperity 'I beg your pardon, I disapproved of it at the time.' After reading the newspapers, he said: 'It was the papers given by Pierron I approved of, not that one.' To which I made no answer.

How could it, when that was the only paper I brought on that occasion, those of Pierron being on another occasion.[62]

3 November

The day he had a good mind to commit some arbitrary act about Bertrand. 'Such a damn fellow as that deserved it.'

9 November

Day Officer, Old Nick [Nicholls], came down St. James. Nincumpoop looking over his letter, observed that the paragraph was a damn impertinent one. If he was Mach, he would give it to him handsomely. He deserved to get a damned good rowing. 'Do you know,' he added, 'what he writes so for? Why, to get his letters published, that they may come before the Parliament.' However when Mach spoke to Old Nick about it, he explained it satisfactorily. (Note xx: Immediately afterwards both Mach and Nincumpoop retired to a distance in close confab, and after talking a long time rejoined us; and after Old Nick went away, Mach said to me there was a good deal of change lately in Nick, that was because he was seen thro'.) 'I see through him now, what kind of man he is. He expects these letters will be brought before the Parliament, that they will be published.' He expressed much regret at having chosen him, but it was the fault of his predecessor Captain Blakeney who left him no peace till he had relieved him. While he was lecturing Nick, Nincumpoop spoke out observing that his predecessor saw him much oftener than himself. All along he was inflaming Mach against him, and said to me before the confab 'what a damned fellow Mach was.'

Giovanni Prete [Rev. Vernon], was the first cause of the gift of the Scatola [snuff-box] being found out, as it was him first told Fisico No 1, [Dr. Baxter] who ran to Nincumpoop [Reade] with it.

Giovanni Prete also repeated to Prete Vascello [Ship's chaplain] what Polyphemes [Admiral Plampin] had said viz., that if Robinson Crusoe [Mr. Robinson] had 4 parchments he would make him lose them all for taking so little care of his store. All of which Prete Vascello repeated on board and to chirurgo of Vascello [Surgeon of the Vessel *Conqueror* i.e. Dr. Stokoe].

9 November

Nincumpoop observed to Mach that R.A. were jealous about new Lieut. Colonel St. Helena Regiment wearing same uniform as theirs,

and that Major Mighty [Power] and his lieutenant were in the
greatest rage about it he ever saw. It was a damned shame that the
Old Fellow should have brought out such a uniform as that. 'It is',
answered Mach, 'damned impertinent.'

'I'll take care they shan't wear it. Order them immediately to
leave it off and assure Major Mighty that I disapprove of it and
have ordered them to discontinue it.' He then added he wished he
had known Major Mighty was coming out before he left England. 'I
would have got him the rank so that he might have had the command
of the whole company but I shall arrange it so that he shall have the
management of the whole.'

A day or two previous Mach had observed that the Archbishop
[Rev. Richard Boys] had been the cause of the Johnny Cos' letter,
in which were subjects of disapprobation again of Polyphemes
[Admiral Plampin], who talked of bringing Giovanni Prete [Rev.
Vernon] to an account for it, and I believe, even wrote to him about
it, and to know his authority. Giovanni Prete was obliged to send
copies of his plichi [letter] from Vecchio Prete [Rev. Boys] to Old
Mache [Lowe][63].

10th November 1818

Fisico Primo [Dr. Baxter] said to me just before dinner at the
Castle how Mach had behaved last time he was at the Pen [? Inn]—
sulky—those freezing looks, never spoke to him or Major Mighty
who was with him but kept frowning in a corner, it was brutal.
Nincumpoop's seizure of Frog 9 November.

12 November 1818

Donna [Lady Lowe] said before Nincumpoop and Phaeton
[Captain of H.M.S. *Phaeton*] that the first time she played loto was
the evening Vignoble got into such a rage with her about something
she said. Observing to Nincumpoop 'Do you recollect how angry he
was?' 'Do I indeed, that I do. I shall never forget his look. How
angry he was, to be sure.'

16 November 1818

His rage when I mentioned to him that Old Frog [Montchenu]
had observed that the Prince Regent ship was at anchor off the town
whereas he thought all vessels, except those belonging to the government or the company, were sent to Lemon Valley. He said he had

also observed another at anchor besides the first, which he knew
had been there 2 days. He would take care when he came back that
he should hear more about it.

November 20

Donna spoke of Mrs. Vignoble, abusing her kit, and saying that
she had only the gown she bought here (that had come out for the
Providatore's figli) fit to wear. She was surprised she had come out
here so badly provided. She brought scarcely anything with her.

About 26th November 1818

Mach observed to Nincumpoop that he would not be surprised if
the note written by the Northern Bear [Balmain] about Magnesia
got him sent on a visit to Siberian Court.

28th November 1818

Donna censured Frightened Rabbit for giggling all the time at
Dinner the day before with Vignoble. They never ceased from the
minute they sat down. She never saw such rude behaviour. As for
Vignoble he had his back turned to Perroquet's second daughter
and never bothered to take the least notice. Quizzing Vignoble's
wife about an old comb with only 2 or 3 teeth.

28th November

Goose given to Old Nick. Said after he went away he saw how to
proceed with such a man, to avoid employing him as much as
possible and when he had anything to communicate to them, to do
it through one of us, through Vignoble or Nincumpoop.

In the latter end of Nov.

Young Polisson (Donna said) had mentioned to her that Young
Rt. [Regimental] staff and Young Brick and Mortar would not
sleep in same room with Grazzioso Giovanni on account of the otto
of to . . . ho, and that Young Polisson had gone into his camera
[room] that morning, after he went away, and found the wash stand
boccale [jug] of water untouched. Her high disapproval of the two
young herres [men] accepting letti [beds] there and refusing to
double up. They should not however be indulged.

She spoke about Mrs. Vignoble, as Polisson inferred [about] her using the Faisca [bottle] of her Pickaninny No 1.

Donna's great displeasure at the Vignobles not sending riscontri [answers] to provocations [i.e. invitations].

3rd December 1818

On letter arriving by Captain of ship *Palmist* complaining of his not embarking plants from R.I., in the first gust he threatened to make a representation to 3rd Polyphemes [Admiral]. He immediately afterwards referred to a letter to 2nd Polyphemes. When he read that part that says: 'In consequence of his good conduct', he said, 'look Captain' (reading it out loud to me) 'what that damn fellow [Admiral] Sir P. Malcolm said in answer to my complaint against Capt. H. What a damn rascal that Malcolm was to be sure.'

9 December 1818

Mach having found some observations in a recent French publication, a fictitious description of our Neighbour's [Napoleon] escape, came up to me with it saying how much this fortified him in his idea about preventing any kind of communication and visiting as much as possible. He added that when designing and ill-disposed men such as 2nd Polyphemes and Magnesia, or [other] fools, thought of such stuff and when they said that being seen before ships sailed was sufficient, and that there was no harm in his going about under less restraint or in his speaking to those he meets or receiving visits, it was necessary to be far more on his guard. He spoke with so much earnestness and so long about it, that it looked exactly as if he suspected me.

10 December

When the Providatore's letter was opened by Cattiva Aria [Fowler] and shown to Mach he exclaimed:—'they had better not remove me or I'll raise such a clatter about their heads that will astonish them'.

11 December

Mach met me in the Library door asking me if I had seen the newspapers, he could not find them, it was really very odd, he had been searching all about the office and could not find them. It was very extraordinary. Had I taken them into my room? I went immediately after this in to the office and the first thing on the long table I saw was that. Nothing else was on that table and they had been there the whole forenoon.

Going to Deadwood to pranzare [dine] with 66th. On overtaking Nincumpoop [Reade] he [Lowe] desired me to pass on as he wanted to speak to Ninny [Reade]. I merely rode up nearer when he first spoke, but on his repeating distinctly and loud so that I could not mistake it, I passed on and trotted off to Camp. On his arrival there he told me he expected I would have gone over to the new building. [He asked] what made me ride off to Camp? [I answered] because he had desired me to ride in front, as he wished to speak to Ninny, and I thought best to come on when I found that he wanted to speak to him in private. He said he had not said that, but only wanted me to ride on, at his side, and that I had mistaken him. I said I understood him to speak as above mentioned. Then I had mistaken him, he replied.

12 December

Mach said the only one to blame was Polyphemes for opening letters. His was the only instance, the only act that could really be complained of, for he opened a letter he ought not to have done. Who desired him? What business had he to do it? He was the last person to have done it.

14 December

Mach on reading Act of Parliament about Post Office, said that he had authority according to that to open all letters thought proper. He was Secretary of State. He was more, he was representative of H.M. and had an undoubted right to open any one that came by post whenever he thought it necessary, and it was a right he should exercise hereafter more than he had hitherto done. He would more minutely ascertain what letters were received here.

14 December 1818

Mach said Sir G. C. [Cockburn] was no great thing, and that on his first arrival he seemed rather inclined to throw difficulties in his way than assist him. Though he behaved better afterwards[64].

19 December 1818

When Polyphemes applied about the Farina [Flour], he said it was a damned impertinent letter, it was damned illiberal, all a trick to get good to give bad in return, it was damned unfair and damn him if he would not throw him on his back for it too.

23rd December 1818

Mach's fuss about old Nick's [Nicholls] letter of 14th December which was not to be found and which, he said, I had. [He said] that he had given it me and that I must have it. I said I had not had it since he put it up with some other papers to take to Town, from where he made Nincumpoop write to Fisico Primo on the subject. That he had not returned it to me since. He said he certainly had not taken it down to Town and he must have put it back in preparing notes if he had not given it me back. I replied, if he had put it back it must have been in one of the wrong pigeon holes as it was not in Old Nick's. I then looked in some of them, but could not find it and Old Nick was sent to for copy.

25th December 1818

Mach asked me about a letter from Old Polyphemes respecting Bruin [?]. I looked in the pigeon hole and examined them all, but told him I could not find it. He evidently assumed he had given it to me the day before. I replied, begging his pardon, that when I took up the letters from Polyphemes which he had thrown on the table, I examined them all and docketed them, but it was not among them. He then roundly and loudly asserted that he had put it down along with the others on the table, and it was doubled up with others in my hand. I casually said it certainly was not among them when I took them up. He said that upon his honour it was. And I again begged his pardon, saying it certainly was not on the table when I took them up. I looked at any papers upon it. He said angrily: 'By your manner of speaking it seems as if paramount to saying I did not put it down, after my giving my word to you I did.

I replied I only said it was not on the table or among the letters which I took up. But, he said, it appeared by my mode of speaking as if I questioned what he said. He again replied: 'I gave you my word of honour that I put it down on the table with the other letters.' And then pausing a moment, he added, putting his hand in his pocket at the same time, 'though I possibly might have taken it up again, and put it in my pocket.' Whereupon in fact he immediately found it with two others that I had not before seen, from the same person. This was after quibbling that notwithstanding that he could assure me upon his honour he had thrown it down with the others upon the table, though he afterwards took it up again.

28 December 1818

Mach said after Old Nick had gone away how necessary it was in general to give one's instructions in writing. Had he done so some time before to Old Nick it would have been enough, without saying anything more, to have removed him from his situation.

30 December 1818

His anger on receiving Old Nick's note saying some persons had seen him. 'I never saw such a damned fellow as that,' he exclaimed. 'It is impossible I can get on with such a shuffling fellow. He wants to throw all responsibility off his shoulders upon mine. It is all a damn trick. I see clearly into it now.' He was sure he had seen Shrug's letter when he said 'une conscience à lui.' Magnesia [Dr Henry], he was certain, had shown it to him or got Roman Candlestick [Lieut. McCarthy], his cousin, to do so for him—for he must have seen it. He would not allow him to proceed in that kind of way any longer and act upon his own opinion. Little Poppleton was the only one who did his duty properly and knew how to do it.

30 December 1818

Donna said she would never go again to a Hop or a Shew. The people here are so rude and impertinent. They shew no attention either to myself or Mach. She however perhaps expected too much, she said.

31 December 1818

Old Mach desired a part to be left out of the copy of Old Nick's letter of the 14th instant, saying that part was not in the original he was perfectly sure. However on my looking in the original which I found, it was there also.

Chapter Three
1819 Feuds and Factions

1st January 1819

Young Polisson told me that Donna had said to him that the Vignobles sent for the Vettura [carriage]. 'It's not mine. It is la Signora Vignoble's.' 'Oh she must have it of course, it's hers.' Was angry because he had got the other [?] mended, saying, because it was for Mrs. Vignoble he did it so soon, not for herself. 'I can't bear the sight of those people, she is a nasty woman and he is a nasty man.'

3 January 1819

Mach said he wished he could have kept Robinson Crusoe here a little longer. He would have contrived to interest him so as to get him to take a share in the business. Crusoe was just the man who could have analysed it for him. He would have assisted him in his answer to the Chronicle. Would have been highly useful to him.

8th January 1819

His rage with Old Nick [Nicholls] on 20 December. Furious gust of passion about Bear's [Balmain] Note and on the 25th December saying he is a damned shuffling impertinent little rascal which same expression had been used by Nincumpoop on 21st.

His observing to me I was as much concerned in this business as himself, and in the whole of his correspondence putting my name as much forward as he possibly could.

9 January 1819

At breakfast as Stercoraceous and Pick Axe were at breakfast he said in a petulant ungracious way: 'It is very odd now that in this island there is not a literary character, not one, who could even sit down and answer [?] this book in the Times [?].' I said no there isn't one.

14 January 1819

He insisted that all letters to Autrichien [Stürmer] were not entered in the book, particularly he said in July about the time of his departure. That he had been looking for two hours and could not find some of those he knew he had written, and they could not have been entered. It was very extraordinary. It was of no use my assuring him all were entered, he still kept insisting they were not. The one he now wanted, he positively asserted to have been in July. I told him again they were all entered and that that letter was much farther back than July. 'No', he said positively, 'it was not before July, it was a very long one.' 'Could I,' he asked me, 'account for it?' I again told him that that one was entered as all others that he ever gave me. After grumbling a little while longer he at last deigned to look farther back, I believe in May, and there found all he wanted entered in regular succession, and tho' he stated he had been searching for 2 hours, he had not for more than $\frac{1}{4}$ of an hour at the utmost.

18th January

He said he would give an order for Followers not to wear tri-colour cockades and if they presumed afterwards to leave Longwood with it, he would order a file of men to tear it out of their hats. It was encouraging a party here.

19 January

His treatment of Old Nick until the poor fellow could [not] retain his tears, flying at him like a tiger—for giving him copy of my letter to Shrug, tho' he had said to me the day before it was of little importance whether he did or not. Contrary instructions given by him in the same breath, one moment asserting one thing and the next completely contradictory.

His telling me there was no necessity for keeping copy of my palavar with Bear and Frog on 18th January. This however was evidently because there was something in it he would not have had recorded and sent home viz. the reproach about his not giving them information.

On first arrival on the island when the pagar [pay] was being settled, his vanity and vapouring, saying it was left to him to settle as he thought proper. He did not care about Secretary of War or the book of War Office regulations. The Secretary of War had nothing to do with it.[1] He was only responsible to minister Bathurst, it was for him to settle it as he thought proper. This was when I argued against the mode he proposed to settle for increase of pay for high service, allowing it double in some cases and only the ordinary amount in others and his wanting to increase drawings of Staff [?] to that of the company which would have given them as much as to Corporals.

Had Magnesia brought the message from Madame Veritas [Montholon] which Lingo [Dr. Verling] did—to know what she owed him—or had he accompanied Shrug's wife and son all round Francis Plain in fact, what would have been the consequences!

Lingo and Shrug [Bertrand] family only came back at 8 o'clock p.m.

20th January

He told me few days previous, Chirurgo Primo [Dr. Baxter] was here for no other purpose than for our Neighbour, and today that he was here for many other purposes.

20 January 1819

When I mentioned to him that Old Brick and Mortar [Major Emmett] had told me about his snub, the rage he worked himself into.[2] He said the latter had held very extraordinary arguments for saying that our Neighbour was right in holding out, that he was very intimate with Lady Polyphemes No 1 and that her husband who was a great visitor there, had the same opinion and talked in the same strain as they did. [He also said] that if he was obliged to write officially to him he would work him up and report his conduct at home, and he would send home copies of all he wrote and his opinion of him, that he had behaved very ungratefully to him, for he had been particularly attentive to him, and had it been any other person he would not have allowed him to have kept his post so long. Though he told me afterwards he had not known for more than a month that he was a foreigner, I am certain he must have known it on board ship or at all events soon after arrival, as I heard the circumstances mentioned in his hearing long ago. He had been recommended to him and he had been very civil to him, and he did not deserve this from him, if he had a bad temper he was very sulky. But he had better take care and not be on his P's and Q's with him. He would sooner send away the whole batch of Bricks and Mortars men [the engineers building New Longwood House] than that he should keep the man. He wanted then to throw all the responsibility upon me. [He said] that it was my business to have it all settled without his interference, as it was me who had pointed out to him that it was not right they should be about the house at Longwood. It was a great piece of presumption in Young Brick and Mortar [Lieut. Wortham] hesitating about it. He ought to have sent him off immediately on the first hint, it was quite [right] for him to know he did not like his being here. 'That note he wrote to me was a damned insolent, impertinent thing on his part.' (This note was addressed to me, marked Private inside and outside, written 'perfectly confidential.' But having by accident laid it down on my writing desk and going to the other cupboard he immediately took it up and read it through). 'I don't know what you may think of it yourself, but damn me I think so.' This was said in his rude overbearing way because I did not answer him in the affirmative when he put for the second time the question, 'Don't you think so? What do you think of it?'—As a snare for my saying yes. He said that it was contrary to his instructions to allow any forestieri [foreigners] to remain here (tho' at this time he had two in his service, had brought 4 with him, one who used to call 'long life' [vive] to our Neighbour [Napoleon] in his own house and where he was kept after knowing it till it became too notorious, and Donna spoke to him in my presence about it). He said that he himself would not bring a French man with him when he left England, and prevented Bear from bringing one, and was very near sending back or objecting to the other two bringing any here. What country was the Fornajo [baker] and Irinetta?

The next morning when dictating for me to write to Brick and Mortar [he said] that he was to send him off because he was a forestiero [foreigner]. I observed to him that there had been others suffered to remain.

January 1819

Mach said Lord B——t's [Bathurst's] duties were all a matter of routine, that it was only the affairs of this place that gave him an opportunity or drew him into notice.

Lord Soo-ta-jin had called on Neighbour; he is informed of this by Fantastico [an orderly].

Speaking of J. C., late commandant at Capri, he said he had no doubt all that was said of him by Count Cla----dri was true, for he was a man of the description to do that, though having just acknowledged the latter as being a bad character. He said that he himself had had a good deal of trouble about him, but he had upset him. He wished that the latter had attacked; how he would have upset him.

January 1819

Mach had given quite a different turn respecting what Old Nick had said about the money paid by Providatore. I said I had not heard it in that light. I understood him to say that it was settled by the bills having been afterwards paid, which were at first pro-tected, and he insisted Nick has asserted that he paid by money they had exclusively received at home.

He was certain it was so. I said I had not understood it thus. A letter which Old Nick had since written out again arrived next morning and confirmed my opinion completely.

He observed about Old Nick 'the stupid fool, he does not under-stand that he is there merely as my instrument to keep me informed of what passes and all he sees or hears.'

21 January 1819

Mach, on seeing some of his own alterations in palavar with Buggiardo of the 17th and wishing to introduce something I did not recollect, said 'we are the most candid and faithful people, in the reports we give of those palavars.' 'By what I saw,' said he, 'of the Polyphemes' notes, he did not seem to be giving particulars or to stand much on the words.'

The rage he got into when I showed him the notes of my palavar with Old Frog [Montchenu]. 'What a damned blasted old fool that fellow is.' Damned blockhead and all this was simply because Frog thought he might have been informed of some of the particulars about Stick [Dr. Stokoe].

His constant abuse of Old Nick.

22 January 1819

Chirurgo Primo [Dr. Baxter]. His insinuating about Domine being always in the company with Magnesia [? Dr. Verling],

Providatore [Ibbetson] and Stick [Dr. Stokoe] and that therefore must at all events have known all they said on the subject of Magnesia and our Neighbour in their conversation—which they could not of course—often speaking before him, as that must have formed the principal topic of their discourses—even if he was not more concerned than that.

Mach's rude tricks of frequently snatching the papers you had before you; turning them over before they were dry, and blotting them and splattering them over with ink frequently by reaching across for ink, when there was some nearer; and shaking his pen afterwards over your paper without regard to what you are doing; using his fingers by way of pointing out something and blotting what you had written with attention; putting some fresh rough over papers prepared with care, and apparently affecting this carelessly or doing it on purpose. His wanting notes you write 2 or 3 times, things merely to introduce alterations of no kind of consequence, and then after all spoiling sheets after sheets, returning to the first and saying it was of no use sending the writings, and not sending them, and keeping you for 10 or 12 days or a fortnight [with] two or 3 persons employed.

His saying to me in January that he never threw responsibility upon any one. He could not bear it. He never had done it and he could not bear to see others attempting it. That Polyphemes was trying to throw it upon him by saying he was of the same opinion with him respecting sending away Old Stick.[3]

January 1819

Young Polisson told Vignoble about Mach's house expenses not being more than £5000.[4]

His repeating that Sultana said she never would have married again if she had thought she would have got Pickaninies—2nd Mach.

Vignoble calling Mach bestia.

Mach's fractious, peevish, disgusting behaviour on 6th March in making up references.

January 1819

Mach speaking of his treatment of Magnesia, said as an excuse that he did not think after all he had done anything so very much out of the way, and that when Lord Stair was ambassador in France in a discussion with one of the French ministers he (the latter) threatened to throw him out of the window. What a comparison. What a similitude of personages and how improbable that they affected it.

23rd January

Mach wanted me to sign some observations on the alterations by Bear, and to say it was so at the moment of his receiving it back. Altho' he received it at pranzo [dinner] he did not show it to me till our going into Library and his angry moods when I explained I could only say so by inference.

26th January

He told me Nincumpoop had spoken to Chirurgo in Primo about his plico [letter] and 'that he was very high about it'. Sultana's [Lady Lowe] constant railing and exclamations against people's rudeness and want of attention to her.

February 1819

Mach's proposition about appointing Young Staff [one of Lowe's staff] to watch and report to him what occurred, and to give him an allowance for giving him information (at this moment in the receipts of an extra 7/6 per day besides his double one of 16/– for doing nothing) from which I disputed. Because he has extracted from Veritas [Montholon] that our Neighbour [Napoleon] had said 'Nous avons fait une bêtise in calling Stokoe'. 'Now that's the kind of information I want, that's of the greatest importance for me to know, and if he was officially there he would bring me a great deal of information of that sort.' I opposed his being so fixed, as it would cause great jealousy to the other officers, and again spoke against the mess established there.

Donna's appropriating 2 dispatch boxes to her use, though always wanted when going to Town to remain even for 2 days.

Donna also said she had overlooked my Giovanni's deliquency for playing billiards, on account of the stewart having begun playing with him, though I had told her I had punished him. As if she had authority over him. And this she repeated 2 or 3 times. She also said once before, that if what her figliola [little daughter] had said about the Commis [clerk] could have been proved, however useful he was to her sposo [husband], she would have had him turned away immediately!!!

Shameful about my knees and la Bella Catherina ordered up to a posta [?] next day.

Donna pushed to make me give an opinion, exclaiming against Mach's delight in writing, and saying my situation was worse than that of a slave. For herself she would sooner die.

February 1819

Mach said that Damned Tuff [Den Taafe] was a very bad hand and desired he might not again be employed, that besides it took him away from other work. And this was the person chosen because he should not be at any expense in living as he had friends to go to.

February, 1819

Donna abused old Vettura [Carriage] to Supracargo Ma-l-ny and condemned Honorable John [East India Company] for not having better. She said they were so shabby as to refuse paying for theirs brought out by Mach. There was an old palanquin found here on arrival, which she had had put in order and turned into a vehicle, but she had not scarcely the use of it as Mrs. Vignoble used it so often. She always dined once or twice a week there, sometime more often and she would never walk to the House or back, but always had it going and coming on those occasions.

February 1819

His proposition of giving German [Janisch] an allowance per diem for assisting us once. Now and then saying you must not call working until 6 or 7 in the evening a common day's work. What was it then? His saying he could take him as seconded, and he could serve as a librarian.

3 February 1819

He said when he got the immense mass of fatras [rubbish] transcribed, it was to send to some friend in England, and Nincumpoop told me afterwards it was for his friend Bun-b-y [Bunbury][5].

4th [February]

His anger about Periwinkle's [Ibbetson] account and sulking because I could not give him an account of what Dz. I.b.n. [Denzil Ibbetson] had done with the store articles, as if I was to be ready with an account to all the questions on that head.

4th [February]

Would not allow Damned Tuff to copy even a paragraph in Expenses [?], as not to be trusted, of course; though [it was] a thing published to all the world.

What would Mach have said to Magnesia if he had gone out walking with Shrug and family out of bounds beyond Francis Plain and not returning till past 8 p.m.; or taken a message to Russian Bear and shewn Madame Shrug to hold fast Tom in company with young Etat Major corps—all which his successor did.

4 February [1819]

When I was entering the immense long epistle, he came up to me, saying there was no necessity for doing that now, there would be time enough some other time. I might ask anyone to do that. The great fatras [mass of rubbish] was the thing he was anxious about at present. It might be very well for the regulating of business to do it but, so long as there existed any record or copy of it, it was sufficient. It would be his fault and not mine at all events. Might get Randal to do it. I had the day before urged his having some of Stercoraceous' commis [Thomas Brooke's clerks] to assist, which he would not, saying these were so few (tho' I believe not less than 5) and he gave me the bulk without coming to an arrangement about who was to help there. Everything is marked that is to be copied, as if I was to do it all myself, and I found that he would not allow me to ask Stercoraceous for assistance though I proposed doing it. I felt again nettled at his coming upon me in his stiff angry style, and told him Randal had 2 or 3 days before begged as a favour to be allowed to return to his duty, not being able to stand so much confinement. And for myself I added 'I beg to submit to your consideration that I cannot stand it, the constant labour and the want of all relaxation injured my health, my nerves, my spirit.

8th February

His rage in taking it into his head that all the Bulletins had not been copied in Book, though he afterwards found they were, and his anger with Chirurgo Primo for not agreeing immediately to analyse and report on the variance of them and necessity [?] of 2nd Fisico Marinaro [Dr. Stokoe].

11 February 1819

Mach after dictating to me for about 1½ hour brought me a large bundle of papers, saying he wished me to set about them and get them ready to send by the present opportunity, [which is] expected to sail in 2 or 3 days at most. At this moment I had enough in hand to occupy me for 3 days at least, which he had told me a few days before was of the utmost importance to have finished, and made me in a most brutal way leave off entries of which there was a mass, to go on with that. On his delivering me this last bundle, [I said] 'Well really I don't know how I shall be able to get through this, and that in hand besides'. Thereupon he got into a most brutal rage exclaiming like a maniac, that he would not even ask me to write out a single word of it (taking the papers away again furiously from the desk). [He said] I was so fond of routine that there was no getting away from one thing I had begun to attend to any other (a shameful, falsehood as this happens everyday, sometimes repeatedly), and that I might go on with my routine, he did not require me to remain writing another half hour in the office. I might walk about or idle, just as I pleased, for he would not trouble me. What he had asked me to do was a thing which required thought and mind to revise and to arrange, but what I was then doing was mere copying (the other was mere copying also and I was well aware my taking it in hand would have been but lost time, and whatever I might have written of it would have been to no purpose, only lost time); it was what anybody could do. But it was the kind of routine I liked however. But he would get some other person to do it. Polisson was in the office at the time. Young German [Janisch] came in to assist, also Vignoble, when he was still foaming in a furious rage, saying there would be 3 hours lost, completely lost by then. I only looked with pity at his outrageous conduct and continued writing what I had before in hand without replying for fear of his taking advantage of Young Polisson having been present, and the others now coming in. He seemed the more annoyed at my silence and called out to me 'Major Gorrequer' in a most official and rude way, 'will you give Young German what you are now writing, I would rather he did it'. I did so and then began the entries he had made me give up a few days before, which with my coolness, appeared to exasperate him

the more. After walking about for some time in a wild distracted
unsettled way, quite lost, he at last went off to Town, and Vignoble
and I rode out a little.

14 February [1819]

Her buggia [?lie] about the long John [a carriage], saying that la
Marchesa [Lady Moira] from Orient had left her one when she
went away, but [she] never used it, and did not even know what had
become of it. She left two, but the one she destined for Madame
Shrug was a very shabby one. The one la Marchesa gave her was
quite superb compared to the other—(buggia) [lie]. The fact was la
Marchesa never fixed upon which was to be sent at all, but left 2,
desiring one to be sent to Mme Shrug [Bertrand], and I was present
when Donna made the selection. She after a long examination took
the best and most complete, sending the worse, saying she had no
idea of keeping the worse for herself. This was done in front of the
House.

Donna's conduct about my knees.

Mach's readiness and eagerness to hear any little nonsense to the
prejudice of our Neighbour and Shrug and his wife without desiring,
or trying to analyse it for fear it might be found false—and communicating such stuff to Big Wigs. Mach's detestable habit of
muttering and cursing thro' his teeth, his brutality in throwing up
the top of the desk, and on other occasions once [when] going down
to town, his saying to me I was grazioso [polite] compared to
Military Secretary of Sir Alexander Campbell (I think) from Isle
of France.

17th February

Mach asked me if I knew whether Chirurgo Primo had sent home
any reports of the health of the Island; as if to insinuate that he had,
and was now wanting to go off for fear of its being known here
before he went away.

19th February 1819

Pick Axe [Col. Lyster] said he was in the little side room biblioteca whilst Mach [Lowe] and Frog [Montchenu] were debating
in the biblioteca on the preference [?] between the latter and

Polyphemes, and had heard them. Mach's cocking up his ears with delight and saying 'Ah I did not know you were there—*perdu*. That's an excellent snug little place to hear things from, without being seen. I'll take a hint from that and make use of it in future.'

21 February 1819

Mach called Bear [Balmain] a damned little snapper rascal, saying 'Merely to gratify his vanity this little popinjay must be sending home all the little trumpery stories he can pick up for Countess Lieven, Nesselrode, Chernicheff and others whom he named but [whom I have forgotten] and such people about the Court of the Imperial Bear, so as to involve me in all his trouble when I ought to be employed about something else; and throwing obstacles in the way of my duties in the care of the man of the greatest consequence in the world. But I know people at that Court of much greater consequence and power than his friends; and if I was just to write a private letter to Lord C———, [Cath-cart],[6] which I may yet do if he does not take care of himself, I could ruin him for ever. He has more weight at that Court than any of Mr. Balmain's friends. He would believe anything I say, for he well knows the principles upon which I have always acted. My account would be much sooner believed than that of such a little jackanape of a fellow.'

He then told me about Bear having told Veritas [Montholon] that if he could mention to him any little anecdotes which he might send his Court to interest Imperial Bear [Czar], it would make his fortune. But they have the greatest contempt for him, both our Neighbour and those about him, and laugh at him.

He also mentioned that Bear [Balmain] had told Captain *Phoebus*, who had repeated it to Nincumpoop [Reade], from whom he had it, that though he was not a young man, he would gladly give up 10 years of his existence to be off. That was, he said, because he was frightened for the consequences of his conduct; he'd do anything to get out of this scrape, and to stand in any other shoes. He was as much alarmed as Autrichien [Stürmer] who, when Pozzo's business took place, had told him, 'Ça pourrait empoisonner le reste de mon existence'; but he had soon got him under his thumb and he would not let him off so easily. He'd be damned if he would. Mach did not say however that Bear had told *Phoebus* that he never came to dinner but in misery. It was the greatest punishment to him. In fact all this said to *Phoebus* was from disgust.

21 February 1819

Whilst engaged in looking over a note he had been dictating to me in answer to letter 2nd of Bear, he desired me to look up a confab book and ascertain which it was he alluded to. Having found it I shewed it to him. He read it and was highly pleased with it saying he would trust to my recollection as to the way in which I had related it before anything Bear might say. Now he saw he had told a damned lie and, after vapouring a little while, and saying that it was the only time he had even spoken to him about it, I repeated (what I had once a few minutes before mentioned) viz. that I did not recollect anything having ever been said on that subject at any other time than this, except at a conversation in October 1817 at Plantation House, where the Admiral was present. He, in a very angry way, said: 'What has that conversation to do with the present matter. What's the use of bringing that forward again.' I said I merely mentioned it as I thought it a confirmation of what he had said. He kept growling a little longer, and left off to again look over the rough draft of the note, that he had just made out, and even dictated me a few more lines, still evidently in a great rage. At last, some minutes after meditating, he burst out in a loud raking tone that he could not conceive what my object was in bringing again forward the conversation here, what could possibly induce me [to do so, and], what are your motives. He would like to know them, it was a very extraordinary proceeding on my part. I told him it was a casual expression meant on my part to strengthen what he had said by instances which I could bring to my recollection of visits to the followers [at Longwood] which had been spoken of. I then resumed the writing I was at when he apostrophised me in that way; but he recommenced however in the same strain about the strange nature of my observation. He could not make out my motives, and was aggravated by those taunting suspicions and attempts at insinuations or some concealed designs on my side. I said it was very hard on me that a most innocent remark should be turned into a crime. He, most sharply gallingly and most pointedly marking the words by a significant emphasis, [and] looking [convinced ?] it was the result of his previous thought, answered 'Not so innocent, I believe either; you had a meaning in it.' This was too much to submit to passively and, though I endeavoured to suppress my indignation and continued writing, I could not. It was too much against nature, and leaving the desk I hurried to him and said 'It is impossible for me, Sir, to stand such treatment. You have wounded my feelings in a most unmerited

Major Gideon Gorrequer.

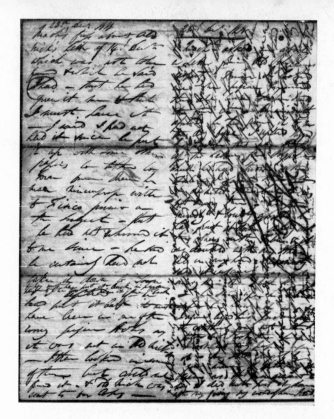

Facsimile of a Page of the Diary.

General Bertrand.

manner such as no man can submit to; nor will I remain exposed to it. I shall leave you. Am I, for using an expression meant in no other sense than merely to strengthen the observation you yourself had made, to be suspected of conniving with or supporting the Commissaires. Am I to be treated in this manner after having toiled and laboured as I have done without any relaxation for these last 3 years, doing my duty and much more than my duty with all the zeal and assiduity possible, and to be exposed to the evident suspicion of joining the Commissaires against you, persons that I have scarcely ever had any conversation with but in your presence, or by your directions, whom I have even never visited?' He went on for some time in a high tone and in a most vexing and irritating manner with the same kind of observations, adding that instead of reverting to a conversation that had no kind of connection with the business in question and said to have taken place at Frog's House and seemed only intended to make it appear he had said something of the kind, I ought at once to have said 'Here, (slapping his hand on the book) we have it and let us work upon it.' He spoke this in the same boisterous tone and I replied that no one else would have drawn such an inference; there was nothing in the expression to justify it or to warrant such suspicion. I walked out of the room intending to immediately pack up and leave the house but immediately returned and said: 'I have, Sir, been long obnoxious to you, evidently, by the treatment experienced, and I here resign a situation which, however flattered I ought to have been by the manner in which it was offered, I never asked for.' Therefore he said in a temperate moderate tone: 'You are now in a state of irritation and when you are cool I shall be very happy to hear anything you have to say on the subject.' That when he had made the observation he had only repeated my own words and that was all. I answered that such kind of explanation as 'that was all' was not sufficient to do away with the effects of his expressions. Something more was required from a person who had wounded, without care, the feelings of another, as he had just done mine. He then said that, in using the expression he had done to me, he had merely taken up my own words and repeated them without intending to attach any meaning to them beyond the mere words themselves. That he had been vexed at my referring to another conversation as if I thought it probable he could have made use of the expressions ascribed to him, and as if trying to justify Bear. I replied there was nothing whatever in what I said to warrant such a conclusion or to support it. He insisted [I should not] be the apologist of Bear

H.N.E.—5

or support him against him. As for my being obnoxious to him he said he did not know why I should think so, for in the letters he had always rendered justice to my services and had always spoken of them in terms of approbation such as he conceived were advisable to him (this is all balderdash as he only did twice, merely referring to my notes of conversation, but never acknowledged the value of my services). That he did not recollect ever having treated me harshly. That he had sometimes been vexed when I appeared to him indifferent about what was going on, and at my changes of temper. I replied that whenever I appeared indifferent it was after having been kept day after day, from morning till night, working unnecessarily, finding in the end it was labour lost. As for changes of temper I could believe I had as uniform a one as any man, when I was treated in a proper manner. That certainly in some cases when he had treated me in a manner such as I never had been, or expected to have been treated, and while I thought no officer in my situation could have been so treated, I had been driven to reply, for it was impossible to remain passive. But I could bring a number of officers, and some of high rank, who would state quite the contrary. Besides I had the consciousness of it. He said persons with whom I had lately associated had spoken of it. 'Persons with whom I have been associated', I replied with surprise. 'No man of honour, or no gentleman has told you so, Sir, for there is not one that would say such a thing; and if it proceeds from one of the tittle tattling persons in Town, of which there are some, they will not dare say so to me, and I despise such people.'

He said it was 'in the family' (Madame of course) it had been observed, besides his having himself expressed it. 'The family,' I said, 'Oh that's all prejudice at what he himself had expressed, and from his treatment of me.'

4 March 1819

Nincumpoop asked me if Chirurgo Primo [Baxter] had mentioned to me anything about an undertaking between himself and Mach respecting 3 years stay. I said he had mentioned to me that he had spoken to Mach about this, hoping that coming out here was not to last as long as our Neighbour lived, and that Mach had answered 'No, perhaps about 3 years.' But he had said nothing about such an understanding having taken place between them. 'Ah but now he has told some people so. However, I assure you there was never any such thing, not a single word of the kind ever was said.[7] It is not the case, you may depend upon it. On the contrary

RURAL LIBRARY
COUNTY WEXFORD
SERVICE

Chirurgo jumped at it the moment it was offered to him and never
thought of conditions ever.' (query? how could Nincumpoop know
not having arrived in Town till the day after Chirurgo had been
appointed). Ninny: 'he says it's for his health, but I know better.
He has other reasons.' I remarked perhaps he wants to get a wife,
to settle down, but this is all conjecture on my part, I said. 'I know
it all,' answered he. Mr. G—— [Gorrequer] has even told him
the family he wishes to marry into. It's all a plot arranged between
them.

14 2059

8 March 1819
Chirurgo Maggiore telling me that Giovanni Etat-Major had
accepted a cadeau from Madame Veritas [Montholon] to the amount
of £7, a seal I think he mentioned.

12th March 1819
Giocando [playing] with Aspirant Sore Eyes this evening at
Bigliardo [Billiards] a few minutes after Lady Ann D . . .ha . . .d
had gone to bed in room over head. Mach came up and desired us
to desist for fear of disturbing her. With his usual disgusting look.

13th March 1819
Giovanni Etat Major came to inform Mach that Veritas had
informed him, on enquiring about tent, that Polyphemes 1st had
hinted he had put it up. But all this Veritas said he only believed,
he did not give it as positive.

Gray R. A. [Captain James Gray].[8] He questioned several times
whether I had had any confab with Bear, Autrichien or Frog. Have
they dined there? His angry questions: did they say anything
particular, had you any private confab with them, what did they
say? and such enquiries.

The delight he expressed when he found Madame First Polyphemes' name introduced in the letter from Shrug to Jesuit [Count
Las Cases], in papers, and adding, his eyes glittering with pleasure,
'more of these names will come out yet.'

His building stables and excluding my Nags.

On reading Providatore's Plicho [letter] to Minister, [he said]
'what a damned scoundrel', because he tried to justify himself.

Recommending two skippers for a lift. Folks out of his profession, known to him but for a few months' services, both equally unknown, one extremely dull. Meaning also Medico Great Gun [Verling] and Chirurgo Primo [Dr. Baxter] after all his reflections at going away. Young Teutonic [Janisch] also, besides Joe Pop'em off [? Poppleton] and Polisson and neglecting me.

[March 1819]

Anything concise, open, fair and explicit; whether in writing or verbal is his mortal aversion. Always some arrière pensée, something doubtful that he may change, deny or admit as circumstances turn out, and as may be required to meet his views. The shortest note that was written to Commissaires or Neighbour's people that did not take hours, sometime days, composing. The P.S. to Bear [Balmain] in long plico took a whole day to merely turn a phrase. His reviling of Bear, his usual nonsensical observation, full of spleen and ill humour, [saying] that it (the P.S.) was the most important thing he had yet written, more so than plico itself.

His constant suspicion as if in league with those opposed to him. after dictating a note or plico to me, when on the point of mounting his horse, he waited till I had written it out fair, then signed it, evidently for fear I should not send it as it had been originally indicated, or that I might alter it. Stopping all the time looking over my shoulder.

His frequently making alterations on copies, duplicates and rushes of plicos, viz. Bear's long plicho in the P.S. tho' both Commis [clerks] and Ego expressed our assurance it was not so, he positively asserted the reverse. Chirurgo Primo's letter about health of Island and his application to be off. Instances in several of his Bulletins. As also when [these were] given to Commissaires.

When Ego accompanied Mach to our Neighbour's domain 31 Marzo 1819 to make a communication to Veritas [Montholon], his harsh acrimonious way of speaking to Old Nick [Nicholls] and his loud vehement angry way of giving out the newspapers I was going to deliver, and, the instant before, his smiling manner to Giovanni Etat-Major, whom he called aside to speak to privately, though only the day before he had told Ego that Giovanni Etat-Major had acted most improperly in telling Veritas that Briars was out of bounds, which had been nearly the ruin to many others. After all that Ego had said in favour of Briars being kept within bounds, he persisted in opposition to it, tho' on the 20th March he told Ego he would not stick to that point at all and expressed his regret he had put it out of bounds.

Oh the tergiversations!!

[? March 1819]

He retorted angrily that he had never shown any humour or asperity to me or anybody. I replied I could not apply any other word except perhaps harshness. His tone and manner to me was such as I never had met with before. I had been near 21 years in the service and had never been spoken to unkindly, before I was on his staff, by any officer under whom I served. I said that the character I had generally borne and the testimony of so many officers as I had shown him, ought to have spared me that; that I was sure no officer in this business could have made any remark upon my temper; that whoever had done it could only have originated it in prejudice and ill-will; that I never had deserved such a remark from any one; that more was required of me than I could possibly perform; that I had no relaxation but continually kept writing; that my health had suffered much from it, and that I begged to resign from the staff situation I held. He then rose from his chair with great violence, walking backwards and forwards, waving his arms and exclaiming he would not submit to be spoken to in such a manner. He had never been spoken to in that way before. He said 'What do you mean, Sir?' and again mentioned there was no such thing as speaking to me, my want of temper being huffed and touchy. Then he flew out, speaking with extreme loudness and vehemence and again adverting to his never having spoken to me angrily or harshly. He said he never had done it so much as he did now. I said no, that he certainly had not, nor anybody else; that my situation with him had long been rendered extremely disagreeable and that I would not remain in it. He sat down and said, as to that, I had no occasion to remain in it, if I did not like it; that it was not him that had made it so to me. These last words (after he sat down)he spoke in a calm tone of voice. He then observed that there was not much time to close the letters, and I said I would write out that about which the discussion took place, which I held in my hand, if he chose, which, having expressed his desire I should, I sat down and copied as well as two others which were all ready before 10 o'clock, and were in the act of being sealed, though they had been closed some time when the captain came for them. He asked me whilst I was writing it, if the enclosures were ready; to which I replied I had them ready the day before. The ships did not sail till late in the afternoon.

April 1819

Mach saying before 3rd Polyphemes that Le Gros Cochon [Louis XVIII] was a blockhead and a fool and old cringing Polyphemes encoring in abject style and re-echoing what he said, with seasoning of his own.

Beginning April 1819

Mach told Stercoraceous [Thomas Brooke] that he had proofs of Reardon being the author of paragraph about distinction of carriages, though there was not positively any proof, but merely a hint of Nincumpoop [Thomas Reade], which Chirurgo Primo had told me he had himself given.

2nd April 1819

Old Mach said that [Captain Knox of] the 'Kitty' had been talked over by them.[9] He told him there was a great deal of difference between Veritas [Montholon] and Poli—[page torn] and that the former always stated that he wrote by Neighbour's orders. His stuffing him with an old trumpery story that Neighbour [Napoleon] had walked round him at one of the first interviews, and at last got completely between him and the door, and that he surely believed he had a stiletto hid about him. He did not know what to think of his conduct on that occasion; it looked very suspicious. Why should not Neighbour suspect him of assassination on the same principle!

He also told him the Government had committed a great error in allowing Neighbour to come with so many attendants—indeed any at all. All he could be reproached with was his having treated him too well. It was Polyphemes 2 and Magnesia that had put all these ideas of their own cause into their heads.

4th April 1819

Old Mach mentioned to me (astonished, as he expressed himself, at not having mentioned it to me when I told him he had not) that Magnesia Terzo [? Dr. Verling] had done things as bad as either 1st or 2nd Naval ones. That he had agreed to the propositions offered by Veritas [Montholon]. That he had been offered £500 a year; and [in order] to insure him the interest, Neighbour [Napoleon] would order a capital to be vested for that purpose in the hands of Drummond or any other banker in London. That it was expected he would be 'l'homme de l'Empereur' and exaggerate his disease. That 1st Magnesia [O'Meara] had done nothing for which he could be had by any tribunal (said Veritas)[10].

Afterwards Mach said 'I do not consider him fit for such a situation. He is not trustworthy, particularly after all that he had said to him, and all his cautions.' There were several things in him he did not like. 'I assure you Mr. Verling is not the person I expected to find. He has been talked over.' (He said he had mentioned the circumstances to Ricketts) [Charles Ricketts].[11] He seems himself ashamed, and as if he did not consider himself fit for the situation now. For he begins to talk of the uselessness of his staying there.

3rd Magnesia [Verling] soon after came in where we both were, and after speaking to him some time, on going away he [Lowe] said to me: 'Didn't you observe his manner of speaking, how short he breathed as if frightened' and again expressed himself very doubtful of his being trustworthy.

He inveighed much this day at Ricketts for involving him in so much difficulty on the subject of the proposals by allowing Shrug to read them over and comment upon them, adding he had no doubt R——— [Ricketts] had given him some encouragement to suppose they might be agreed to. 'Depend upon it,' he said, 'I wish he was now here to see the trouble he had misled me into'. I on this occasion mentioned Giovani Staff's note to Old Nick and hinted that though I now could [not] think of saying a word which might prejudice him in his opinion or to say a word against him in the minutest degree, yet I thought he had not sufficiently thought of how to assist Monsieur Shrug. He said that he had trusted him too far, but he would give him a hint not to visit them, but not let it be inferred it came from him.

6 April 1819

Sultana [Lady Lowe] after dinner, (after speaking of Chirurgo Primo [Baxter], Young Brick and Mortar [Lieut. Wortham] and Giovanni Etat Major not being on palavaring terms) observed to me: 'Vignobles [Wynyards] are your great friends and you may be of a different opinion, but I will say, notwithstanding, that his manners are extremely unpleasant, and I have never been treated with so much rudeness in my life as by him. He has often, as you were both coming up from the office for tiffin, passed close to me, looking at me full in the face without taking the least notice, bowing or speaking to me. Frequently at dinner he has looked as sulky as possible without scarcely deigning to notice or even answer when I spoke to him. I have heard a number of people speak in the same way of him.'

'Chirurgo Primo has mentioned to me he has treated him in the same way, and there is scarcely even common acquaintance between him and several people. He will scarcely notice Nincumpoop [Sir Thomas Reade], tho' they were such friends at Madeira [?] where they met. I never saw such affection on shaking hands and embracing one another.'

'Many people if they were treated so would leave off speaking to him altogether, and he would get cut by almost everybody. For it is not always that people can put up with those kind of things.' I defended him saying it was a natural way he had; sometimes he was cool without cause, and I had perceived it myself. But as I knew that I had given him no reason, I attributed it to a peculiarity.

But I was obliged to give up for I saw a storm was gathering over me. Polisson was there and met Old Mach [Lowe] and me.

This very morning it was that Old Pick Axe [Lyster] had observed to him a few days before, as they were walking in from Plantation House, (Giovanni Etat-Major and himself) that the former observed to him that it was very well for Sultana that she was in the first place here, otherwise she would not be suffered to abuse and run down every body, as she did, with impunity. Pick Axe himself inveighed strongly against her.

6 April 1819

When O. O. (Nick) [Nicholls] sent in his application for removal, in the private letter to Nincumpoop [Reade] enclosing his official one, he said it was in consequence of his not being able to please Mach.

On reading this he flew out into a violent rage, more particularly at the expression which he said ought to have been for the disgust he felt at the conduct of Shrug [Bertrand] and Veritas [Montholon] which is really and actually the case, added Mach; and not on account of what he says; and this he must be brought to say too. He must declare that to be the cause of his quitting. Then he abused and cursed him for his stupidity and folly etc.

The hostility he began displaying about Great Gun Magnesia [Dr. Verling] and his angry remarks at his not having reported to him sufficiently of his palavers with the satellites of Neighbour [Napoleon]. His reflections about Ricketts, and then on this day he said. 'Oh if he only had remained and was here now how much use he would be to me in answering the proposals'—which he had been at that time working at for 2 days incessantly.

On two in particular, it seemed that one moment he would answer it one way, then another moment he would answer it in another, then not at all. Every sentence he uttered in contradiction in the same breath. Observe he had sent back the original of these proposals.

How delighted when he was up to his chin in papers from morning to night, taking out books of entry to friz about and opening all the papers; his groans and smiles of demon-like origin when he read over his composition, and so self sufficient. He constantly declared that whatever was then in hand was the most important, serious and interesting. And that it had got to be answered. When he went to Town was the only moment of ease I had. His appearance became like nauseous medicine to me. His affectation and strutting.

He showed me (6th) a passage in Lord B———'s [Bathurst] letter and when I observed His Lordship granted it, he said: 'Ah but I know they do not wish me to authorize it notwithstanding.' Tho' this was as plain (that he was allowed) as it could be.

If he was accused by Government as to authority he would take care to show to the world he could not avoid communicating Lord B———'s letter.

7th April 1819

Great Gun Magnesia [Dr. Verling] came, and Mach asked afterwards 'Did [ever] you see a man in your life so embarrassed.' Finds a great deal of faults with him for having indulged [?] Veritas [Montholon] on the expectation of a Bulletin of his. Spoke and said he could not be trusted in that situation. He also observed he should have knocked down Veritas when he made the proposition he did, and then came and told him what he had done. It was also perfectly plain by Lord Bathurst's plico[12] that he was authorized to issue Bulletins (as it merely said 'you are not required to demand them if he objects to it') if our Neighbour [Napoleon] did not oppose it, though he insisted it was against his instructions to do so, and made that one objection to one of the articles of our Neighbour. He explained this day, before Great Gun Magnesia, about one not being cunning enough; tho' he afterwards boasted he had, he believed, allowed him to get much out of them, and that he had succeeded sometimes.

H.N.E.—5*

7th April 1819

He again assured me in the evening, after dinner, that Great Gun Magnesia [Dr. Verling][13] had told him he left Veritas under the impression that he agreed to the proposals—that he did not object to them, in fact saw nothing in them to reject.

10th April 1819

He asserted to me, whilst dictating, that he never desired Magnesia to report malaviso [? maladies] to him; that he never had kept back numeros of journals of Morning Chronicle from series and had not kept books and newspapers of theirs. Tho' at the very time in the room over him, were books he had retained of those sent out, and a pretty large box nearly (if not altogether) full of Morning Chronicles of 2 or 3 years, piled up, sent out for them, which he would not send saying 'what's the use of sending old papers to them. It is not those they want!!'

11th April 1819

He asserted that the warrant to keep fast Neighbour [Napoleon] was put by him in a pigeon hole, and tho' I carefully examined it and assured him it was not there, and that I had not had it, he insisted that he had not, and never had, touched it since he put it there, and therefore it must have been taken away by some person, not him. Some hours after deigning to look into his portfolio, there it was, but he never made the least apology. The same with Pick Axe's letters [Colonel Lyster], for months denying his having them, tho' they were the first thing to be seen on opening his cupboard.

14th April 1819

Whilst writing to Bear, he frequently called him a scoundrel, ('did you ever see such a rascal') and he repeatedly put me such questions: 'Don't you think now he is a great scoundrel, a damned rascal?' He looked at me with looks portending some mischief when I did not answer, which I NEVER DID ONCE to any such question, whether applied to the people at Longwood or to the Commissaires.

15th April 1819

His brutal way, insisting that he has not touched 1st Magnesia's [O'Meara] letters after having replaced them in their proper place and, after searching an immensity of papers, finding them where he had crushed them in a wrong packet. He insisted upon a particular confab with Bear, saying positively it had taken place before me, tho' he well knew every one was in the book.

15th April 1819

When he told me of Bear telling him Frog [Montchenu] had orders 'de voir les choses de plus près', he said in his triumphant style, 'I wish he would dare write or speak to me on the subject. I'll settle him in a short time. I like that, his Court pressing to interfere in my views here of what I consider right or wrong. I would very soon put his Court right upon that point. I shall take care neither his Court or any other Court shall interfere with me here.'

His bravadoing on a former occasion that, if he was restricted in his discretion, he would not hold the situation and his saying, soon after 2nd Polyphemes [Admiral Sir Pulteney Malcolm] left this island, that if he had remained he would not have stayed here to act with such a man.

16th April 1819

Mach showed me Bear's [Balmain] letter and on my observing there was nothing in it to irritate, or anything of severity in his moroseness, he however acknowledged it; but observed it had made an impression upon him. I said it apparently had, as it was written in a more serious tone than normal.

I remarked he had mistaken the date of confab.[14] 'Yes,' he answered, 'but purposely, but I'll take advantage of that to write to him tomorrow. He is frightened, I am certain, and he would give anything had I not written that letter to him. But I shall not let this opportunity slip. I'll not let him off so easily.' All this and much more of the same strain of bravado. It was said with the demonlike grin of satisfaction at what he supposed a victory and the hopes of further persecutions of a man he thought frightened.

16th April 1819

Primo Chirurgo [Dr. Baxter] told me he knew of the hatred and malice of Nincumpoop and that he knew he irritated Mach against me. His frequent exclaiming when he saw Bear [Balmain] returning from a ride, 'Oh I suppose the rascal has been again conversing with the followers of our Neighbour' [Napoleon], and of his telling Chirurgo of XX [Dr. Arnott], when he applied for more pay, 'Oh wait until Chirurgo Primo goes and then you'll have no cause to complain.'

16th April 1819

Obliged again to spend an hour looking for papers about rations of the Troops and their health, and find it in his clothes, tho' his shouting that he had given them to me.

16th April 1819

His finding two of Pick Axe's letters, which he often repeated afterwards he had not in his possession [but] had returned to me.

17th April 1819

He said what a damned piece of impertinence it was of Gros Cochon [Louis XVIII], what a damned blockhead he and his ministers must be to send such a letter to Frog [Montchenu].[15] 'What damned stuff it is, did you ever see such nonsense?'

22nd April

His brutal way of going on, when I spoke to him of Chirurgo Maggiore's passage and the allowance. It was a hugger mugger. He would rather pay it out of his own pocket. What was he to pay for his cabin?—He would pay that himself. It was for his own convenience. Besides, he went away. At least will he wait to be spoken to privately about it, and told not to mention it to any one; it must be settled after he goes away. First refusing, then granting it to officers of 66th; but [only] on my urging it to Nincumpoop and quoting 53rd and 2nd 66th.

Same day, I believe, or thereabout, he said he would not let that fellow (Bear) [Balmain] slip through his fingers—He would blow him up in Europe in every court, and in England, if he went there. He would blow him up all over the world. He would follow him up and if he could not do it publicly, he would privately. For he considered him one of the greatest scoundrels and rascals

that ever lived. The fellow would lie through thick and thin. He
was a fellow that would stick at nothing.

He asserted that no officer was obliged to write except stating
at the same time, by whose directions he wrote. . . Ego's letter for
instance to Magnesia Primo about his Journals going away. That
nobody had ever been dictated what to answer B——— [Blakeney][16]
for instance, and Joe Cole to Magnesia's letter. The former dictated
to by me at Mach's desire, who even dictated a sheet of what I
was to suggest to him, if he did not show himself ready to say what
was required.

His comments and animadversion on Great Gun Magnesia's [Dr.
Verling] embarrassment when he brought him plico and palavar.

29th April 1819

Mach told me about Frog's palaver with him at races, that he
began to bully him and ended like a dirty sneaking fellow which
he was.

29th April 1819

Medico Primo [Dr. Baxter] telling Ego of his bruzo with Mach;
that he gave it to him well. He first found him very high, but he
soon cooled when he told him he had observed he withdrew his friendship from him, that he had devoted himself entirely to him and that
he had lost the protection of x x x (his capo) who would now no
longer countenance him, that he had avoided writing anything
about this place, that his name had been slandered in consequence
of the share he had made him take in the Bulletins, that he had
rendered, even by Mach's own representation, important services,
that he thought his services respecting the General Hospital entitled him to something more than mere acknowledgement, that it
would be much better not only for himself but for Mach also that
he should go home with a recommendation to H.M.'s ministers,
than to go as if it were under his displeasure, that it was in his power
to get him promotion, if he thought proper, which would involve no
additional expense to Government and no emolument to himself.
In fact he made it out he had completely bullied Mach into a
promise of recommending him for promotion. He also said that on
Mach's telling him Ministers would put many questions to him
for information he answered he meant to go and live retired at
Cheltenham, and go near nobody, that besides he knew nothing of

what had passed here and how could he expect he should give any information?[17]

April 1819

Mach's delight in putting all your papers in such a state of confusion as often as possible (3 or 4 times a week and frequently oftener), cramming them into the wrong buca di Piccione [pigeon hole] purposely, to give you additional trouble. Leaving them about the room in various places, carrying them upstairs or stuffing them into his coat pockets, and on enquiring of him for them his invariably beginning by denying most strongly he had not them, did not know what had become of them, had not seen them, had given them to Ego, he was positive, and had most certainly never seen them and touched them since, or he was sure he had put them up in their proper place and since then had not displaced them. Then breaking into exclamations of astonishment: 'It is very extraordinary, who could have taken them, somebody must have them, they must have been taken out certainly, who could it have been', and such ridiculous stuff, and then constantly ending by his finding them in his coat pockets or upstairs when he chose to take the trouble of looking for them—or crammed in some other place by himself.

Giovanni Etat Major [Captain George Nicholls] kept for no other purpose at Longwood than to pick up all manner of little tittle tattle to bring him. What rogue Magnesia was. In with Sultana [Lady Lowe] when he gave her some of our Neighbour's [Napoleon] locks. Donna's [Lady Lowe] letter to my Commis [clerk] and saying when Mach and Ego ordered him [to do so], not to attend on figlia. The abuse she gave him and the complete authority she assumed over him as being under her orders.

1st May 1819

Nincumpoop told Ego he did not consider Chirurgo Primo [Dr. Baxter] as entitled to recommendation for step, he did not deserve it. He said he had begun so wrongly in his confab with Mach, but soon cooled and ended by asking to be recommended. What a damned Scotch trick that was to be sure, he added. He said Ego was now the person for whom he ought to ask promotion, that he already had spoken to Mach about it, that he would again urge the matter; and on Ego saying he meant to write to Mach about it, he desired him to wait until after arrival of *William Pitt* and assured

Ego that Mach had already written strongly in Ego's favour to Earl Bathurst.

1st May 1819

On race ground Nincumpoop told me of part of confab which happened between Chirurgo Primo [Dr. Baxter] and Mach, and that the former finished 'like a damned cunning Scotchman' by asking him to recommend him for promotion. [He said] that the confab was a very warm one but Chirurgo Primo was soon brought down. He then went on that Chirurgo Primo had no right or claim whatsoever for promotion, that he had told Mach so and, in consequence of what he had mentioned to him, he had declared his intention of not doing anything for him whatsoever, but to his great surprise the next morning, the day of the ship's sailing, he came down hot about it and whatever he could say, he was determined to do it and even read the letters to Chirurgo Primo to his great astonishment.

He [Nincumpoop] told me I was the only person who was entitled to it, that he had already spoken to him [Lowe] about it and he would again. On my saying it was my intention to write to Mach concerning it, he desired me not to do it till after arrival of Billy Pitt.[18] This was of course to his own taste of improbability. He added he knew that Mach had written about me in the strongest terms to Earl Bathurst, and asked me if I had seen the letter. I said NO, well aware that he had never done it, and this was all.

3rd May 1819

Dottore Great Gun [Verling] used the term Napoleon in speaking of our Neighbour in his report of confab on 1st same month. This was one of the charges against Stokoe. Humble Spine did the same also several times in his reports, and so did O. O. Nick [Captain George Nicholls], as Polyphemes 3rd [Admiral Robert Plampin] observed to Ego one day pointing it out to him in one of the notes given before the Tribunal of Stokoe, saying: 'Better have it altered, for' said he, 'it is one of the very charges against Stokoe and here is O. O. doing the same.'

[May 1819]

Sultana asking Secondo Cappellano's wife if she did not think Cadetta [Lady Lowe's younger daughter Susanna] beautiful—she was in earnest— So Primo Medico's wife told me.

Capo Flago Vascello's [Captain of the Flag Ship] dudgeon at the infrequent provocations [i.e. invitations].

9th May 1819

Finding the letter from Veritas of 2nd April and bringing it to Ego altho' he had so often assured me he had not got it. His shuffling about the business of aprire i plichi at casa sua [opening the letters at his office], as Portsmouth Journal of 1st Marzo mentioned. He said it was false, for it was done in Citta [the Town] and he would make Curbone [?] deny every part of it publicly.

The fact was they had been opened in Town, and the packet contained an original plico of Providatore of no consequence— powers of attorney executed at Home to be acted upon here, principally about Crout's (Chirurgo) morte [Dr. Robert Crout died 1817].

10th May 1819

Mach said that Tulip [refers to one of the Commissioners. ? Balmain] was a most intriguing character, a fellow that would make a dispatch out of anything, out of a song, a man who was always engaged in espionage, who had people continually on the look out to spy about and pick up information of all kinds to bring him, that he might send to his Court. Disliked by his Court and thought very little of by the people who were with him, when attached to the Prussian Army, tho' he had been to him personally very civil.

13th May 1819

He sent to me to know if I had the Edinburgh Magazine and in the evening questioned me as if he suspected I had it and concealed it, though he found it next day.

16th May 1819

Mach said Bear was a most perfidious fellow. There was no honour or integrity in him, he would tell a lie as soon as not, he would assert anything or disclose facts in any way, so long as he could do it without being exposed to immediate refutation,

21st or 22nd June 1819

Sultana [Lady Lowe], in a most ungracious ill tempered manner, called out in the middle of pranzo, molti personi a tavola, that the ragazzo Giovanni was standing in dietro di sedia [behind the chair] of Ego staring about, doing nothing. She called the attention of Mach to it, and spoke out loud enough to be heard all over the room.

26th June 1819

Mach's anxiety to turn off all the acts towards 2nd Magnesia Navale [Dr. Stokoe], being sent home, upon the Polyphemes [Admiral Plampin] saying it was all his doing, and that he had no business to send him home; and that as for himself he had no hand whatsoever in it. It was very badly managed of Polyphemes. What hypocrisy when everything was at his instance and active instigation. The next moment he was abusing Polyphemes for shrinking upon all and every occasion from any share of responsibility.

27th June 1819

Captain *Phaeton's* [the ship] insinuations against commandant of *Larkins* for bringing out opposition feuilles and crying down his principles to Mach in consequence.

27th June 1819

Mach's suspicious questions to me as to what I had written to Bear, tho' only a few trifling words and according to his dictation. And this because I did not wait to show him the note before I sent it off. He tried to shuffle off upon me for this act (tho' he had first desired me to send it off). His difficulty in sending les feuilles publiques to our Neighbour [Napoleon].

19th July 1819

About 11 o'clock Captain Lee came in to the office where the governor and I were writing. He said he had come to know whether he had any further commands as he was going to sail, and to thank him for the attention he had shown him during his stay on the Island. The governor asked when he was going to sail. He answered 'immediately', as he had got the gov. dispatches and his sailing orders. 'What, so soon?' said the governor. 'Why, I wanted to send some letters by you, but they won't be ready for some time.' Captain Lee replied, 'I may stay for 3 or 4 hours longer.' The governor said he would thank him to do so, and that his dispatches would be ready by that time. In the afternoon about 3½, a signal was brought in to the governor from Ladder Hill by Major Pritchard that the *Moffat* was under weigh. All the official and private letters and Dispatches had been ready before tiffin (that is before 2 o'clock), and after coming down from tiffin at about 2½, there remained nothing to do, as I supposed, but to compare the rough copy of the last written letter (a private one to Earl Bathurst) with the original as, in writing the latter, the governor had introduced some alterations. This took me about ½ hour, and every thing was ready before the signal from Major Pritchard was received, except a private letter the governor was then writing.

Sir Thomas Reade, who had come in after tiffin, had gone up on the terrace to look at the *Moffat* 15 or 20 minutes after Major Pritchard's signal was received, and came down saying to the governor the ship was under sail and would sail in probably ¼ hour more. The governor gave me the private letter he had been writing to seal, which I did, and put it in the bag observing as I put it in that it was addressed to Messrs. Currie, London. I closed the bag, sealed it and as I was going to dispatch it the governor desired me to open it again and give him back this last mentioned letter. I then had to open the bag and having delivered it to him he re-opened it, cut about ½ leaf and wrote for some minutes on it. He took a half sheet of letter paper, which he appeared to substitute for what he had cut out, and enclosed it in the letter, sealed it up again, and I then once more closed the bag, sealed it and handed it over to Sir Thomas Reade who said he would take it himself. On his going up however with the governor, the latter called out to me through the office window, as I was still there, that the ship was off—this was past 4 o'clock, half past four I think. On going up, she was starting away under easy sail, nothing I believe but top sails, which were going before the wind. I could not exactly tell. The governor asked what was to be done; when I said better make a signal to the *Conqueror*, to make her lay to; which after a little hesitation was done. Sir Thomas Reade by this time was on his way to the wharf, and we saw him soon after rowing off towards the ship. The *Conqueror* had now a flag of recall hoisted, and she fired some guns with blank cartridges to windward, her stern being then to the sea. Sir Thomas Reade went on board the *Conqueror*, but I could not however see him go beyond, tho' he afterwards said he had, which must have been a short way, and he would have been seen clear of the *Conqueror*. Soon after he got on board she fired a shot. The *Sophie* brig of war (anchored a little to the Eastward of the *Nautilus*) soon afterwards also fired a shot; and Ladder Hill, where the flag of recall was also flying, likewise fired shots. Six shots at least must have been fired before she finally brought to. But immediately after the 2nd or 3rd shots I observed she had hauled to her leeboard side of her fore-top sail, which was afterwards explained to me was a preparatory thing for laying to. As she had been going very slow all this time, and particularly after this preparation business, had the boat continued rowing towards her (which she then could not have failed to see), she would have backed her sails, and let the boat come up. This was an opinion expressed to the governor at the time, and he expressed surprise that Sir Thomas Reade had not rowed on, instead of going on board the *Conqueror*. The *Moffat* was, I suppose, better than 3 miles off when she finally lay to. A boat of the *Conqueror* was then sent for, with an order from the Council to the Captain to come ashore; which he did about 7, and was received by the governor in the office in the Council Room, before Mr. Greentree, Sir Thomas Reade and myself. The governor reproved him severely, in a loud and angry voice, for having persisted in standing away after the signal of recall was made. He said it was treating him and the government with contempt, as also the admiral, when shots were fired from the British Flag Ship and other vessels, and that a brig of war had even got under weigh to bring him to; (this must have been a mistake, no brig of war or other having got under weigh). Captain Lee [of the *Moffat*] excused himself as not having known that signal, conceiving it to have been intended for the *Conqueror*, particularly as the first guns from the *Conqueror* were fired to windward. But that the moment the *Bridgwater* had made her the Company's signal to bring to, he immediately did so, most earnestly protesting he never meant the least disrespect; that on the contrary he would have immediately brought to had he known it was for him. But finding on his arrival on board two boxes, as he understood, of dispatches marked 'On His Majesty's Service' (these were Post Office) he conceived they were those the governor had spoken of to him, having already got those of the island government and thought then he might make sail. He said that he saw no man of war get under sail; that the question was for some time agitated on board whether his ship was meant; and that Captain Wyburn of the Marines,

late of *Conqueror*, a passenger on board was of opinion it was not.
He said that he himself was in his cabin when the first guns were
fired, arranging some papers, and it was only after hearing them
repeated several times he went on deck, when soon after a shot was
fired and he then began to think it was for him and prepared to
lay to. He dwelt upon the confusion there is on board a merchant
ship for some time after getting under weigh.

Wednesday 11 August 1819

Special session on murder of Chinese.[19]

The governor after the Grand Judge had been sworn, addressed
to the following effect, that before they proceeded to examine
witness upon this Bill, he thought it incumbent upon him to declare
to them what he had thought his duty to declare to the Coroner
before, that the officer who assembled the party of soldiers, had
acted without any authority whatever, either from himself, from
the Government, or from any superior officer; that he had taken it
entirely upon his own responsibility. He did not mean, however, to
arraign the right of an officer, or other persons, in certain cases of
riot or tumult, to interfere to quell it. Although in a Colony composed
as it was, all laws do not equally apply, yet the Grand Jury was to
be given for their proceedings the general principles of the laws of
England. That according to that law a presentment might be made
by the Grand Jury against any other individual, though not in the
presentmentation [*sic*] against others they judged sufficient evidence
was produced to implicate him. That he would again repeat that the
responsibility of a Military Force did not emanate from him, that
it was not the spontaneous act of the soldiers themselves, and that
Captain Shortis (A.D.C. Major Gougun) had not repeated the
circumstances to him until after the matter had terminated.

15th August 1819

Mach, Sultana, Cadetta and Primogenita on a marooning
expedition to Neighbour's palazzo,[20] but no invitation to Ego,
merely Mach saying long after vehicle was at the door, he was
going there, and then adding that Sultana was going also. Ever
since this, Neighbour's residence was called una Reggia [a royal
palace], and the magnificence of it a constant topic; and the
beautiful situation and view from there. Sometime ago nothing but

abuse of it. How cunning. Would now willingly change Plantation House for it.

His this day ordering Teutonic 8/3 per diem, viz. £150 per annum, with retrospect to June 1819, the date of Young Polisson giving up his berth of nominal commis. Teutonic scarcely was to be found.

His calling the arcivescovo [archbishop] a damned scoundrel, rascal, etc. . . . .

21 August 1819

The joy demonstrated by Nincumpoop on opening the plichi by *Abundance* [arrived 21st August] and finding that Magnesia de la Marina 2nd [Stokoe] was to be traduit [indicted] before Maritime Tribunal.[21] How he jumped and raced all round the table, clapping his hands and shouting on Mach's telling him of it, and the ferocious grinning of the latter about it. Soon after opening of private plico about Chinese, his vexation [?] and showing it to Nincumpoop, [he said] 'did you ever see such fulsome stuff and nonsense after what he has done'. And the latter saying after reading it: 'what a rascal the fellow is.'

Sultana's reflexion on Mrs. Schmidt saying that she abused Plantation House; she declared there was something gloomy about it; it seemed as if something very bad had been committed in it; and mentioned whether it was not troubled with revenants [ghosts] (this was said, she observed, to Majordomo); that she wished the whole of it would tumble down and not a stone left standing the moment she and the fanciulli [the children] left it.

She then told [the Captain of the] *Phaeton* that Mrs. Schmidt had declared she was under the control of no one, not accountable to any one, and might do whatever she thought proper after her hours of lessons were over.

22nd August 1819

Mach's asperity and ill-natured expression to Ego about some alterations of dates which I was about to make, and that according to his orders; and which he reproached me for not having done, though what I was doing was perfectly right, and was what he acknowledged most rudely to be the case the moment he gave himself time to look over it. Also his harsh ungraceful manner of reflecting upon my not having observed whether our Neighbour had, in his own name, demanded Marine Magnesia [Stokoe was asked to attend Napoleon in January 1819].

6th September 1819

On this day he directed upholsterer to send him a list of what things were here, out of the English stores, for himself, for Nincumpoop (saying these would be paid) and for Polyphemes 2nd [? 3rd Admiral Plampin] (never would have been however had not Magnesia's letter referred to them).

Nincumpoop did say, certainly on Monday, that Bear's man came to him that day.

7th September 1819

In a letter to Bear (the first rough draft) he wrote encomiums about Nincumpoop and about the attack upon 'the first officer of his personal staff' [Reade] to whom he was most indebted in the particular line of his duties for his zeal and activity and the great assistance he had afforded him in the discharge of his own duties. The above was with the assistance of something even more disgustingly fulsome. But after considering it and as if ashamed of such gross trumpery, he tore up (what I never saw him do before) that part into small pieces and threw them away. This was said of a person of whom he had that day and 2 or 3 times before, expressed himself doubtful of his word; and who, he was certain, no doubt had misrepresented things. For he at first said he had heard Alfred [?] was to sail Saturday, and denied it afterwards; and that he had been asked on Monday, and afterwards positively asserted he did not; though both Mach and Ego heard him assert again to Bear that he wished to know at once. He coaxed him at dinner to applaud the report of Medico Primo [Dr. Baxter] however badly composed and [after] upwards of a fortnight's work, merely because the cunning Scotyese [Baxter was a Scot] had profited by his hints and stated what he wanted. What an excellent, what an admirable report. I am devilish [glad] he can make out these kind of reports.

8 September 1819

Mach said Magnesia Great Gun [Dr. Verling][22] had played a double part. The rancour he showed against him. His jealousy. He said that any other [doctor] should be chosen in his place—and the vingtième [20th] Magnesia [Dr. Arnott] in particular. His labour to propose to Nincumpoop to disentangle him from what he knew was a false assertion about the Monday. He himself stated to Nincumpoop he had first mentioned Monday and had frequently referred to this to me and wanted me to say whether he had or not; which I evaded.

10th September 1819

The extraordinary way he talked over the Cappellano about his answer to Magnesia Primo [O'Meara], and got him at last, backed by Stercoraceous, to change the greater part of it. Little thanks I got for my labour about answer to provisions, and his wish to take advantage of it to find faults and attack me on some point, which he however could not do. But tho' ready to express himself indebted to others on trifling matters, always withheld it from me. [Spoke] to Vignoble this day on some trifle about Magnesia's letter's broken seal, after all his assertions of suspicion of the Giovanni Cappellano.

20th September 1819

Stercoraceous exclaiming 'Oh what a complete unprincipled vagabond the Primate has shown himself,' or words to that effect—if not even stronger.

20 September 1819

His paying no attention to any complaint of the insolence of Nincumpoop's Myrmidon on inspections of baggages of Pub and Medico.

22nd September

Mach's wanting to bring in names of Magnesia Primo [Dr. O'Meara] and Polyphemes Secondo [Admiral Malcolm] in his letters to Lombard St. Great Folks and Stercoraceous [Brooke] applauding all his violence.

22 September 1819

Making it appear in his letter to Secretary Big Wig, Lombard Street that he, with difficulty, spared Young Polisson from his office for an engineer in 66th. (This was when answering that no notice had been taken of his recommendation to captainship, as he had done in his letter to Horse Guards.)

22 September 1819

Sultana [Lady Lowe] said she had offered £20 for a collana d'oro to Jew Lewis [Lewis Solomon], which he asked £50 for[23]; and on my laughing she said 'why, they only cost that in China. He did not pay more.'

My being asked 6/- in payment for hemming a black silk handkerchief!

28 September 1819

The violent brutal way he broke out on receiving the professor's [Dr. Antommarchi, who arrived on Sept. 18, 1819][22] letter complaining that his rooms had not been completed in furniture. It was damned hard upon him that he never could get anything done, that he not only must order things to be got, but must see them brought to the spot. There was not a soul about him to assist him. There was something, he believed, in the air of the place that contaminated everybody. In any other place where a word would suffice, here orders upon orders must be given before it was done, and at last he must do it himself. It was damned hard that to his other duties he should have this additional labour, but he never saw such a place as this. There was a torpor and indifference, a want of feeling, that he had never seen before. He kept raving for a while, tho' after coming home and abusing Darling he found almost everything was done, and the delay was his fault in having ordered Chinois to be got from Rock Cottage[24].

3rd October

His rude answer when I asked him the hour his dispatches would close so as to inform Vignoble. He said that he could not tell till they were finished. I was obliged to explain for what purpose I asked him before I would get an answer, tho' working like a slave all this time. His brutal way to Dean Turf [Den Taafe] without any reason when he merely asked him the meaning of some of his scratched words.

Query: Were all those articles of furniture and shirts ever paid for?

Governatrice told me about Sultana's telling her youngest

fanciulla that when her eldest was sullen it was from jealousy; and that she (Sultana) was paid more attention to. She said that mothers like to marry off their oldest figlias, not liking to see grown-up girls in some parties, as it made them look so old.

7 October 1819

He told Vignoble of the match, never mentioning a word to me about it, though I gave him an opportunity the day before. When speaking to me about Bear's not going to Neighbour's people, he replied he could not do that when he was riding the whole time with the heroine of his choice[25].

7 October 1819

His breaking out with his usual violent fit of rage with the Magnesia Statico, when the latter observed to him our Neighbour said he could not go out without running the risk of being interfered with by the factionnaires. Vociferating that he did not believe it. He did not apprehend it. His eyes red with fury, his face inflamed, spluttering, frowning and his muscles and body in a state of frantic agitation. His misery, and his regret if by accident he ever committed himself in anything open or acted handsomely and with straightforwardness; and how he would lament at not having left himself a loop hole.

17 October 1819

His candour in telling me Bear made a confidant of him.

17 October 1819

Donna's encouraging him and highly annoyed because he did not, at her suggestion, abuse Majordomo. Her look and spite about it. She quoted Bear's good sayings, [whom] she used to abuse so much.

18 October 1819

He told me that he had been deceived in writing to Big Wig Ministers at Home about Navy sending back Magnesia's books; that none of them had, and that Kent had pretended his was lost. His eagerness to find out whether he had sent it ashore, and who got it,

He wrote to Nincumpoop about it, from whom he heard it, and who had it, no doubt, from the pompous commodore.

18 October 1819

His liberality in lavishing away money to those who did nothing; and his saying he would get Medico Primo of XX [Arnott] 15/- daily extra; and his saying that 15/- was so little for Great Gun Magnesia [Verling] that he would give him something in addition to the £1 per day whilst at our Neighbour's [Napoleon]. He wanted two days before, to continue his allowance till he embarked.

20 October 1819

His tirade against Polyphemes No 2. [Admiral Pulteney Malcolm]. He said he had been the cause of all his difficulties and the trouble he had experienced in his relations with our Neighbour. He buoyed up their hopes, made him believe the Senate would take up their cause, and that he would be supported at home. He came here in fact for that purpose and as a spy, but he had done for himself, and he would never be employed again. He railed in this strain against him for a long time. He said that the Foreign Commissaires would not have given him trouble only for Polyphemes. That if our Neighbour had consented to see them they could not have been more troublesome. He had played a bad game in not seeing them. This was in opposition to my observing that if they had seen him they would have caused him more trouble than had done Polyphemes. Polyphemes had done an incalculable deal of mischief and was sent out here for that purpose.

20 October 1819

Mach opened a note to me from Frog's adjutant [Captain de Gors] without saying a word to me about it, before or after, tho' bearing the mark of its being a private one, as it was an answer to an invitation to pranzo. This he was in the constant habit of doing. Whenever I received a note, [he said] 'who is that person? What is it about?' Without enquiring if it was on service or not. Or if I myself wrote one, his side glances to see if he could not make out the content. 'Who are you writing to?' Sultana constantly exclaimed against the extraordinary impropriety of the conduct of Long Adjutant [Captain de Gors][26], and Frog and Miss B being so often together. What was then passing in her own house? He said that Old Kentish friend Moggy's brother and Cairns had returned the Magnesia books. *Vide* note of Nincumpoop 18 October.

His dissatisfaction at la Signora Molinodelre [Mrs. Kingsmill][27] paying a visit to Lady Shrug [Bertrand] of upwards of an hour's length, tho' she was one of those included in Signora Shrug's list. What could they be saying all the time, he observed?

29 October 1819

He insisted that the soldier of the 66th had said 'going out', and on finishing Old Nick's [Captain George Nicholls] report not mentioning it. He said 'I am quite sure it was so', and added that it may easily be altered. We can cut the intention out. It was however contrary to reason they should have required to have gone out, when their object was to get in.

He then asked me if I did not recollect Mark Anthony saying our Neighbour was ashamed of what he said, and the matter of his representation. To which I answered I did not. 'No, then I do perfectly.' This was the first time he mentioned it, tho' he had carried away notes of confab, and made such alterations as he chose without mentioning it.

30th October 1819

His harsh way of speaking to Stercoraceous [Thomas Brooke] (who kissed the rod the whole time) about Captain del Porto. His working himself up to the highest pitch of rage and then going out and falling foul of Majordomo in the most outrageous way.

In the evening his looks, his flushing, his smothered rage when I did not tamely coincide with him when talking big that he would make our Neighbour [Napoleon] give up all his connections with Magnesia [O'Meara] and Providatore [Balcombe]. And before he would show him any consideration or attention, he would insist upon his giving them up. 'Damn me but I'll not allow them to keep up their connections with him, or keep up their pecuniary concern in that quarter. But XXX he shall declare himself, and that against the clan, before I show him any consideration.' Vapouring in this way.

I said I thought from the game they had been playing, and however bad their policy, that they would keep up their connection, were it only for the sake of conveying clandestine communications though they most likely would not entrust him with such[28].

1st November 1819

Mach himself knew of Magnesia having received some of the prints and newspapers he said he lost—what a rogue he was in them! What does this paragraph allude to[29].

He wrote to the Secretario Grandioso 1st November 1819 that the carrozza had been borrowed from him by Donna Veritas [Madame Montholon] and Old Mexico. [Father Buonavita] The former was offered by the Sultana in a note asking her to mercantare [sell]. In the other case the newcomers never asked for anything but uno carro to convey baggages. The carrozza was sent down to them [?], and offered for their use, which was the first thing that he heard of it. He also wrote to Secretario Grandioso that he intended to have recommended Magnesia Great Gun [Dr. Verling] for advancement had he gone home.

2 November 1819

After having copied at least 30 times alterations in limits, he made up his mind too and changed it as often. He took upwards of 3 weeks and worrying us all the while composing 6 lines. He said he would not make any alteration; and having repeatedly said he did not see that safety of his custody would be in the least possible degree affected or endangered by it[30].

Then putting on the same footing that Mme Shrug might be coming with her children to visit them, and might expect to remain there to spend two or three days, or make her visits too long—or our Neighbour might send his people into the grounds to insult him.

7 November 1819

Bear's [Count Balmain] turncoat proceedings in sending Consul's [Russian Consul's] letter and newspapers, forwarded to him, to Nincumpoop, who was expected in a ship to call en passant hourly. Also his general obsequiency ever since his becoming 'amouraché' [in love with Lady Lowe's daughter]. Mach's contumacy against Consul. The fuss he made about not finding some note of his, breaking open and cutting up drawers to find it out. His suspicion saying 'what can have become of it', with his frequent applications to me asking if I had seen it. A whole day was taken up by commis [the clerk] and a good deal of my time in searching for it, though he had it and found it when he took the trouble of looking.

7 November 1819

He showed me a letter from Consul to Stercoraceous [Brooke] about Shrug's own case [?], soliciting payment (dated 19th July, but never acted upon till 22nd November following). He showed it now, all in a fuss and fury, then finished by wanting to pack a copy of it off to Shrug [Bertrand], desiring him to settle for it. Both he himself and Sultana [Lady Lowe] tried to enforce an impression that what escaped povera pazza[31] in her delirium of ridiculous accusations against herself, were true.

Two plichi of recommendation, which [Magnesia Glory?] sent to him for the Padrone of the galera [galley] who brought him out, and who was to make a voyage to Livorno to some of his friends there (dated 24th September 1819). But they were never given to Padrone.

13 November 1819

On receiving Old Frog's letter about Histrion's [Theodore Hook][32] attack expressing his astonishment he said, 'how could he have heard of the remarks made by our Neighbour [Napoleon] to Magnesia Primo [O'Meara] about him.' But added after a moment's pause, 'his adjutant heard it, I have no doubt at Mrs. S . . .'s, to whom Old Kentish's acquaintance must have mentioned it after hearing it from Magnesia Primo.

Now that he found Histrion assailed in his turn (who Old Frog threatened also to castigate saying Bear Consul [Russian Consul] was gone home to do the same), he began drawing in his horses about him, and having myself commented on his unjustifiable attacks on individuals, he began to lament that Histrion had written it, saying it had done an incalculable deal of mischief. But on reverting to the book about what he said of Bear Consul he laughed innocently, saying it was all true, that he had said nothing against him but what was correct.

He then wanted some letters, which we were getting for upwards of an hour, and which I knew nothing of, nor would he explain, but he expected I should guess at his meaning. These letters could not however be found, and must have been some of his secret ones; a whole drawer full (at least 100) of which he then shewed me, which he kept concealed from Vignoble and me. Only Nincumpoop had seen them. He showed them to me with an air of triumph. 'Look at all these that have never yet been entered.' Whilst looking for it he said to me 'you should find it there, it was written to Big Wig statesmen before my quarrel with Autrichien [Stürmer]'. (Mark my word that he had so frequently asserted he never had any misunderstanding with these folks.) He then answered Frog saying: 'I must at all events make him understand I never had any hand in Histrion's production [publication] nor even knew anything of it's being intended till it came out; and I must say something flattering to him in answer, tho' his first emotion was that of rage.' Notwithstanding his often saying he knew nothing of the publication, how often have he and Nincumpoop talked about the probable time of its coming out? I have heard him with Ninny saying 'are you sure he will publish?' 'Yes to be sure I am, he assured me he would.' And whilst Histrion was here his anxiety that Ninny should explain this and that, so as to introduce it into his publication; and Ninny's frequently answering he asked him 'Has he been told this and that.' 'Or has he left me alone for that?' He stated he was then furnishing him with information, and that Histrion was taking notes on the subject. He also took him in the country to stuff him along with his better half (Naval Hero). Also after he had sailed a sufficient length of time he would look out for the publication, with the frequent exclamations of 'I wonder if the next ship will bring us Histrion's publication?'

He ascribed to Bear in sending him Consul's letter, the best motives. It was to show him he had no connection with him, and would have nothing to say to him, and anything about Bear was mere fulsome approbation.

14 November 1819

His rage when he remarked it was very extraordinary (this was on the receipt of a conciliatory plicho from Frog that day) that they, the Commissaires, never would understand their real situation, that they were here as mere cyphers and that all they had to do was to live as well as they could and pocket their allowances. I observed that it was a pity their governments did not themselves see the uselessness of their being kept here, as in placing people here in their situation it was really making the individuals conceive themselves people invested with a certain character and having certain functions dependant upon it and as persons therefore of some consequence. No answer to this, but evident high dis-satisfaction at my remark.

The evident determined and consuming hatred to Mercanthors, manifested on all occasions even so trifling.

19th November 1819
Sticking it into Bear about Bear Consul [Russian Consul]

21st November 1819
He said that he would upset Consul by attacking Polyphemes 2nd,
which he did most furiously in letter to Big Wig at home. Brutality
in sending me to the bottom of the table again and Vignoble at top,
tho' [there was] a round one for a small party where he ought to
have sat at the head himself.

Old Frog's cringing to Mach after his vapouring about 'Histoire'.
Mach's delight in having people or horses for himself and staff
kept waiting for him for hours. Could not bear to see me a moment
disengaged or away from desk. Old Polyphemes No 3 [? Admiral
Sir Robert Plampin] cringing to him by making notes on books to
read in the sense he knew would please Mach.

23 November 1819
Domiciliary visit to all the stanze cercando l'ancella [rooms looking
for the maidservant] and Sultana's prevarication when relating
story next day to Giovanni Grazzioso. Her tirades against Capo of
Tees [saying] that he ought not to be asked any more by Mach to
his house, and her attacks on Capo of Caffo for having remon-
strated on the visit.

The indelicacy of Nincumpoop bull dogs of Police prowling continually about the streets, spying on the insulaires [islanders] as well
as Lobsters, and both these fellows of known bad character. Smells
not a little of tyrannity.

25 November 1819
Again his suspicion on missing some plichi of Polyphemes 2 which
for a long time he wanted to insinuate I had; but which were produced at last where he had left them.

26 November 1819
He taxed me with having in my possession a plicho from Bear
Consul to the Sapient King of the Hebrews, and after my saying he
had not given it to me but had it still among his papers, he persisted

and said that he had given it to me a few days before, desiring me at the same time to have put it in a secure and safe place and a copy of it taken, that it should not be lost. I said he had spoken of it but had not given it to me. He in a serious sullen mode said 'What? Didn't I give it to you to put up carefully. I am sure I did, and never put my hand upon it since'. All this time I was searching among the papers and continued to do so, until he at last thought proper to look into a bundle he had taken with him to Town, when he was there last, where he immediately found it. Notwithstanding I had before indicated that it was among those, as I was well convinced it was. But it was no use attempting to argue without being exposed to some harsh language, as he was then working himself into a rage. When he found it I said: 'I am, Sir, extremely careful of official papers and never have mislaid one in my life.' As I said this under the impression of wounded feelings, he interrupted me at the first word saying 'I know your are,' but at the last gave me one of his black menacing frowns.

The hour before this only, he had acknowledged to me that he had found in the possession of Stercoraceous 2 letters which he insinuated and hinted as good as assertion, I had got them in my possession.

October or November 1819

The affectation of sending mobile [furniture] from Plantation House to our Neighbour to save the best in stores, evidently as a set off and to have it to boast of hereafter, after having taken such a quantity for himself from the Neighbour's stock ,and for Nincumpoop and Polyphemes Primo.

(Query: Were those about which Magnesia Primo made the fuss ever paid for after all? No appearance of this ever having been the case. Why take them at first? And now find the scarcity and being obliged to send home for more? Pretty foresight, only to keep what would do for 4 or 5 years, as if Neighbour was to hop off the hooks in that time.)

Pretty expense brought upon E.I.C. [East India Company] at first starting to ask for set of microscopes large and small scale, large mounted telescope on stand with glasses for nocturnal observations of high price, globes, maps (an immense number), ice machines, electrical or chemical machine credo also. And all these things to make himself appear a man of science, none of which were used after all. The fowling pieces also were unnecessary to him immediately after he curtailed bounds. Did not the government's sanctioning the guns express the idea of greater latitude.

Continually building and levelling, doing and undoing, making useless rooms, painting one colour then over that another. Getting painted floor cloths, then soon becoming tired of those, must have new ones, papering rooms, disliking them and putting others over, and all for lack of space for all to settle. Never building a place for one officer. Never having [anything] but a nasty hole for commis [the clerk]. Then constantly finding work for artisan and beginning on a pigeon hole case, and not even leaving time to have a lock put on them.

[Probably] December 1819

Mach bad payer; difficult to get anything out of his hand [which] he owes. Witness Chirurgo Maggiore's £20 on arriving here not paid till long after and upon my application, tho' it was borrowed on board on arrival. The Ritratti [portraits] of Royalty Chin-Chin and other things of that description from the Padrones of Legnis perused by Young Polisson.

Sultana's qualms about the chastity of her servants, tho' one had a bambino in the House, and she allowed her partito [husband] to remain in it, and offered to give sleeping accommodation to the Bella Caterina and her amico within the House, thus sanctioning their proceedings; and allowing fornication to be going on at Rock Cottage between our Neighbour's [Napoleon] domestic [Gentilini] and a woman, altho' all the time the fuss about the [illegible] man.

December 1819

The number of old trumpery things sent from Plantation House to our Neighbour's [Napoleon] house as soon as Magnesia's No 1 [Dr. O'Meara] book was published, and how Donna [Lady Lowe], in comparing, always tried to make it appear he was sending everything there and would have nothing at Plantation House.

7 December 1819

His observing to her, asking him if the plicho had arrived in time for the CIGNO [the ship *Swan*] that had andate via [gone away] the evening before. 'No, it was the fault of VINCITORE [the ship

Conqueror], not however the Amiraglio or Capo del Vascello. It was like them.

11 December 1819

His particular charge to Darling's Menuisier [Carpenter] to specify every article, not leaving out anything of what he sent from his own casa to our Neighbour. About something that it appeared by Darling's account he had got, he said, 'Oh, I never got those. It does not signify about them.' The extraordinary amount made out of a scatola [box] of instruments relatively to the price, tho' a thing given to him by [? the Surgeon] who had received it in public reward (£10). He admitted himself in credit.

18 December 1819

Recollect the extraordinary account he made out of Dr. and Cr. about bringing in box of instruments (mathematical), then all at once doubling it from £5 to £10. He struck out a vast number of articles he had secured for his own use, saying he would replace them, which would have made a heavy balance against him, instead of in his favour. So he made it out at last. The articles given to Nincumpoop's House from Fantastico's [an orderly] room, and after all making it out in his return that nothing, at least a steward's bedstead, had been supplied to him out of our Neighbour's stores, and his saying 'you may put down all you can bring against Polyphemes 2nd, don't spare him, but little against me.

25th December 1819

Nincumpoop said (meaning Knox of 'Kitty', extra ship EIC [East India Company] after abusing him for charging so much for the viaggio [voyage] of the donna), that it was imparava [not fair for] the fanciulla [child or girl]: 'it is now too much by half. [Susanna][33]. If I had known that, I would have taken good care he should not have landed his damned traps for sale here. But I have noted him; I have made a remark opposite to his name in the Register Book, and I shall not forget him when he comes again here, I promise you.' And this notwithstanding Captain K—— [Knox] had reduced his original claim one half and that there were 3 attendants and 1 piccinina along with the donna.[34]

27 December 1819

On his receiving the answer to my supplica, the unfeeling manner
in which he threw it down on the table to me. 'Here, here,' said he,
'the answer about your business or supplica. You had better keep it.
You'll see it's a promise.' Without saying a single expression of
disappointment or concern. I read it and said 'I hope you will
allow me, Sir, to address you again on the same subject.' He muttered
ungraciously an assent saying, 'Very well', adding 'I hope you are
satisfied however with what I have done.' I answered, 'I am much
obliged for what you have done certainly and thank you for it; but
I cannot however help feeling it, after all the labour I have gone thro'
and after seeing Captain Poppleton promoted for merely 18 months
attending at Longwood, a duty of very easy and trifling nature
compared to the duty I have had to perform.' 'You have seen the
letter I wrote again; I hope you don't think I could do any more, and
that I have done all that I could. It was impossible for me to do any
more.' I replied I was satisfied with what he had done on that
occasion[35].

[End of 1819 ?]

Lord Bathurst's idea about a Jury as his reasons for not prosecuting
Magnesia Primo [O'Meara]. That one dissenting voice and one bad
character, among such men as London juries are composed of, might
perhaps clear him.

When Madame Shrug [Madame Bertrand] sent the list, his
observation that C—ns and Pear—n [Cairns and Pearson][36] were
objectionable characters to visit there. No man in the Island had any
business to have any opinion but himself about the people of Longwood, and much less on his own actions or duties here.

Tearing a leaf out of a book sent by Lord John Russell to our
Neighbour [Napoleon] on account of its having written upon it. . . .
[Gorrequer leaves this blank]. The book was entitled [this also is
left blank]. He desired me to cut it out, which I could not refuse
doing.

Notwithstanding what Mr. Ricketts[37] had done in his favour in
England, as informed by Lord Bathurst, how he had taken every
opportunity after his departure to condemn his acts and ascribing
any unpleasant correspondence to his having listened to him, he said
he was but as vile as most of the others coming from India. How often
he abused him and reflected upon him in his letters home.

Sultana (as Governatrice informed me) said Bear [Balmain] was the only gentleman on the Island, when she began to smell out his feelings about her fanciulla [daughter][38]. How different from some months before, when she complained so much of his rudeness and his ungentlemanlike conduct to her, that he never bowed or spoke to her, and she in consequence (as she said) took no notice of him and they had not spoken for several months, and that they were all (the commissaires) rude and ungentlemanlike in their behaviour to her in particular.

How Old Mach changed his tone after Bear's proposal [engagement of Balmain to Lady Lowe's daughter]. Everything now was proper in him, even the extraordinary confab on the grounds 29th September 1819 was correct. High praises to *Eurydice*, on him particularly, and Old Frog [Montchenu].

Chapter Four
1820 Island Society

14 January 1820

Mach asserted most positively I had got Secretary of War's plicho about Morali's vedora [widow], that he perfectly recollected having asked me for it but I had not given it to him (this last assertion was in reply to my answer that some days back, after having before given it to me, he had asked for it again and I had returned it to him). At last after my repeated assurance I had not got it in my possession but returned it to him, he took the trouble of putting his hand into his pocket and as usual in almost all these accusations, there he found it. A few days before he had in the same manner insisted I had Polisson's letter to Existing Stone [Dr. Matthew Livingstone] to come up to Longwood to consult about Shrug's [Bertrand] child. Nincumpoop, he said, had sent it up and it had been given to me, tho' I had never seen it nor knew anything about it. On my referring to Nincumpoop, who did not at first acknowledge his having it but said he was sure Mach had, Nincumpoop found it, and 2 or 3 days after sent it.

15th January 1820

The rows of Sultana if any libidinous matter was going on, and notwithstanding suffering our Neighbour's valet [Gentilini] to come wh——g at Rock Cottage, and the Signorinas frequenting the same on Sundays.

15th January

The cunning turn given to the desire in Foreign Magnesia's letter [Dr. Antommarchi], not to send him 'pantaloni d'été', viz. that this was too cool a climate, when probably it was because he could have them so much cheaper; at the same time mentioning in his dispatch to Big Wig that thermometer never had been, since that Magnesia's arrival, above 71, when it must have been certainly above 74 at least frequently here and at our Neighbour's, and I have no doubt 75 or 76⁰.

He asserted in most positive terms on my showing him a letter I had prepared to Military Secretary at Home, that he had desired nothing should be said in favour of young D.T.'s [Den Taafe] obtaining the Alfiere's [Ensign's] post, tho' I had particularly noted his words and immediately put down verbatim what he desired me to say on the subject. His cavilling, fractious behaviour about the simple return of offiziale de la Stato Maggiore, made out 2 times, exactly according to his own directions, and at last after the fourth time, saying that it had been conned and conned again. He got up the next morning after the 'expeditions' had been sent off the preceding evening, [in order] to get back the sacco for the purpose of making it up in some other shape; but fortunately [the ship] had sailed. First he wanted to deceive about the amount and make it appear less, then put in the very same words he had objected to as prepared by me. Then he would act openly and show all the expenses made under this head by bringing in both Nincumpoop and Grazzioso Tomazo. Then 'no', he would not bring in Nincumpoop but merely Grazzioso, as he said it was an appointment of no efficiency or use. At last he sent it without Nincumpoop's name. Extended enceinte not fixed upon till 31 December 1819, three months after he began about it, and his writing masses of paper for a matter of 10 lines.

His vexatious trick, when plichi were all put under signed covers, directed and ready to seal, of opening them all to look at details if all present, which he did in a hurried way without convincing himself, putting them out of their envelopes, throwing them all about the table, splashing ink over them, dirtying them, tearing some, notwithstanding he was assured they had been all previously carefully examined. And by this means keeping them back for frequently upwards of an hour to get them all right again, scratching the blots and dirt off, while ship was waiting. Then fussing and confusing everything, growling to get them off quick; and to give a colour to his vexation making some little marginal notes of no sort of importance, and declaring that without that, they would not have been understood, or some such nonsense. Sometimes for minutes (ships under weigh, messages sent to know when ready and complaints for being detained) reading over some of his, as he thought, well turned phrases, smiling and drawing himself up with all the vanity of a peacock, admiring his clever phrases, self sufficient coxcomb, constantly ordering dispatches to be got ready, though evidently not necessary, and when the greater part were ready, saying it was of no use sending them, and leaving them on your hands.

16th January 1820

His tergiversations of the answers on examination of Sergeant and Gunner of St. Helena R.A. about firing, in order to twist them into the meaning he wanted them, and so completely, by his harsh exclamations, bewildering them that they knew not what they said, but answered just as they thought he wanted.

His anger at restoration of smuggling Captain when talking to Nincumpoop about it. 'Did you ever hear of such a thing? Was there anything so unjust'. His constant hints at Polyphemes No 2.

His never ceasing introduction, on the most nonsensical matters, of Nincumpoop's name in letters to Big Wigs as if he did everything in terms of recommendation and approbation. The expression of his readiness to forward Dan's [Den Taafe] views and application, his intention of repeating it and of leaving no stone unturned to get a reversal in his favour, compared with my case.

18 January 1820

His saying to me today how Nincumpoop got everything from Sn——llo's moglie [Snell's wife] that Gentilini told her. The husband repeated to Nincumpoop all his wife got out of Gentilini. Also how Ninny got hold of everything that Polyphemes had said about firing at Naviglii, and of Poly having taken an urgent part in making the Padrone of Men—ai urge the complaint. Mach added 'I don't know how he continues to get his information, but he gets hold of everything.' He boasted that he had made Stercoraceous see things in a different light in the letter from P——rr——y than Stercoraceous at first did, or was inclined to do. He said that he first seemed inclined to see them in a modified light, but he had made him feel for his own dignity, and that he had furnished him with suggestions to answer it. As he had done all others written to P——rr——y by Stercoraceous, though in his own name. (This I was aware of by seeing the rough sent to Mach to revise or approve).

Donna's locking up all the good candelieri [candle sticks] herself,

by her own acknowledgement (boasting of it), so that I was obliged
to put up with any old broken incomplete thing, and advising an
inch or two of lume [candle] alone. Such was the explanation given
me when I wanted more.

Donna's constant encomiums of the Prima Fanciulla's [eldest
daughter's] beauty and accomplishments, to her own face. The two
fanciulle's abuse of people they met with in their rides, was repeated
by Donna to their faces with pride to her company, without checking
them for it. Her delight in telling every one of the suitors the Prima
had, and of the offers of marriage.

Locking up Negra Kate whenever she would hear of her wagging
the coda [tail], and her partiality for H——n——h, and not punish-
ing her sh——gg——g with Polisson.

19th January 1820

The rows Sultana was constantly kicking up if any libidinousness
was going on, always so seeing among the servitu [servants]. Notwithstanding our Neighbour's valet G——t——i [Gentilini][1] is
allowed to go to Vignoble's old abode for the avowed purpose of
fornicating with Mrs. S——n——ll [Mrs. Snell] living there with
her husband. This being the place where the Ragazzi always went
to walk and sit on Domenicas [Sundays].

To me the only moment of comfort I had was when he was out of
the house.

3-4-5-6th February 1820—Confined to my room 3 or 4 days; no
inquiries after health nor any offer whatsoever of anything; or
question asked if I wanted anything.

19 or 20 January 1820

Bear's [Balmain] new plan of operations. Being now in the habit
of going towards Neighbour's domain, and falling in with the
Sultana's [Lady Lowe] daughter [who was engaged to Balmain],
telling her, in order that she might repeat what he said to Mach.
That Madame Shrug [Bertrand] was continually talking of Mach,
praising him and saying how much they were obliged to him, which
Ragazza [Lowe's eldest daughter] repeated to Sultana, and she to
Mach. At pranzo one day 22 or 24th, Mach's ridiculous vain way
of going on with his new paraphernalia from London schneider
[tailor], strutting about like a peacock, admiring and looking at
himself in specchio [mirror], buttoning and unbuttoning abito

[coat], strutting up and down and admiring the reflection of himself in specchio, and for 2 or 3 days doing nothing else at dinner than buttoning and unbuttoning his coat and admiring the aiguilettes [epaulettes], and asking Donna what she thought of it.

About 20 January 1820

His side wind attempt to show me at fault in having said to Veritas that they had new enceinte as old, tho' it was so expressed in the order. He said that had not this question been put and an answer given, he might have turned it into such a meaning as he thought proper about the attendant.

26 January 1820

His suspicious insinuating hints on not finding a portfolio of correspondence 1819 he was looking for. 'Have you seen it? What's become of it? I left it on this table and never touched it afterwards. I did not take it away nor have I seen it since. It is very extra-ordinary. Somebody must have taken it away. Who could it be? Did you put it up? Is it in that cupboard? It is a most extraordinary thing. Someone has taken it, there can be no doubt, for I never touched it. It was left upon the table'.

I merely observed that if it had been left there I would have seen it. I did not suppose it could have been touched or meddled with, had it been left there. Most probably he had put it up himself. No he had not, he was positive. I had by this time looked everywhere it could have been put by accident, but it was not there. He again began his suspicious innuendos, evidently trying to throw it upon me. I said 'I have not seen it, Sir, nor have I touched it'. Then in his rude brutal way he retorted 'Altho' you may not have seen it, that's no reason why you should not assist me in looking for it.' I replied 'I have already looked for it, as you saw, Sir, but have not been able to find it'. 'Oh that's another thing'. He then called commis [the clerk] whom he interrogated, and the Orderly Sergeant, neither of whom, of course, as he well knew, could give any account of it.

He himself had not thought proper to make any search whatever for it except first looking into his cupboard. After however blasting away for another hour the first moment he thought proper to look for it in his dressing room or some of his other sanctuaries, there it was.

H.N.E.—6*

Tho' he never said a word about his finding it, or expressed concern about his side wind reflexions.

27th January 1820

When writing his private plicho, he made me repeat what Bear had said, and notwithstanding, he gave a totally different account of it, tho' he was as it were, writing down my own words viz. 'Je les ai toujours trouvés raisonnables', leaving out 'Toujours' and representing it as on that occasion only. He made Bear [Balmain] appear to act a prudent and friendly part, though on this occasion he acted worse than he did on others when he wrote queries to him and attacked him so rudely. He represented that he had advised Mrs. Shrug [Bertrand] to pay a visit (for so many paid to her by Sultana). Of what is within this circumflex, not a word was said to me.

28th January 1820

When abusing Neighbour [Napoleon] for his rudeness to Old Lord Bear [Lord Charles Somerset][2] of the Ethiopian Coast, he exclaimed in a rage, 'I'll work him up for this yet, damn me but I will! I'll not allow him to give himself such damned airs, to be so damned important. I'll not stand on any further delicacy about it. If they do not send an answer in future when anybody asks to see him, I'll give leave to go and walk all over the grounds and about the house'.

28 January 1820

He made me search again for letter from Mr. Goldfish which I had told him was not in my possession. He did not take the trouble to look among his own papers tho' he knew as well as I did it was there. After an hour's search on my part in the place he had looked for it, there it was. Even going so far as saying Nincumpoop had it.

He told me how delightfully he had stuffed the Old Bear from Ethiopian Coast about Polyphemes Second [Admiral Malcolm]; that he even expressed him self completely convinced, and that he saw entirely through the business. He had said all his difficulties and troubles proceeded from Polyphemes; that he had considered him an open plain sailor, but now found him an intriguer. In fact that he had perfectly satisfied him on every point that Polyphemes was completely wrong, and had behaved very ill; and that to him was to be attributed all unpleasant occurrences. How he stuffed him with all sorts of trash, making him see everything through his own medium, and then after he found the bait so easily swallowed, saying he was a man of strong judgement, had a good head; and, heavens, what a different account [there would have been] had he been a little less credulous.

Sultana also pleased on account of Old Mach's success and passing over Old Bear's horrible, angry looks, want of dignity, and manners.

Crowing over Polyphemes 3rd [Admiral Plampin], saying he had ventured too far in the business. How much would he give not to have it taken up in the way he had. He had outdone himself completely; he'd take care not to venture again into a thing of that kind, and such sort of vapouring. How different from his funking irresolution on receipt of the last plicho.

30 January 1820

On desiring a large caraffa [water bottle] to be put in my room, I was told by the ancella [maid] that the larger ones were for the best cameras not for those in the part of the casa where I was.

1st February 1820

His brutal manner about Ego's plicho to Paymaster 66th Regiment after the trouble Ego had taken about taking steps to have the refund of overpay matters put into some train to prevent any unpleasant matter hereafter happening. He asked abruptly in an indistinct manner for Treasury Papers which could only be understood as I minuted. And on my bringing them to him he gruffly said it was not that he wanted, but the enclosure in Secretary of War's last letter, which all the time he had in his hand.

His claiming so much merit for having sent a plicho to Reverendissimo [Abbé Buonavita] about the defunct figliola of Veritas [Montholon] telling him to break it to Veritas; and triumphantly sending a copy and riscontro [answer] highly flattering him to Big Wigs in the original favella [speech], putting it all to the account of the great delicacy of his proceedings, altho' he had in the first instance desired Ego to put up the foglio which contained the articles among those to be sent to Veritas direct by O.O., when Ego suggested its being sent to Reverendissimo.

3rd February 1820

Mach said to Tresorier 66th that by persevering in your application to be relieved from payment to Secretary Guerra and Trezzoreria, and not giving up the justice of your claim, you generally got the better of them and they gave up at the end. That for himself he had frequently had a great many battles of this kind to fight with both, and generally had got the better of them by showing them he was determined to persevere in maintaining his rights and asserting the justice of his claims. What different sentiments to those he expressed in Ego's case on refusing the second application, and saying that at no time of his life, when even a subaltern, would he have persisted or made a second application; for all that I could expect to get relieved from was the small sum of £30.

3 February

His readiness to fight the battle of pay overpaid at St. Helena, and his boast to the Pagatore [Paymaster] how he would attack the folks at home about it. Contrast this with my case. How vauntingly he spoke about recovering that of Le Poer Royal Artillery. His brutal way of calling out when I went to the shop, and he was in. Never answering until after rapping and finding nobody answered, I tried to turn the latch to ascertain whether anybody was in. Of a piece with his brutal manner once in London, when I rapped at his room door.

7th February 1820

He told me that it was very extraordinary the little interest that was generally felt about the situation of Orderly Officer, seemingly so little prized. That, however, there was not another situation in the service offering such prospects to a man for distinguishing himself or to make himself so much known or bringing himself forward; particularly if he wrote well and could relate anecdotes to give an interesting turn to what occurred, by the impression it would make in his favour with the government. It is the most important and most confidential situation in the duty near to our Neighbour, next to his own.

10 February 1820

Donna's abuse of Vignoble saying that he would know people one day and not the next, and passing her without notice. This said before fanciulle and sola ajutenta. Quoted when riding with me by Primogenita [Lady Lowe's daughter] when I gave her some hints on his own mode of proceeding.

Mach's rage at the appointment of Polyphemes' brother Grande Croix.

12th February 1820

On Angelbright [Capt. Engelbert Lutyens][3] reporting to him that Mrs. Shrug [Bertrand] had pointed out to him the ritratto [portrait] of Magnesia Primo [O'Meara], his anger at her, saying this was the consequence of granting these people the least indulgence; that this was a plan adopted by which to feel the sentiments of strangers calling there towards him, and everybody who now went there would be sounded in that manner. It was highly improper and very indecent in Shrug and his wife to hang such a pittura in their room.

14th February 1820

Calling Polyphemes 2nd a 'damned son of a bitch' for interrupting Neighbour when he was in the act of relating what passed in conversation between him and the Hocuspocus Colonel [Colonel Keating, Governor of Ile de Bourbon].[4]

His observation was made to me when he was looking over the correspondence he had on that subject to send it home to Secretary Government.

16 February 1820

Being the day after (as it appeared by a rough draft of a note from Mach to Bear) that the business was off with the 'Petite lutine'. How furious he got with Bear for asking him some information about Neighbour's proceedings. It was damned indelicate, indecorous and impertinent; damned impertinent fellow for asking it. He wanted in fact to oblige him to furnish him with some reports. Vapouring and strutting about assisted by Nincumpoop [Reade] with a little hit now and then at Bear. 'Think of his asking to be furnished with such reports', and he'd do this and that, all highly approved of by Mach. His then setting to answer 3 or 4 lines, labouring half a day over a biglietto in Gallic, calling it a chiarian chiosa [? a clear error]; and horrid bad grammar and composition.

Fury at all times and his philippics and tergiversation and misrepresentation in his plicho to Big Wig.

17th February 1820

This is the first day he appeared willing to acknowledge that Histrion's [Th. Hook] book was an improper publication. He said that it was Polyphemes No 2 and his Galatea that had provoked all the animosity of the Edinburgh Review; that they and their friends had instigated the Editors to write against him.[5]

Recollect Histrion's boasting that he disliked foreigners of all sorts on his arrival, and that he never allowed a Frenchman to come within musket shot of his house. How opposite to his book. Nincumpoop and Phaeton stuffed him altogether. Calling the great ——— of Limerick 'a damned son of a bitch' for his gulping rum out of the ship Marquis Hastings Indiaman, a thing constantly done by all of them. His rage with the Captain and the Dandy in Cut Glass for not coming to pranzo.

12 March 1820

Donna's extraordinary conduct to Ego when the fanciulle and all of us were pelting pellets during her and padrone's absence. Her violent looks at me tho' apparently quite easy about Grazzioso [Lyster] and Dean Tuff [Den Taafe], tho' former had begun throwing before me. This was one of the strangest instances of her hostility towards Ego, in which it has persisted during the whole of the following day. Her looks as full of ire on entering the billiard room as on the preceding day. It only wore off by degrees. Her rage with ragazze.

14th March 1820

Vignoble [Col. Wynyard] informed me Nincumpoop [Reade] had promised, so far back as the races September 1819, the situation of O.O. [Orderly Officer] to Angelbright [Capt. Engelbert Lutyens].

Sultana's abuse of [blank in the diary] and calling him a nasty, dirty, mean little fellow and other such genteel appellations. Mach said the Archbishop [Rev. Richard Boys] would rue the day he went home, that he would not spare him, he had done for himself etc. He called the General's [?] plico [letter] from the soccii of Leadenhall a rascally, scoundrelly, infamous (and much worse) composition.

18 March 1820

Donna's anger evidently in consequence of the fanciulle's [children's] misrepresentation of their rudeness to me at tiffin.

25 March 1820

Sultana's violent tirade against Vignoble's servant passing her vehicle without doffing capello, notwithstanding Ajutante dell'Isola [Thomas Brooke] was riding alongside. Then attacking the Ajutante about his want of spirits in not immediately sending him prisoner to his corps, which it was his duty to have done (even putting herself out of the question), for his own sake and respect to himself. But he had not the spirit. If he had only hers—here touching him up on the metal. But she had no doubt, in fact she was sure, the man had been instructed to do so. And whenever he passed her vettura [carriage] he never took any notice of her or touched his hat. It was a shame, as he knew perfectly the livery, the carrozza and herself, but he was directed to do so. But she met with nothing but insults here. She then launched out bitterly repeating with all the ill nature possible, that the man had been ordered and desired not to do it. And all this evidently, by her manners and not turning towards me, to annoy me as Vignoble's friend; and saying perhaps that I might tell him again. Then she launched out, but at whom I don't know, whether at Ajutante or me (most likely however at me), for not taking a part in the conversation which they all did (Ajutante, Mach, Grazzioso and Tomaso [Reade]) abusing apathetic people but who, she however did not doubt, would break out at anything that personally annoyed them. Old Mach then joined his voice saying that the man ought to have been punished in some way for it, and that he was fully aware (which indeed I just before mentioned) that it was quite customary among the soldiers of the garrison. His ill humour (strongly shown) because I said Old Taff [Den Taafe] had exaggerated the extent of Yiddo configuration 9 × 7 miles. Why should I doubt it, as so many people had asserted that it contained 6 million of inhabitants.

26 March 1820

Sultana teaching her muchacho [boy] to drink:
God help the King!
God Save the Queen!
And Damn our Neighbour!

2 May 1820

Mach having given me plichi to write and seeing him preparing
to go to Town, I went to the Hall in hope of meeting him as he
went, to ask him his instructions about the plichi; if I was to go
down with them or if the expedition was to be finished in the
country. But looking towards the sentry where he generally mounts,
and seeing no hurry, I asked the sentry if Mach was gone. He
answered yes. At this time he was so far away that the sound of his
horse's feet was not even to be heard. At this very instant the
Adjutant Dragoon made his appearance from among the trees on
the Public Road close to the sentry, and I asked him which way he
(Mach) had gone. Seeing him I immediately called out to him to
stop a moment for a note. I ran in and scribbled off 2 or 3 lines—
which did not take me more than 2 minutes certainly—(it was to
Nincumpoop to let me know by signal what I was to do; come down
or wait). Just as I was folding it up the O.S. [Orderly Sergeant]
came in and told me there was another man ready to return to
Town, and asked whether the other might not follow Mach without
waiting. I told the O.S. to wait for my note, which caused no
additional delay, having only the short address to write. I immediately
gave it to him and running out with it he instantly dispatched the
O. Dragoon [Dragoon Orderly], who had on the whole positively
been detained 3 minutes. I would not even make him wait for Old
Frog's letters just arrived by storeship. I waited and sent them off
by the returning man. Vignoble who was present all the time and
looking at the window, soon after this said: 'Here is the O.D. riding
full speed with some message for you I suppose.' Going to the window
where he stood, I saw Mach looking furious, coming up to the window
at a gallop and calling out to me and asking why I had detained him.
I answered that as he had left me no instruction, I [had detained
him] for about 3 minutes, whilst I wrote a line to Nincumpoop to
know what was to be done about the plichi. He went on in the same
furious way saying I had no business to stop his O.D.; that he had
ordered him to go on by a different road when he started, and make
all the speed he could. I said I was not aware of that. 'Did not O.D.
tell you I had given him orders to set off immediately?' 'No,' I said.
He then turned to the O.D. and asked him whether he had not
informed me of it. He said he had not, but that he afterwards
told the O. Sergeant to ask me whether he might not go without
further waiting. Mach then went on spluttering and foaming at the
mouth saying he had been put to great inconvenience by my detaining
the O.D.; that he had not thought it necessary to give me an

instruction before he went away; that I had detained him altho' he
had given him such positive orders against it. He went on in the
hardest manner vociferating like a Billingsgate porter and screaming,
repeating about the inconvenience, the disappointment I had
caused, and that he had been obliged to ride back to the house in
consequence. Soon after his going off I wrote him a note on the
subject, and at 2 o'clock, not having received any communication
as to what I was to do, I sent off the plichi that had been prepared,
and followed myself. But just as I came down to the foot of the stair-
case a signal was brought that I had no occasions to go down that
day, But having dispatched the plichi, I went down notwithstanding.
His asperity, vehement tone of voice and gesture. The scolding
attack was in the hearing of O.D., O.S. and Orderly Man and
Vignobles and heard all over the grounds.

3 May 1820

Mach this morning came up to me in the Library and said: 'You
wrote me a plicho yesterday about the delay of the O.D. Perhaps
you are not aware of all the circumstances and therefore I shall
explain them to you.' He then went on saying that on going away
he had ordered the O.D. to go round the stables while he himself
went the other way to make all the haste he could to overtake him;
that he had done that because he had written to Nincumpoop to
know if the ship would sail that day certain; that there were 2 boxes
(I think) of letters from the EIC on the road for him; and that the
O.D. was to stop them if he met them the way he rode and bring
him those letters; that when he got beyond High Knoll he looked
round seeing no O.D. He rode back and only met him when he
came near the house; and on asking him why he had stopped he told
him he had been delayed by me. He said that the consequence of this
was the O.D. had missed the letters, as the man who was bringing
them was already come to the house; that it marred and upset all
his arrangement and was the cause of the Young Signoras going to
Town which they otherwise had no occasion to have done (how could
this be of any influence on their going down, as he found the man
with Ninny's letter on his return to house, by his own acknowledgement, on which their going depended; that it was when he returned
to the house only about 12, and the Signoras did not go down till
2 o'clock). [He said that it] had produced all this embarrassment
and inconveniences that had occurred that day. I repeated to him

how the circumstances had happened with regard to me, that I only did then what I had done before without being found fault with, that it was the high tone of his voice and anger of his manners which had hurt me. He said he would have done the same towards anyone who had been the cause of so much inconvenience to him, and that he did not understand being obliged to regulate himself by the feelings of others, and that it was what he would do upon all occasions. That I might like it or not, he did not care. I might take it just as I liked. This he said in a very irritated way. I told him he treated me in a manner I had never been exposed or used to. That no situation or rank however high could justify any person treating another in the way he had done me. That it was treating an officer like a servant. He went on repeating the derangement of all his plans, and that when he came up and spoke to me about it where I stood at the window, instead of my expressing my concern and saying I was sorry for it and begged he would excuse it, I began to justify myself. I said was it not very natural I should do so. Was I to acknowledge myself meriting to be spoken to in that way without explanation, when I had done nothing whatsoever to deserve the harshness and sharpness of his expressions, that Vignoble was present all the time, and that he had no idea of studying the manner in which he was to express himself. [He said] he did not understand being obliged to use all this sort of delicacy in turning his expression and that I might take it just as I liked and act just as I pleased. I said every one expected proper treatment, and that the way in which I had acted only showed my anxiety to do right by immediately writing to know how I was to act when he went away without giving me his instructions. I then repeated how I had acted, that when I went to the door on hearing the O.D. asking the sentry which way Mach had gone, I could not foresee in that way, particular haste and as he appeared to me to be coming from the stables. He said how could he possibly have asked the sentry that, when I had just left him there; that he saw me set off, and that I had particularly ordered him to follow me? I told him most positively that he distinctly made that enquiry in my hearing, which he still disbelieved by saying it was impossible, repeating what he had just said. I explained that I conceived he might rely on my veracity. He said 'Well if that is the case I shall discharge him from being my orderly.' He then rung and sent for him, and the very first thing he asked him was whether he had said so or not. The man acknowledged instantly he had. On being asked after he had received such positive orders to go round and meet him and seeing him start, how could he have

asked such a question. He said he did not understand, and did not
perceive which way he was taking and therefore asked the sentry
which way he took. He then asked the O.D. whether he had not
first been somewhere else. He said NO, and that the sentry would say
the same thing. 'How long were you detained?' 'About 10 minutes.'
Old Mach then walked away triumphant without waiting for another
remark though I immediately said (which he plainly heard):
'What, 10 minutes?' The O.D. immediately answered to correct
himself 'I beg your pardon, Sir, I may be mistaken.' He did not
however turn him away.

I was told in the evening by Yamstock Ajutante that the day
before he was told by the Cadetta Ragazza at 10 o'clock that the
ship was not to sail that day, and that she had said they were only
going down to tiffin and would be back again in the afternoon to
Plantation House. Bear himself had told me the preceding evening
that the next day at sunset would be that of the departure. How
does this accord with the digested leisurely fabricated buggiarderia
[lie] of its being owing to me that the Ragazza had gone down,
which had they known the ship was not to sail, there would have
been no necessity for!!!

4th May 1820

His sending up O.St. [Orderly Sergeant] to know what I had done
with the papers he had put in the portfolio, which O.St. brought to
show me, as he had himself put several letters in it. Positively false,
as I packed up the portfolio both going to town and the last time
returning, and there was nothing in it but what I put in.

27th May 1820

Some observations having been made by Sultana of Playfair's
book, Sir H. Lowe said he was well pleased with the preface. A
few words more being mentioned by Sir H. Lowe, Lady Lowe said
'Miss J . . . had read her some of it and she did not think much of it.'
It was tiresome and appeared to be chiefly a critique of Lady
Morgan's France, and that the author appeared to say a great deal
too much against her. Sir H. Lowe vindicated the author again,
and said he had not said too much of Lady Morgan. Lady Lowe
having again observed what he said, she thought it did the book
more harm than good.

I remarked he had been a great deal too severe, I thought, on

Lady Morgan; that the commencement of the book was entirely an abuse of her; and that he (Playfair) had taken her up on one point where it recorded about herself; and that the way which I had mentioned the circumstances was much more against the author than Lady Morgan.

Sir H. Lowe asked me what was the passage, and I said it was that part with respect to La Villette, and that at all events Lady Morgan's book had proved amusing and had been through several editions.

Lady Lowe expressed herself as having read it by saying 'Oh it's that part, I recollect it.' I said nothing more, but after a few minutes pause Sir H. Lowe began in a most angry way by attacking Lady Morgan's book as instilling the worst principles, advocating the cause of the French Revolution, [and being] written with a view of making an impression in England, representing all the infamous characters who had figured in the Revolution. He was extremely severe against the book. It was a book against morality. That because some ignorant people read the book and were pleased with it, it had 3 or 4 editions, and that as it was written by a woman, she must be spared.

Lady Lowe joined in the answer on the head of supporting revolutionary characters, and Sir H. Lowe proceeded by saying in a very violent way that, as for the marquis de la Villette he was one of the most infamous characters in France, and many other epithets of this nature, and that Lady Morgan had not been treated half severely enough on that point, and he entirely disagreed with me on the subject. This was said in the most violent manner. I replied I had not attempted to defend Lady Morgan's book, but that the subject of La Villette appeared by Playfair's book to be only slightly mentioned by Lady Morgan, and people in general on reading it would either have known his character or would not have adverted any further to it, but the manner in which it was brought forward and dwelt upon in this work was extremely indelicate and disgusting, that he had [? distorted it].

June 1820
about 5th or 6th

Sultana's observation to Mach about Young Brick and Mortar. [Lieut. Wortham]. Looking at him very significantly. Think he is staying at the Vignobles . . . Her religious affectation and church going (commencing a few weeks back) and her tirades against the whole society of the Island for not going regularly. How different a turn, when she perhaps had not gone to the country church much more than a dozen times in 3 years. Her high enthusiasm which broke out about this time about the Giovani Cappellano [the Young Chaplain Rev. Vernon], his admirable delivery, (tho' a short time before so monotonous), his evident goodness—in fact a demi-god. How little she would think of a severe illness if she was so good as him, and had as little to answer for. Not long before often severe upon him, and his donna particularly, whom she now again was beginning to patronise.

Beginning of July 1820

He remarked about letters being detained. He said that had it not been for the unfortunate delay of the *Tees* going round by the Cape, and consequently not receiving his letters as he might otherwise have done had she come here direct, all the last unpleasant discussions with Autrichien might have been avoided. For, by the dispatches she brought, he was ordered to give him all the information in his power, with regard to his relations with our Neighbour [Napoleon], and communicate to him his correspondence with that quarter.

The umbrage taken by Donna at Young Brick and Mortar's way of speaking to the figliolas [daughters], asking them whether their mama had lately scolded or whipped them, and asking them to speak to Young Polisson; partly evidently trying to set them against her, and making her an object of dislike to them and setting them in opposition. Her annoyance at Mrs. Vignoble saying, as had been repeated by Young Brick and Mortar, that she never more would chaperon any more young damesellas to collazioni [luncheons] in maroon parties.

22nd July 1820

Her rudeness again, all at once at Dinner, shunning speaking to me, and her caresses to Yam, who did nothing in return but breathe like a porpoise, following his usual grunt.

24 July 1820

(Yamstock [Den Taafe] was present as well as Ego)

Cadetta having observed when Donna was speaking of her, about Madame Vignoble having frequently remarked on Cadetta's rapid growth and great height for her age (the subject being then on this point), said that when Colonel P——g——tt was here and he was sitting next to Madame Vignoble, she heard the latter say to him that Cadetta was in her fifteenth year. Hereupon Donna flushed up with indignation and said this was exactly like Mrs. Vignoble's children, Cadetta not having mentioned it at the time, and that she might have made her explain what she meant. She spoke of the malice and enmity of Madame Vignoble and how she took every opportunity of showing off. (Note: Her saying how cold blooded Signora Vignoble was). That she had treated her with the greatest rudeness and impertinence. Had it not been for Mach's connection with Vignoble, she never more would have noticed her or associated with her. Madame Vignoble never would have entered her house again. That notwithstanding all the advances she had made to her, and of which she ought to have been proud, she had only met with rudeness and impertinence on return. I said there could be no object in such a remark, and was going to put it on the footing of a misconception when she broke out interrupting me. 'Object, there was an object, a very malicious and vindictive one; but it was only a piece with all the rest'. Colonel Vignoble's house was always open to their enemies and shut to those who were intimate.

28 July 1820

Old Stercoraceous again found fault with by Mach, as mentioned to me by Teutonic, for always answering YES.

29th July, 1820

Sultana professing great affection for Forgeron XXth [Blacksmith of 20th Regiment] and her encouragement to Cadetta [Lady Lowe's younger daughter] to fall in amore with someone or other.

Abusing Blackstairs [Dr. Baxter][6], and Mach saying he thought he would come back here, and Ninny who was then chiming [in] said he would repent all his life going away.

Whole of this day working without cessation with Stercoraceous to turn a short phrase always ending it much the same, moaning and every moment pestering me, asking my opinion about it.

30th July 1820

Sultana asking Yam [Den Taafe] languishingly at tiffin to biberete [drink] with her; and her rudeness to Ego then and at pranzo [dinner] same day; and the Old Mach also (no doubt urged by her) asking Yam to biberete with him and taking no notice of Ego, nor had he asked the latter to bevere [drink] with egli [him] for a long time past.

6 August 1820

Sultana's tirade at Mach and Ego when former was speaking in praise of nuovo commis scrivenning [The new clerk's writing], saying that in consequence of having brought that famiglia (viz. commis's) to this neighbourhood it made commis's cognata [the clerk's friend] desirous to return to Cappellano secondo [Second Chaplain Rev. Vernon] in order to be near her sorella [sister]. 'You see what inconvenience will therefore be the consequence to that family (Cappellano's) by bringing those people here. This was said with spleen in her sulks with Ego. What reason was there, because cognata wished to be near her sorella, to take former back in to Cappellano's family! ! ! On return from Citta in 1819 to villa, they began to have only one pranzo di compania per settimana. [one dinner party each week].

7 August [? 1820]

Old Scratch [Col. Charles Nicol] sent a note saying this was the third day he had not seen our Neighbour [Napoleon], and his not having seen Veritas [Montholon] himself to deliver a message, as he had been desired, on account of sickness. Mach exclaimed in a furious rage 'what a damned stupid fool the fellow was, damned idiot;' and then wrote his blackguard, rascally notes to throw the blame upon him. His gesture, his furious (foaming at the mouth) manners and the billingsgate expressions, in a style even worse than the above, continued for a considerable time. When Ninny arrived he recommenced about the scoundrelly, rascally stupidity of that ass, that damn rascal, his damned rascally insidious notes to throw the responsibility off his own shoulders and to throw it upon him. But he would make him rue it; he would take the full responsibility. He bewailed his unfortunate choice in him and Great Gun Magnesia [Dr. Verling][7] who, the moment he had found he could not become our Neighbour's [Napoleon's] attendant, became perfectly indifferent to anything else, particularly towards him, besides his being 'orbo' [blind]. Again in the evening about 11 when over those writing to Old Scratch he said to me: 'what a scoundrel, and rascal he was'.

It is impossible to follow him in the strain of low abuse he went on
with.

The side hits he made at Ninny and Ego because he wanted us,
particularly Ego, to volunteer to go to our Neighbour's settlement,
adding 'and there to exercise your judgement and act upon your
own responsibility and discretion'. A number of mean innuendos and
insinuations of not having a person about him who knows enough
and is sufficiently active and willing to set off to see the business done.
As for him, his going was not to avoid the trouble, but because he
thought it beneath himself. But he wished me indirectly to go. On
his saying he thought I ought, I said it was very well for his A.D.C.
to go if it was to our Neighbour himself; but to go to his two followers
I thought it was a duty for him. To which he then agreed, but again
indirectly. When he canvassed the proceeding to be taken with us,
he reprimanded us for our opinion by saying: 'There you are both
sitting and speaking in such a manner, when you both know as well
as myself that neither Veritas [Montholon] nor Shrug [Bertrand]
will receive the letter'. Fool, idiot, rascal, scoundrel, blackguard, ass,
animal (about Old Scratch).

10th August 1820

The reflection on Vignoble for making such a bad ill-judged
comment, completely contrary to i suoi advice. But it was Vignoble's
doing—all his own.

Mach said to his Sultana that Teutonic [Janisch] was almost
every day working in uffizio, on purpose, to distract from Ego in
favour of the other, who was not there so often as one day in the
settimana [week].

12th August 1820

How proud at her primogenita (Sultana was) being toasted by
the [flag] captain who did not even know her.

Sunday 12th August 1820

Donna, in a soft tender strain, said to Yam 'it's very seldom indeed
we have the pleasure of your company at pranzo [dinner]. You
seldom favour us indeed on Domenicas [Sundays].'

16th August 1820

Mach never introducing me to il Cavaliere Duck Re consequently
my not being asked to the fete à bord. Indeed never did introduce me
more than about 3 times since leaving home.

His now scarcely mentioning Ego's name, notwithstanding the long late confabulations. Though whenever Tenente Croad[8] had any report full of dullness, and half of it being to say he could not recollect more, he was mentioned 3 or 4 times with a degree of ostentation. Nincumpoop's aid was mentioned as 'through Sir——[Thomas Reade's] effective assistance'.

Old Noto's passage money though going on licenzia.

Notification in August 1820 of promotion of Yam Maggiore Long Shanks dated 27 May 1820, after enjoying £1200 a year for a long time since [? Grutan's] removal in July 1818.

22 August 1820 or thereabout
When returning from the spectacle, never asked me, though inviting Nincumpoop, though we were all standing together, to go to the Castello to bevere [drink] Negus. No bed prepared for Ego, tho' nothing but bed clothes for it was necessary at the Castello.

29th August 1820
Sultana's ill humour at pranzo [dinner] after returning from paying some visits, and having a merendare [lunch] at Nincumpoop's country house, where Ego was not invited, because she had no adjutant with her as an outrider, Yam [Den Taafe] being out of the way. She said Mach had therefore been obliged to do this duty. But it served him well as, notwithstanding all she said to him about it, he would not take another person for adjutant. It was very hard upon her, she must go out without being attended by one (or parole simile). This is, Ego supposes, what Mach alluded to on giving him the last appointment, that he very often felt the want of a sufficiency of adjutants. Oh pride, oh vain glory. Would either of them a few years before have been warranted in anticipating all this high rank and honours, and to have gentlemen to follow them as staffieri or palafreniri.

September 1820
Cadetta [Lady Lowe's younger daughter] taking parrucca [wig] out of band box of Signora Cerceuil [Madame Pine-Coffin][9] and carrying it to la Madre, who took care to tell everybody.

Sultana's behaviour to Ego 2nd September 1820 in all at once old style, leaving me out of confab and confining it entirely to Yam [Den Taafe]; and tho' Ego went to the door, flouncing out without the least notice of Ego.

On the 3rd at tiffin continuing similarly, but returned to civility again at pranzo; but expressing her regret that Yam so seldom favoured them with his societa on a Domenica. Mach's wanting me to agree to his having said to Frog, and proposing to have it entered in confab, what had never been mentioned, Ego could swear, on 28th August 1820. Several alterations in confab of 25th and 28th with Frog, and in that of 27th with Veritas. Never saying 'Good morning', saluting or taking any notice of Frog on taking leave at his Casa [house], 28th till he was in the middle of the street when, suddenly turning round, he made the most ungracious, unmannerly sort of bow-nod possible, looking as black as limbo [hell], though Frog had repeatedly bowed as he was retiring.

Sultana observed that la signora Cercueil had the naso of uno scold.

Sunday 10th September 1820

Had not seen Sultana and Cadetta for a week in consequence of the latter having been enrhumée [had a cold] and Sultana keeping her company. Two days before their retirement to the room, Sultana had been molto cortese and the ensuing day, at a large pranzo, had merely given an inclination of capo [her head]. I never saw her, or had anything to say to her after, till 10th when she would scarcely speak, in the middle of dinner, merely asking if I had gone to Chiesa [church] that day. Old Scotto Chirurgo (Pietra Existenzia) [Dr. Livingstone][10] present at pranzo. Scarcely answered and then most angrily and looked with most hostility on my inviting her to bibere with Ego. Flounced out of the room, going out without casting a look at Ego. Next day 11th did not see Sultana, being at pranzo with X X. But second day, 12th, Sultana more kind. Yam [Den Taafe] was not of the party but on speaking of the Bello Tomaso's [Sir Thomas Reade] annoyance (upon what Primo Bombardiero had told me evening before) about invitation and speaking of Bombardiero Primo, Sultana took an opportunity of saying how amiable and good a personage the latter was. You were always sure of him, not capricious and full of whims or a moment one thing and next another—meant as innuendo at Ego. The rest of the time however more kind to me, better than usual.

13th September 1820

Pranzo Amiraglio [Admiral's dinner]. Stiffo but spoken [to] and biberando [drinking].

14th September 1820

Being in Town I called on Bello Tomaso about 4 p.m. or after. He mentioned to me what had happened towards him and that he had declined invitation to pranzo that day at Amiraglio, but had sent excuse soon after getting invited. He enquired if I had heard anything about it at Plantation House. Yes, I said, and that Mach had been surprised he had not been provoked [i.e. invited] on that day with him and desired me to take an opportunity of mentioning his feelings. I did so at pranzo, at which Yam was not present, and repeated what Bello Tomaso had said. She agreed but Mach was furious about it and never spoke after Sultana retired.

Next morning, 15th, Birro Capo [Police Chief] of Madras had arrived.[11] He was civil and Joli Tomaso after dining called in my room and asked me if I had mentioned it; when I repeated what had passed.

15th September 1820

Sultana's rage with figlia primogenita [daughter] of Birro Capo Madras at her wishing to provoke [i.e. invite] mia conoscenza [my friend] to come up to Plantation House. Next day, 16th, vehicle going down, but no provoke from Sultana; and my conoscenza, hurt at the proceeding, would not come.

Then in Citta (this day) standing in company with Amiraglio, Nincumpoop and Flag Commandant, the latter said: 'Do you, Reade (Nincumpoop), know what Sultana says. That you are the governor (Capo) and Mach is your deputy. That as for herself she is a cypher'.

This Sultana said in company. Ego never asked to go in carrozza, despite rainy weather, on coming down to Citta to hear recitare [the speech] though badness of tempo [weather] was the cause of preventing him coming down. There being plenty of room; and her primogenita did the same when Signora Rogers was the one and only [passenger] besides herself.

She also said she would not like to stand behind Dandy Gold—e [Captain G. L. Goldie][16] in such position, meaning lest he should let fly. Only an old derelict candelabra allowed Ego, tho' lots of them in House, but all kept always under lock and key and he was not allowed one. No letto [bed] at Castello for Ego though nothing in the world was wanting but linen, there being bed and washstand and a room ready, and I was always considered as Adjutant. Sultana's conduct to mia conoscenza corso, [my friend, at the races] when taking her up to presentation. A most supercilious haughty scornful disdainful angry look; and [she gave a] curtsey but [received] not a single word. When she came however (against Ego's advice, with her friends on the way to P.H.) the fawning way, the hit at Ego and the ribald wit [?] of the Madras party. Speaking of Polly's cavallo [? Nylan] restrainingly, [she said] 'Oh she has lost her good breeding since they came from England like many persons here'.

First attack at Ego for accompanying the Indiana Brigatta [Indian family] to Old Yam Knight when Primogenita expressed her acknowledgement at Ego's attention. 'Oh, then you may think yourself very fortunate I assure you (meaning Ego). He is not so gallant to the ladies'. And something else I did not hear. Attack upon all the Brigatta on their departure, which was joined in by the figlia accasata [married daughter] of Stercoraceous [Thomas Brooke]. Comparing her Cadetta to the females of the Brigata and extolling her over them and the altra Cadetta [other daughter] in beauty and manners. The famiglia was well aware of her dislike to them. She told figlia di Stercoraceous how happy she was that the Brigata family was gone, and the flood of abuse of every individual of them (except Padre whom she spared for Mach's sake). The fuss about their position on the canape [couch], [and her] reflecting on this and the partitos [husbands] going upstairs to visitare them.

The powerful efforts at popularity on the Scoglio [The Rock].

16th September 1820

On Corso [race course] Bello Tomaso [Reade] mentioned Bombardiero Primo [Major Power] babbling to Billy what I had told Jolly Tomaso on 12th.

23 September 1820

Sultana said before Old Stercoraceous and his figlia and her sposo [husband] (the Knight of Joy Mount and sposa were at Tiffin),[12] that if Old Chief of Madras had flogged his figlias well, they would have been much better behaved. This was said in consequence of her son showing some cunning about a rod Old Chief of Madras said he had to flog him with. On which occasion figlio showed some wit.

Mach so uncomfortable when Ego was not for a moment over head and ears in business. Even on my going to Citta for a day and night, he said 'Can't you take something down to travailler', though there was nothing in particular in hand but entries to bring up. And 'Can't you take down something, I would say anything to copy or duplicate'; though none was required. Confab of extraordinary length of which originals and some duplicates had been sent home 3 or 4 weeks before, and then after making a great fuss about it, as readily giving up the idea.

Sultana this day, at pranzo di famiglia, addressing herself to Yam, said how extraordinary it was the general dislike Madras females had inspired in so short a time. Everybody seemed to hate them. That her own Cadetta had told her everyone she had spoken to at the Corso [races] had expressed to her the greatest dislike of them.

24th September 1820

She wondered how Polyphemes [Admiral Robert Lambert] could have given Madras famiglia the colazione seconda [second dinner] after their rude behaviour to him. Never suffering him to have any of them to pranzo (how was it possible when he always handed in Sultana on all those occasions). They certainly did not deserve it. Her sudden great dislike to Walshwig, after a very short time before praising him to the skies; then his gentlemanlike manners, and now how rude and unmannerly.

28 September 1820

Sultana visited Shrug's wife [Bertrand], and the delight which she had with the whole of them on return. The encomiums on Shrug's civility. Her anger with Angelbright [Engelbert Lutyens][13] for inattention to her whilst there, but adding 'he has never shown me any attention, he is never civil to me'. Yet it was only a few weeks before, 'how good-natured, amiable, cheerful and good humoured etc' . . Her kindness to Ego today.

Mach's furious way of going on, on my showing him a note from Angelbright before dinner respecting a servo Soldato for our Neighbour. Swearing he should not get him; it was sufficient [reason] to refuse it, that he was being employed by Shrug. He threw the note most vehemently on tavola. Notwithstanding this, the next morning he asked me about it; and I said I thought he would do no more harm with Neighbour than Shrug. He answered that he thought so to, and most readily let him be so employed.

Allowing, without hesitation, for Shrug to draw for £250 when a
few months before he would scarcely suffer what was really necessary.
And at the commencement of this year allowing them to draw £50
per mensum more than before, though there was such a piece of
work to allow them to draw for £480 before.

30 September 1820

When Ego was presenting to him the warrants to firmare [confirm]
he enquired how Ego now drew. 'You don't draw paga [pay] for
both?' 'Yes, the same as Vignoble did, the allowances of the former
having now become mine, and his therefore returned in the same
manner as he had done.' 'But not the full, surely, for both?' adding
some foolish remark, which he knew to be unfounded that there was
some objection to drawing the full of both. Ego mentioned that it
was allowed, when both situations were permitted to be held.
Altho' there were some further ungracious observations tending to
evince his desire to curtail Ego as much as possible, he said: 'Well
it may continue as at present then', He also tried for a good while
to see whether he could get the paga [pay] of the other ajutante
per lui, and in fact appeared very desirous to take for both, saying
he had before received pay for one of Ni——lls men, Lt. M. G.,
and given it to a servo in the 20th Regiment, which had been
effective.

September 1820

The astonishing fuss which the sposo [husband] of figlia of
Stercoraceous got into completely. Courting with Donna absolutely.
Tho' neither her nor Cadetta came down to take leave of the Madras
family when they went away. Her constantly coming down to Tiffin
set for the forenoon table. Sending signals for vehicles at all times
without previous warning when they wanted them. Both frequently
at pranzo, and spending 2 or 3 days at times, and she always down
with them. Donna's incessant attention to him, and his constant
dangling at her elbow. The Cadetta was with the figlio of Stercoraceous in an equally affectionate way. Cadetta publicly wearing
Gorch's racing colours and mentioning it. Madre's publicly speaking
of him as Cadetta's partito [husband] and meeting at times, 6 or 7,
as such. Her astonishing efforts for popularity. At the 3 days races
always present there, and often with the figlia. Her repeating about
Signora Cercueil's parrucca [wig] before the whole party assembled,

to me and the Madras family (28), and turning her into ridicule.
Donna's last note to the povero scaminato. Her writing to anybody,
(for instance Corporal Moyce [? Mosse] who had written about his
sposa something which she conceived in a disrespectful way) and
her answering:—'Lady Lowe's most humble duty to Corporal
Moyce and begs to say . . .' And again the private who used to be
hankering about the brown damigella of the camera [chamber
maid]. Her writing to him about marrying the damigella, as she
understood. She wrote congratulating [?] and cutting out the
correspondence with him about it. Constantly writing thus to
Cuocote [the cook].

1st October 1820

Sultana cutting Ego again all at once at pranzo after half an
hour's friendly chat, without the least cause whatsoever.

2nd October 1820

Cadetta's behaviour at Ball when Ego came in and made a bow
to Madre, then turning to figlia to do the same. The instant she
caught his occhio [eye] she turned her head away immediately.

2nd October 1820

At Ball her taking off the Giovanettas to their very faces. Mach
spoke of the affair of [the Manty] fund row, alluding to General
Cercueil [Pine-Coffin] and Commandant Old Nick [Nicholls] and
finding fault with their audacity: He said 'They ought to have
consulted Nincumpoop, and referred everything to him, who knew
more about these things than any of them.'

Ego was sent the next morning after this to General Cerceuil
at 9 before pranzo.

Next day Donna said to him: 'I believe I did not see you yesterday
at pranzo'. Her dirty simile of Neighbour [Napoleon] pinching
noses. 'That would be very dangerous in England where colds in the
head are so frequent'.

13 October 1820

Sultana, on Ninny saying the Cercueils were no favourites of
Polyphemes Quarto's Old Woman [Admiral Lambert's Wife][14]

exclaimed: 'How can such people be liked by anybody who live entirely for themselves.'

17 October [? 1820]

After working hard for a week, being the only one engaged in it, (viz letter to Great Guns Magnesia) and at last leaving it for me to write out, he said: 'Vignoble had better do it'. On my offering to write the second one to the same, a draft of which had just been made by me after a couple of hours work as it was about an allowance, he said: 'No, they ought to be both by the same hand, or instead by Ninny, in order to give then the highest official form.'

He told me of the Commis [clerk] and that he was to have to write in the new office, (or rather a young officer). He said, they were to be adjutants, which he said was the case in other offices. He began to mention some, but said they would do very well if it was not for having any other person living in the house. I then offered to show specimens of writing of a sergeant and a soldier I had; which having done he said he wanted such a hand as those, pointing out some scribbling bad examples of officers and NCOs in the guard reports, and pretending to depreciate what I showed him as not good enough. He said he wanted all letters written and received entered in regularly. I told him that it was impossible to do any more, or even to continue doing so much as had been already done, as I found myself often sinking under it. 'That is the very reason why I wish to have more assistance, and therefore mean to have 2 or 3, or 3 or 4.' After going on in that strain for a while he ended by saying it was time enough to talk about it, though they were not wanted then.

18 October 1820

The fuss made by Mach and Ninny about the note Ego received from Brick and Mortar senior [Major Emmett][15] about the two pieces of oro offered by Veritas [Montholon] as a regalo [present] to two of his préposés [officers]. The number of knowing speculations and guesses about them, both as to the object; the suspicions all at once existed of some grand plot. 'Depend upon it there is some meaning in that. Something more than you are aware of. Why else should he have delayed so long mentioning it. It is to pave the way to something else. It is the forerunner of a present to themselves (including in the plural the young Brick and Mortar) [Lieut. Wortham].

Napoleon dictating his memoirs to General Gourgaud at St Helena (reproduced by kind permission of Baron Gourgaud).

Dr Barry O'Meara.

Longwood House. Napoleon's Residence.

Sir Thomas Reade.

'You may depend upon it they expect some gold snuff boxes inlaid with diamonds,' says Ninny. 'Ah that they do, you are right, there is something very remarkable, something very extraordinary in this whole business. There is something in the wind depend upon it. It is very odd but those people are cutting their own glass. They will not stop till they have done their whole business. Let them run on, they will soon be brought to a full stop.'

Ninny afterwards told Mach that it would all be found out at home and their names would be marked. They would get no further advancement.

Then the knowing reflections of both on the amount of Young Brick and Mortar's [reward] for accompanying Shrug and his consort. And the insinuations of Ninny at O.O.'s mistake in omitting to say Shrug himself was among the party in the ride.

The Sultana's inconsistency in having Young Polisson four days staying in casa after all her accusations against him for dishonesty, and for the indecency of his proceedings towards Cadetta (as inferred by the latter) in their walks, and as told by Cappellano Giovane [young Chaplain Rev. Vernon], and his proceedings with Ebony damesella.

21st October 1820

Sultana again recommenced (after sometime past taking little notice of him) to pet and caress Yam, and during a great part of pranzo treating Ego in the old way. But restraining or correcting herself, she resumed some attention to Ego.

Mach's ungracious rude manner to Ego when he merely represented to him the inconvenience of leaving such an immense vacant space between entry of plichi of commissaires by Teutonic, which he was proposing and in the most surly wrong way, ordering it to be done as he desired.

22nd October 1820

Mach's lashing out at Dandy Occhio d'Oro [Captain Goldie][16] and Grazzioso Tomaso [Lyster] for being hurt at Polyphemes's Old Woman not inviting them except on the second day of the feast.

His uncandid and unfair way of arguing and his comparison between the Polyphemes's service [naval service] and il nostro [ours]. His tergiversation on the subject, put up to it no doubt by Ninny, as a few days before he was of opinion Grazzioso Tomaso ought to have been asked primo giorno [the first day] and now upbraiding him for refusing a second time in the most angry mood. And also Occhio d'Oro, saying (Ninny's words of course as Ninny made the same remark to Ego) Polyphemes would not trouble those who were then annoyed, hereafter with invitations to pranzo.

27th October 1820

Sultana boasting that Shrug's wife had spoken in the highest terms of her to the capitano from Rio della Plata. How ill this accords with former tirades. Also saying she would like to go to Rio de Janeiro[17] for the purpose of seeing Autrichien's [Stürmer] wife. Her loud praises of Madame Grido y Miles began after the attack of 27th May . . .

Extract from Ninny's plico [letter] about the letter of Corpo 66th which brought the latter the sub.

'Sergeant Jeffries, who was employed by me as an assistant-Provost-Sergeant confidentially at Longwood, was given up to him.

I think his plicho [letter] is most disgraceful, and he ought and I hope will, get checked for it'.

1 November 1820

Ninny on returning from Cercueil's pranzo where Honorable Capitano of Rio della Plata had dined, immediately told Sultana that Cercueil had everything under lock and key. That he opened every bottiglia and in ferretting about he had by accident put his hand on a liqueur bottiglia, and Bristol acqua, and turned the latter beverage in great ridicule. Sultana's strange conduct to Ego on returning from this dinner, avoiding as long as possible looking at him and then giving a cold formal nod. And on Honble. Capitano saying that Ego was the only one who kept them talking at pranzo; in a deriding manner she said something about Ego's attractions (which he did not hear) but which had the effect from its ill nature to draw all eyes from the circle surrounding her on to Ego, who was at a little distance.

2nd November 1820

Cadetta came to merenda [lunch] after being some time with Castor and Pollux whom she had come down to meet. A thing she had not done for upwards of a month.

Favoured Subs. asked to meet the Honble. Captain and his noble

squad two days running to dinner whilst Pick Axe [Col. Lyster] was
left out.

3/4 November 1820

Sultana's repetition of rudeness to Ego at pranzo. Cutting him
and addressing herself to Yam, without any cause. Cadetta returning
from little Joey's christening. Mountjoy Squire[18] attacking every
guest. How sulky some of them were. Mark Madre's word how well
they were copied.

16 November 1820

Ninny asked to be remembered to Bear in so earnest a manner
after all the irritation and the epithets lavished formerly upon him.
Sultana remarked on the H.E.I.C. [Honorable East India Com-
pany] not paying Mach for his appointment as Capo. Reflecting
upon them for not paying him all arrears. He was appointed 2nd
August 1815 and arrived 14th April 1816 which would have made
at £1000 monthly, £8000.
After Tulip's departure it appeared that Sultana heard, probably
from Sally, that Mach had been after pagatore [paymaster] and
deputato giudice-avocato [deputy judge advocate Major Hodson].
How he gave it to him. What would you have done in that situation
(Pagatore)?

18/19 November 1820

Affection returning for Yam [Den Taafe] after a little miss.
Chiding Cadetta for not taking his braccio [arm] (Cadetta only
being jealous of him; thought he did not pay her as much attention
as usual). 'Do now, Susanna, do take Mr. Den Taafe's braccio.'

20th November 1820

About P.M. of Marina's [Paymaster of Navy] lodging money.
Insisting he never knew till now of Brevt. F.O.'s having retained
that of effective F.O.'s, though he had written to the P.M. that it
should be so when additional pay was struck off. Tho' Ego told him
of this operation he said that he never intended it, or knew anything
about it. Decided upon no sort of principle whatsoever, that P.M.
of Marina should only receive as Captain a sum of £30 per annum

on the whole expense of the Island, tho' as much entitled to it as any other P.M. Threatening to take it off from all P.M.s.; but that Great Gun F.O. should have it, as commanding a corps—as much a corps as Engineers, [it was] nothing but a company. I said this would only create a subject, and a just one, of jealousy. He was only Captain commanding a company as all other Brevet F.O.s were. He then gave it up; but never did Ego see such tergiversations. Want of candour, and favouritism. He did not wish to have it said, added he, 3 or 4 years hence by the inspectors of accounts that he acted uncandidly and unfairly.

27 November 1820

Cercueil [Pine-Coffin] said of costive Old Scratch [Colonel Nicol] on review, 'Having principally served in India he is not a very good drill, and some of his notions on the subject of military discipline are antiquated and exploded in the modern practice. He is also rather tenacious of his own opinions and averse to having his errors pointed out. His words of command are often at variance with those presented by H.M.'s regulations, and he is wanting in attention to many minutiae on the part of his officers, which so much tend to give neatness and precision to the movements of the Bn [Battalion]. Hence it comes that the improvement of the Regiment's service, it has fallen under my observation, has not been commensurate to the drill to which it has been subjected.'

Note: Cercueil arrived 22nd August, never saw the troops, till a month or more after, and the regiment had at the utmost 7 or 8 days drilling before inspection.

December 1820

Ninny was constantly making unfavourable remarks to Old Mach about Old Constipation [Colonel Nicol]: about excess of drill, and his being always complaining and dissatisfied and crying out about excess of duty of the men.

December 1820

Ninny's observation, when he heard of Vicino [Napoleon] having stopped some time whilst his carrozza was nearly upset and looking so pale, as reported by Croad [Lieutenant Frederick Croad]. Addressing himself to Mach with self-sufficiency and importance:

he said 'Oh it's all a damned trick. It was all done on purpose to show off. Nothing but a trick so that his pale face might be seen. All pretence to make people believe he is ill'. Also when he heard he had been eating in his carriage remarking brutally to Mach: 'It was all for effect. Depend upon it he took an emetic in order to make him sick when in carrozza, and that he might thus be seen by the English grooms, vomiting'[19].

Ninny in October or November, 1820 said to Ego that Pick and Axe and the other gentleman (who had refused dining with Polyphemes' Old Woman) had better take care, for Polyphemes would not ask them again if they did not mind. Mach's perseverance in getting his private plichi copied by Ninny. Taking him upstairs into his sleeping room at Plantation House and upstairs in Castle for that purpose, so that they could be copied with more security.

Bear's [Balmain] fulsome adulation and praise of all Mach's great measures in writing to him after arriving home. His abuse of Old Frog [Montchenu], who never had abused him, or Autrichien [Stürmer][20].

Sultana's taking a great liking to Madame Autrichien upon the praise of her by Madame Bear.

Padrone of Flago Vascello [Padre of the Flag Ship] was called by Sultana a vulgar creature, a disagreeable man, expects a great deal of attention.

2 December 1820

Sultana beginning to get out of conceit with Stercoraceous' daughter and her sposo [husband]. The latter a pompous fool.

3 December 1820

Mach's observation about the Jack Corse Magnesia [Antommarchi] being vergognoso [abashed] at meeting with Mach, and having a guilty look. Did not like his countenance, had the appearance of guilt, was certainly employed in some intrigue. I would not at all be surprised if Neighbour [Napoleon] had been doing and taking something to make himself ill, as it would upset him for ever if, after all that had been said on the subject, it was found out there was nothing the matter with him. It was his last game. He had no other resource, and it was necessary his appearance should follow the letter written by Shrug [Bertrand] to the Pond of Liver [Lord Liverpool].[21] How different from the opinion expressed so recently to Big Wig Cabinet that Magnesia Corse [Antommarchi] appeared dejected and out of favour, probably for refusing to lend himself to Neighbour's view.

Mach's inflated vanity in speaking of Hume of the House of Representatives, St. Stephens, on the speech of the latter about Ionicum [Ionian Isles]. 'Had I been there in my place as representant, how foolish I should have made him look by getting up and saying I was his chief, and dissatisfied.' Mach's observation that our Neighbour's illness, if real was all in consequence of Captain S . . . . . from Plata not having fallen into their views. Nothing else. It was the severest blow he had ever received. It upset all their manoeuvres.

His annoyance at O.O. ordonnanza's [Captain Lutyens] remarks whenever they applied to Neighbour's health, or when he particularly dwelt upon it. If he was worth his salt he would form his own observations, and make his reports not from that of others.

His denial of what Old Brick and Mortar and Dandy Lt. Colonel asserted he had said to them.

Sultana's constant encomiums of Bear, and affectation about young Bearess being in high favour, and back at Imperial Court, even saying he was an excellent judge of horses. Nothing too good.[22]

3 December 1820

Mach's remarks about the meanness of Shrug in putting his name to a letter of Neighbour's dictation.[23] That no man should be called upon to do that, so long as it was against his own feelings. That in cases of that kind it was always stated at the beginning: 'I am directed' or 'by order', and that nobody ever called upon an inferior to write his own sentiments without such commencement. If otherwise, that inferior ought to object, and it was proper and necessary he should do so.

He then instanced a case of his own, when he objected to the orders of the Prince of Orange, and carried it through; a circumstance which he afterwards brought out with a memo in order to forward his interest in an object of importance. A recommendation which had its effect. That he at another time refused to follow the same prince's orders though backed by M.Sec. and Adjutant General, except in writing.[24]

How different from Ego's own experience, when he was so often made to write in his own name, and in some cases in a very ungracious way, particularly once to Providatore, which Ego had

made up his mind not to have signed, had he insisted. But that one
was not sent, though one had been sent before less fierce in Ego's
own name by Mach's dictation with a very unpleasant retort to
Ego. Wanting also to make Ego write in same strain to Young
Brick and Mortar [Wortham], explicitly expressing his opinion
that he ought to write about his Fantesco [servant] in his own name;
and endeavouring to throw the whole blame of the business on Ego,
merely because he had observed upon the Fantesco's having been
in Neighbour's service. Wishing to make it appear it was Ego's act
and not his own.

4 December 1820

When Ego showed him Periwinkle Providatore's [Denzil Ibbetson]
account and pointed out the comparative increase of the 2 years,
Mach said: 'I really think I ought to give him the whole.' Was on
the point of giving it to him, notwithstanding his not having a
fraction of responsibility, having all his commis [clerks] paid,
altogether amounting to perhaps as much more as what he got
himself, occupation of a house in that capacity formerly let at £100
per annum for which he paid nothing, tho' all Regiment Officers
did, and his high pay otherwise, and scarcely any duty.

4 to 10 December 1820

Sultana's constant hits at Polyphemes 4 [Admiral Lambert] for
want of attention at pranzo on 4th, and the high disgrace he got
into. Comparison of Poly, his Capo di Bandieri [Flag Captain
Thomas Brown] and Ninny with the 3 Rei dei Brentfordo. Ninny and
his commis the two greatest men on the Island. Her tirades about
Ninny's greatness, and being everything. Her change with regard to
Yam Den Taafe again, his uselessness and 'quinta mota de la
Carrozza'. And notwithstanding this, next day on his making his
appearance being greeted in the most affectionate manner. Mach's
way about Ego's moneta [money] advanced to Signore Rogera,
and Sultana's asking him about it a couple of months after she had
repeatedly desired him to replace it. He said: 'Why he never asked
me for it.' Was it for Ego to ask for it after she had so repeatedly
put him in mind of it, with the risk of some rude apostrophe had he
done so. And as Sultana said, why should he have asked you for it,

when I myself demanded you to do it so often. But this was of a piece
with his debt to Capo of Ospedale Primo [Dr. Baxter].

                                                          Horse Guards
Extract from M. S.   5 December 1820

His Royal Highness has ever felt anxious that these sentiments
should be impressed upon every officer whatever may be his rank.
'That the discipline of the army and the subordination between its
relative ranks upon which the preservation of that discipline and
the character of the army depends, cannot be more effectively
maintained than by constantly avoiding harsh, brutalising or
injurious expressions upon occasions when reproof or even punishment may be necessary. The dignity of the superiors is lowered by
the use of the expressions, and by intemperate manners the feelings
of the inferiors are hurt, and with others, respect confidence and
affection towards the superiors are destroyed; nor does His Royal
Highness wish by any means to confine the restrictions to the
principle which should guide the conduct of the inferior officers.
He considers it applicable to all ranks from the General Officer
to the Corporal, satisfied that in the lowest or in the highest ranks the
use of coarse, harsh and intemperate language should carefully be
avoided, that reproof conveyed in terms which are not insulting and
humiliating will at all times and upon every individual produce a
more beneficial effect.'

                                                       5 December 1820
When Ego told Sultana of his reception by Polyphemes' Old
Woman—of not noticing him on entering drawing room the
preceding day and once before—she observed to him, after a
terrible tirade against Old Woman that Old Constipation had
significantly moved backward the chair of Capitano Benetto
[Captain James Bennett]25 (who always made it a point to sedere
on her left, next to her), as if to call her attention to the position of
Capitano at her side, as much as to say 'he is always there'. She said
that having repeated the circumstances to Old Mach, he answered:
'Then he is a dirty fellow for doing that.' Sultana said at the same
time, 'You see the feeling, and it is impossible to say anything about
the N-v-y; they are everything here.'

Sultana received Ego on the stair case when he sent up word to
speak to her about Rogera's bill; not condescending to ask him
into the princely boudoir.

7 December 1820

On my asking him this day whether he had spoken to Teutonic [Janisch] about the days to attend, he said NO, he conceived that was settled and understood. (Though I had told him only 2 days before that notwithstanding my desire, so repeatedly expressed, that he should come 3 times per settimana he now came only when sent for, and that he had only desired him, the preceding week, to come not later than 11.) The very day before this a Dragoon had been sent for him at Arno's Vale, a message to Town and another to his own place, and to the latter also the evening before; altogether 4 messages before he came and then it was nearly 12 o'clock the day he came. But he began to attempt to justify him for not coming two days before, on account of returning from Town. 'But then he never offered himself or came near me to know if there was anything to be done.' I replied, 'and then I was employed from 6 in the evening till 11 at night. That he had shown a great deal of reluctance in coming (two days before I had told him, he appeared very indifferent about it). That I had been once three days unable to hear from him and had written him 3 notes, and had 3 or 4 messengers searching for him in different parts. That he appeared now not inclined to come except part-timely, and by this only coming little more than once a week.'

9 December 1820

Mach's tergiversation about Ordonnanza No 4 Angelbright [Engelbert Lutyens] (whilst awaiting to hear from Ninny respecting his conversation with Ordonnanza this day, to whom he had written about it). First telling me he really believed he heard of the matter from Captain of Rio della Plata, and second very uncertain whether it had been mentioned to him at all by Ordonnanza, and was quite confused in his recollection. But the moment he got Ninny's answer, just such a one as he expected, he said, Oh, he was then quite positive that it was from Ordonnanza, who did not speak of it as at all doubtful, but as a matter of positive and actual personal observation. His bitter reflections on him and his unsuitableness for post. On Ego's proposing to Mach, that Ordonnanza should give a written statement of the circumstances, he replied, as if I had a scheme in view, 'What do you think would give him the advantage of making a statement or report?' I said he had told me he had made one.

H.N.E.—7*

9 December 1820

The governor asked Captain Lutyens (referring to one of his notes where he states General Bonaparte to be ill of so and so) who had given him that information. He said it was Count Montholon. The governor observed that by reading his note it would convey the idea it was an information given from his own knowledge. Captain Lutyens repeated that it certainly was not; but upon Count Montholon's information. The governor observed it was perhaps just as much to be relied upon as the information given by Bertrand to Captain Lutyens viz. that General Bonaparte was assisted back from the house by Counts Bertrand and Montholon when at the same time Captain Lutyens had seen him returning by himself, walking without assistance. Captain Lutyens said he was assisted, and then explained that in consequence of what Sir Thomas Reade had said to him, the day he dined on board the Owen Sandown [?], on the subject, he had, the next morning, spoken to Taylor (one of the gardeners), who informed him he had seen General Bonaparte returning from Count Bertrand's house with Counts Bertrand and Montholon, and that he was assisted by them. (It could not be made out whether he stated by both or only one of them, from the uncertain and confused manner Captain Lutyens related it.) That he himself had afterwards seen the top of General Bonaparte's cocked hat over the sod wall, as he was returning home through the gardens, and was pretty sure there was some one with him, but could not tell if there were two. This appeared also to be a very confused recollection of Captain Lutyens of this part of the matter. At one time it appears as if he had, or might have, seen two, and at another as if he had only seen one, and even that was uncertain; but he concluded being under the impression that General Bonaparte was accompanied. However, it was difficult to reconcile with his having only seen the top of the cocked hat. The governor said he had mentioned to him his having seen General Bertrand returning home alone, and believed Captain N/c [George Nicholls] had also told him that Captain Lutyens had stated the same thing to him. Captain Lutyens mentioned that he was so occupied about the circumstance of some slaves having got to the stables without a pass, and his mind was so full of it, being then endeavouring to ascertain the matter, that he was not so particular in his observation as he otherwise would have been.

10th December 1820

His boisterous exclamations and language about Ordonnanza for writing a Note objecting to peeping.[26] No doubt put up to it by the

Young Brick and Mortar [Wortham]. 'There was damned intrigue going on in that quarter, there was no doubt. Damned impertinent note.' Then obliging Ego to write to him in his own name, notwithstanding the remarks at Shrug's submitting to writing for Neighbour in his own name. He also was having a side-wise hit at Ego. Should ask the gardener yourself. Should be oftener at Longwood among those people. His shifting and quibbling to throw all this on Ordonnanza, and, if he could have done it, on Ego, and asking him: 'Don't you recollect my saying so and so to you yesterday before receiving Ninny's note?' Which he had not.

Same day [10th December 1820]

On looking at the entry of Magnesia Primo's notes to and from, he said he was sure there was one written in answer to the first one Magnesia wrote to Ninny, and that he was certain he had seen it among Magnesia's notes in pigeon holes. Not the case, and Ego had taken the precaution to enquire not only of Ninny, but Mach himself, to know if they had any of these plicos [letters]. To which both declared, most positively, they had not, and Ego had searched among all the papers and books, and had not found any such, nor is it likely it ever was answered, otherwise than verbally. His jealousy at Polyphemes No 4 paying a visit to Shrug's consort, and not mentioning a word to him tho' conversing with him a long time the preceding day to his going.

12th December 1820

His vapouring and anger about Polyphemes Old Woman's [Admiral Lambert's wife] visit to Madame Shrug [Bertrand]. How he would be at him (he said) if it continued. He would first attack him by showing the contempt in which he held Polyphemes' No 2 character [Admiral Malcolm]. That he would expose the latter to him (as they appeared to be such friends) and let him know everything about him. Expose his whole conduct here, and his intrigues. How he pretended to discuss his (Mach's) duties and actions here, the acts of government etc... and worked himself up, going on in this way to a perfect frenzy. How he despised and held his character in contempt.

13 December 1820

Mach's brutal look at Ego when on laughing out loud at something he was reading, and turning round expected that because he laughed, Ego would also. But, finding he did not, stared in his savage way for sometime. Most likely in consequence of Ego not making any remark on ordonnanza's note received a short time before, which he observed he thought was a very short one, and he conceived might have been a little more explicit.

Sultana more courteous than ordinary by asking Ego to have piccolo ligno sent for Chirurgo in Citta on his complaining of having been amalato all day. She was however molto piu cortesa towards Yam Aide [Den Taafe]—whom she advised to avoid exposure to sole [sun], and enquired into all assertions of his complaints: a thing never done to Ego.

14 December 1820

When Mach showed me the anonymous plico, and asked Ego 'what do you think ought to be done'. I answered I thought it would be well to endeavour to find out if the Fantesco [man-servant], who found it on the stair case of his Padrone's quartieri, was not concerned with it. That Ego thought it would not be difficult to ascertain that point, and by that means form some judgement how the matter originated. That Ego himself thought it would not be the production of a combined set of people, as it had been so thought of, as appeared in plico. Something of it would have been heard before this. That Ego however would be strongly inclined to suspect the Fantesco to be concerned; that he had such an idea of him that he believed that when there was any trouble he would be one of the first to place himself in the front of it. If he was found connected with it, send him off the Island.

Mach asked Ego who he proposed should ask Fantesco, as himself of course could not do it. Ego said the Capo of the corpo. Mach fired at this saying he was not a person he ever would think of for such a purpose. How did he act in presence and hearing of his own men when meeting with a fatigue party carrying flour casks? Did he not order them to throw them down and say he would not allow his men to be worked in that manner? He would be the first man most likely to say: 'Oh, it's no wonder when the men have had such hard work'. How did he act when he desired him to speak to Tenente Croad? He was not satisfied with him on that occasion. He had not repeated what he had said to the Tenente, but merely that the latter should not do so again. He did not know what he might not have said to him then. He would not be surprised if the plico was in consequence of the way in which he had fagged his men

by marching them up to Chiesa, Terra Francisco Piannina,[27] and
working them as he did, and he would be happy at any opportunity
of throwing it off his own shoulders by ascribing it to the fatigue
parties. (As he had already made a piece of work about the fatigue
duties.) The proper person to question Fantesco was his Padrone.
Ego answered that he had merely mentioned the Capo as he thought
the Fantesco would be more likely to be awed and alarmed in the
presence of him, if guilty, than of his Padrone (who was, as it
appeared, very partial to him, particularly if he supposed he was
a favourite of his) and was more likely not to be appalled, and by
that means deceive him. That the plico being found where it was—
where none but services and orderlies, or persons having business
there, could have access, and the caserne being entirely detached and
at some distance—agreed strongly in favour of the supposition that
some of the servi must have had a hand at it. That if nothing was
done about it, and should Fantesco [man-servant] be of the party,
he, of course, should not have failed to acquaint them. Seeing no
steps were taken, they might be emboldened from an idea of his
having been intimidated, and caused no apprehension to investigate
it. That I should think it right to ascertain whether any promise had
really been made to them on parade, as stated in plico. All this time
Mach's face was flushed with anger; he spoke to me in a tone of
asperity and resentment because Ego had recommended something
should be done. Though he had explicitly declared [upon it] merely
in an incidental manner at first and disavowed all idea of éclat, he
observed that such things generally got consistency and arrived as a
consequence by not being sufficiently early investigated. He simply,
the whole time, objected to anything being done in the business except
the mere enquiring by the Padrone of Fantesco if he knew who had
put it there but nothing more—of all things to avoid giving it any
importance. [He said] that there was nothing disrespecful in it;
it only referred to past opinion which had been entertained. There
was nothing to be apprehended now and certainly, at all events,
not till after a reply to it had been received from England. That
there was no threat, no menace, nothing which seemed intended to
intimidate. Should the authors even be discovered, what was to be
done? It only involved a great deal of embarrassment how to act.
They only solicited to be removed, and it was most extraordinary,
after them having been so many years in India. They could not well
ask it less offensively (meaning to that effect), and he was sure it
would be granted immediately. That the government would see the
propriety of it immediately on sending plico home. That perhaps

they had over-stepped the proper boundary in doing so, and had gone greater lengths than solidati ought to go. In fact the whole of his argument tended to show it in as favourable a light to the authors as possible, because he was buttered in it. [He was] 'the father of soldiers', they had no one to look to but him. They would all die for him. If they heard he was going home next year who would stand their guide after he was gone; and such sort of stuff. He eyed Ego with suspicious a look, as if he really knew something of the business, or had some sinister views in what he said, which, after all, was principally what he himself agreed was proper to be done, and he was evidently delighted at the balderdash it contained about himself. It was no wonder after five years (he said) they should be anxious to leave it. There were none of five years, except those condemned to foreign service of 53rd, and only such of 66th who came out with the 2nd battalion, the 1st having been only 3½ years. This was another scene of his old hostility.[28]

16 December 1820

On Cadetta's [Susanna, Lady Lowe's daughter] returning; she had been invited da sedere on a fauteuil of our Neighbour's [Napoleon] in the Temple Chinois by Madame Shrug [Bertrand], the latter saying, 'Would you not like da sedere on the same sedia after him'. She had answered that she did not, and declined doing it. Sultana [Lady Lowe) observed it would have been much more proper for her to have done so, that her proceeding showed a want of feeling and contempt towards him, which she thought very wrong towards a person in his situation; that the last time she was there and that Madame Shrug had shown her the Sanctum Sanctorum, she, in like manner, offered her a seat, of two there were there, saying it was Neighbour's own, and that she offered it to her in person on that account and that she immediately accepted it, saying that anything belonging to such a person involved particular interest, and again asserted her disapproval of Cadetta's manner of answering. Mach observed that, for his part, he thought the answer was a very good one. He approved highly of it. She could not have acted better. Her conduct was perfectly natural. Sultana immediately retorted warmly, 'Many unnatural things were done every day which met with approbation', and that for her part she wondered his liking anything that was natural. 'I am surprised to hear you talk in that way, that *you* should approve or like anything that is natural'. Disdainfully and with a look full of contempt and triumph, rising

from her sedia and quitting the room, Mach looking pale as a sheet,
absolutely ghastly, lips quivering with rage and resentment, with
at the same time an expression of humiliation as if conscious the
rebuke was justly merited.

Cadetta had before observed that Madame Shrug had expressed
her belief that a Chinese fauteuil in the little pagoda had been
sent for from Mach's residence[29]. He fired at it immediately, exclaiming against the cunning and artifice of Madame Shrug in
endeavouring to tempt Cadetta, and insinuating at her dangerous
and intriguing disposition.

Mach's delight on a former occasion on Sultana's observing she
would be afraid lest her primogenita [Lady Lowe's elder daughter
Charlotte] should see Neighbour, for fear of his saying something
rude to her, or using the phrases he was wont to do of his being a
coward, a butcher *che gli tagliare la testa*, and in thinking him right to
do it, expressing his wish he might, and that he would be glad of
it.

Mach's constant change of mind about whether foolscap, post or
note cards should be used. One moment directing that such sort
should be used for certain object, and the moment after finding
fault and getting in a rage with one for doing so, saying he did
not mean it. And, when told he did, either answering he had not
said it, or, if he did, did not mean it. Long plichi sometimes six a day
to Ordinanza [Orderly Officer Lutyens] at Vicino's [Napoleon's].

23rd December 1820

Mach and Sultana boasting it was at his recommendation Domine
Padre Wales got himself posted.

Her now saying that her primogenita [elder daughter] did all
she could to attract the Bear [Balmain].

25th December 1820

Old Frog [Montchenu] being asked to his Christmas, though long
before proscribed, and his giving out to the world that he never
would be again invited.

25 December 1820

Mach's brutal proceedings towards Ego on showing him the answer
to his prega [request] for exaltation.[30] After having read it, bringing
it up to Ego along with Plichi book: 'There's a letter about you. It's
very odd they will always view the matter in a totally different

light from that intended.' He said that it was refused on the plea
of its being asked as a consequence of the application of Mach, which
was not what he meant, pointing out at the same time a paragraph
in his letter where he mentioned that the first application was made
for anterior services (a construction of Mach's own part upon it to
give it weight, as Ego never meant to confine it to former services;
but on the contrary expected Mach would have warmly advocated
it on the grounds of those [services] he had rendered him). On which
Ego observed: 'Yes, Sir, but that only mentions former services, not
those here'. On which Mach flew out, 'What, do you mean to say I
have said nothing else? That I have confined myself to that'. Ego
said he did not mean to say that, and checking his fury Mach added:
'But see what follows'—which he read. He then began again very
violently, saying that instead of being satisfied with what he had
done for Ego, he found me discontented, reproaching him by my
looks and manners for not doing more. Ego replied, the whole time
perfectly mild but gravely, that I meant no reproach, that I found
my situation considered in a totally different light from what it was,
and that there had been nothing said at all satisfactory about me,
as it appeared by Vignoble's letter when he saw Sir A.I. [?]. I said,
of course I felt hurt and dissatisfied at it, disclaiming again any
idea of having meant any dissatisfaction at his manner of recommending Ego, but that I found in this instance as well as in the first
when Sir George Bingham interested himself about me with Sir
A. I., that my situation and particulars were not considered in the
proper light. Mach retorted in a fury that he had watched Ego's
countenance and manners, all the time, and that by what I said he
was sure I meant it as a reflection and a reproach against him for
not doing more for him, whatever I now said. 'That, I can assure
you, Mr. Gorrequer, that impression will not easily wear off my
mind'. After all he had done recommending me in the strongest
possible terms, that he could not have done more for Ego had he
been his brother, and the return was nothing but discontentment and
dissatisfaction. Ego again disclaimed all this, saying that he had
duly felt, and with proper gratitude, what he had done for him, and
did express himself so on those occasions, but he had not regretted
having tried to explain to Mach.

                                                    27th December 1820
After all the abuse of Old Frog [Montchenu] for his plico to
Veritas [Montholon], being proscribed her tavola [table] by

Sultana as well as himself. Abused to all the world for those plichi, and giving it to be understood he never was to be again invited. All at once reinstated into high favour and grace of both, by his writing to Mach in answer to his congratulations on the parturition of the Duchess de Berry: 'J'ai reconnu la noblesse de votre belle âme, et je la conserverai avec soin'. After that immediately invited to pranzo. Not a word now heard against him, but kind notes inquiring about his health—which had never been even verbally enquired into for months, of his indisposition; he had even avoided Old Frog in the strada [street].

30/31 December 1820

Working hard whole day fabricating a short biglietto to Old Frog [Montchenu]. The frequent bursts of 'scoundrel, rascal, blackguard etc' let off at him whilst composing it, and the frequent observations of 'this is a most important note (to ask him who the persons were who had spoken of the wish to have Giovane Vicino [young Neighbour i.e. Napoleon's son][31] on the throne of Frogland [France]), one of the most important I ever wrote; it requires a great deal of consideration'. This was when he was puzzled what to say, or how to turn his phrases in French. Several of mine he was obliged to adopt after all. Not knowing in fact what to say, but determined to pick a hole in Frog's coat and to harass him. Saying he had completely committed himself, and he'd be damned if he would let him out of that trap. He would make him feel, he would work him, and not let him alone till he got fairly involved. Then all at once giving up writing, saying he did not think it worth writing about. But the second day, at it again with revived vigour, and full of the high importance of doing some thing on it. At last sent it off with imprecations on Frog.

December 1820

His constantly increasing dislike of Capo 66th Regiment [Colonel Nicol], long urged to it by Nincumpoop. The 15th, showing me Cercueil's letter, enclosing one from sudetto chiamandola [the above mentioned]; most impertinent. When Cercueil [Pine-Coffin] had found out Capo was not a whiteheaded boy of Ninny, nor consequently of Mach, he began to show a prejudice also. His remark on the revista [review] of Capo was unfavourable, and he showed that feeling not a little, compared with the revista of XX Regiment by so inferior a Capo as Jack's figlio [Major Edward Jackson], who was exalted above Capo, evidently from knowing the feeling of Mach, and the gratification that it would afford, and also probably from pique that some of the soldati de corvée of 66th employed by Cercueil had been ordered on duty and called away from this job one day about the time of making the rapporto. Cercueil [General Pine-Coffin] pretending to be a judge of Pivot's maxims and rules. When did he learn them? Swell [Sir George Bingham] used also to be prejudiced and to shape his views agreeably to Mach's ideas. He was satisfied with his lame accounts and garbled extracts, swallowing them as facts.

1820

Indelicacy of Sultana showing Madame Vignoble [Wynyard] ritratti [portraits] of figli naturali of [illegible] . . .

The tortuous manner of putting me off from taking a drink.

The *General Harris* retained from 25th April, though ready to sail (for the purpose of taking Bear and She Bear), till the [3rd] May[32] and waiting to put off if lead from Mach to make it a matter of official attention and conditions of the character of the Company, though he had plenty of opportunity to go before, being under his order of recall, 8th March. What chance would Bear have had of such attention a few months before.

Date about 1820

How regularly applicable to Mach's steps was the following remark (as relating to his conduct towards Ego) when writing a goosy wissy to 20th Regiment respecting the behaviour of Noto on 17th August 1820:

'It is a most serious transgression of the proper bounds of authority to substitute personally injurious, insulting or humiliating expressions in the place of reproof or of punishment, even when offence might appear to furnish a just motive for either of the latter; nor can there be hardly any proceeding which had a more direct tendency to deprive command of its proper dignity or to weaken more the feelings of due and real respect towards it. The delicacy of an officer's own sentiments ought to present the best rule of his conduct on such occasions'.

Chapter Five
1821 The Death of Napoleon

1st January 1821

Sultana's conduct to Ego, who bowed twice on her entering the biblioteca without any notice (tho' apparently in favour next day). Wishing 'bonne année to every one, almost, and only about the middle of pranzo condescending to notice Ego. And because he did not smile or seem delighted at her deigning to observe him, working herself up into a horrible rage. Directing her eyes with violence from him, and smiling and looking so affectionately at Yam [Den Taafe], and on leaving tavola bursting away in fury and passing round by Yam's end, for the first time since arrival on the Rock. The preceding day, returning from Chiesa [church], leaning so affectionately on Yam's arm, without even looking towards Ego, tho' Yam had come to Chiesa late, and tho' Ego had accompanied Sultana there. This was done by moving out of pew previous to Ego.

2nd January 1821

He broke out in the same strain at pranzo [dinner], before Sultana, observing Longwood had been fatal to all medici [doctors]. Sultana observing 'Yes, to four viz: O'Meara, Stokoe Verling', and adding 'Dr. Baxter fell away in disgrace at least with you'.

5 January 1821

Mach's rage with Old Brick and Mortar about lime. He would lash him for it. It was damned impertinent and presumptuous in him to behave in that way to him. Was he nothing but a cypher? This was all because Old B. and M. had adhered to former instructions about giving out so many days per week or month.

Ego's Bill of quaranta livres [£40] paid on Sultana's account, March 1820, only repaid January 6, 1821 (11 months), after several times, within 3 or 4 weeks, been prayed to do so by Sultana, and his

[Lowe's] ungracious remark to her: 'Why does not Major Gorrequer ask me for it?' To which she replied, 'And why don't you pay, when I beg of you so often to do so. Why should he ask you, when I ask you?'

Great renovation of the threat of Sultana taking herself off, all beginning of January.

Old Constipation in deep disgrace with Mach, Cercueil and Ninny. The latter always stirring up Mach with his insinuations against him.

7 January 1821

His peeping into Cappellano's [Chaplain] plico which arrived from England in Leadenhall's [?] box of plichi to try to find out the contents, and immediately thereupon writing a note to Ninny, no doubt to give him some hint about the plico; and he sent it down to him with others immediately. Previously to sending it down, he showed it to Ego squeezing it all over, examining it and the sigilla [stamp or seal], his fingers itching all the time, as if impatient to have it open. Asking Ego, 'Who do you think it's from? I should like to know,' and then continuing to paw it.

Old Costive left off about this time speaking to Ninny. Had he but known his obligation to him he would have done it long before. Mach's admiration of Brougham (whom he used to declare against), the moment he heard from Ninny that he had abused Neighbour in his speech of 4th and 5th October.

8 January 1821

Two more dispatch boxes appropriated by Sultana to her private use. Mach coming down in Ego's absence, emptying two of them and telling him Sultana wanted one. That he would take both up for her choice. But on coming down again saying she wanted both. Same evening Cadetta telling Ego Sultana was determined to go to Inglaterra the ensuing month. The dispatch boxes, no doubt, being meant for her own use as packing boxes.

Mach's grin and demon look when telling with delight and emphasis about the fate of the victims of the medical tribe at our Neighbour's. 'None of whom had had one solitary pleasing reflection in looking back to their approach to that quarter'.

9th or 10th January 1821

Cappellano Secondo [Second Chaplain Rev. Vernon] came to show him some plico from Cappellano Primo [Rev. Boys], not before

shown him, in order to show him so little variation about what he
wrote, and what he had said to him in his attempt to stir up Mach
against Cappellano Primo. This was a matter of some months back
(about the affair of Magnesia Primo) but Mach, to his surprise,
seemed satisfied with Cappellano Primo's letter, and it tallied better
with what he himself had in view. Cappellano Secondo's behaviour
scurvy and scandalous about Cappellano Primo, and himself the
sole cause of that blow up.

Mid January 1821

January 9, 11, 12, 13th continually reflecting on O.O. for his
observations about Neighbour's [Napoleon] looking ill, in his
rapporti. 9th: his brutal manner towards Ego when he found he
would not join with him in falling foul of Angelbright [Engelbert
Lutyens], tooth and nail, about the Aspirante at Neighbour's. His
justifying the latter at the expense of Angel. Saying it was the pomp
and overweaning conceit and self sufficiency of Angelbright that had
been the cause of it all, and that made him now ask to be replaced.
His vain and pompous importance. His rage at Ego for advising him
not to push the matter of Aspirante further, and finding fault with the
latter, but finishing, however, by taking his advice. Ninny's endeavour
to make him push the business against Angel and the terrible dislike,
for some time past, of him.

16th January 1821

Mach's brutal and pursuing boisterous bellowing breeze at
varleto for not telling him aicuiescosco's [?] son, Captain namesake
of Cappellano Secondo [Rev. Vernon], had called.

16th January 1821

Sultana's coaxing ways to Yam continued, tho' sometime clawing
him behind his tergo.

Wednesday 17th January 1821

Signal made to Yam [Den Taafe] by Constipation [Col. Nicol]
about mancanza d'acqua [lack of water] at the monti di scala,
received by me in his absence and that of Mach. About ½ hour after
it arrived Mach was shown it, he seeming in a great rage at first,

not with Ego, but at the signal being made. Soon after however turning round to Ego sternly: 'What did you do?' 'Nothing, I waited your return, having reasons to expect it, being nearly dark when signal received.' Which tho' marked 5½ it was near 6½ when delivered to Ego, as Yam had gone home. 'And why did you not order a supply?' 'Did not know who to apply to for the purpose, or who was in charge.' 'What,' continued he in a sulky, stern, violent manner, 'did you not know it was supplied from 2 springs in the garden, and why did you not apply to Chota, the gardener?' 'I was not aware that it was supplied from that quarter.' (Ego being under the impression it was supplied from the tank or some intermediate reservoir at Red Hill—and not that the gardener had charge of it.) Mach kept harping, chicaning and fuming, and Ego went away. A few minutes after Mach sent back for him, desiring to write to Constipation and Ispettore of the Telegraphi [Captain Henry H. Pritchard]. Then avowed that he was aware of the lack of water in the forenoon part of the day, and had given orders for as much to be supplied from the 2 springs (which had been flowing in fact), as the springs allowed, ever since 2 o'clock. The next day further acknowledgement: he said he knew of the want at 12 o'clock, noon. Where then was the necessity for his brutal mode of treating Ego? His violence during the whole of the correspondence with Constipation on the subject and pretending he knew nothing about it till the signal.

17th January 1821, after pranzo.

(Polisson present) Began a long and angry violent tirade against the Lungi [Dr. Shortt] family for not going into her [Lady Lowe] loggia at the teatro; but instead offered preferring to go into Amiraglio's [admiral's]. Altho' the reason for not accepting this was that they and the Cerceuils [Pine-Coffins] had taken one between them. And as the Cerceuils did not go, perhaps afterwards they gave it up and went into Amiraglio's, not wishing to take the liberty to go into hers. But this was always the case. The more you tried to be civil and attentive the worse it was, and that was the return you got for your civility. She would however take great care this would be the last in this or anything else she would show them any attention. Also about rudeness and impertinence. But there had always been a party against her in the Island: first the Swells [Binghams] and the Vignobles [Wynyards], then the Cerceuils [Pine-Coffins] and their adherents. But she was above all that. She scorned and despised all such little dirty intrigues, she cared very little for any of them. Whatever the Swells had done and however they might have been against her the affectionate plichi of Madame Swell, which she so often received, showed how much she must have regretted it, and how different she even felt.

19 January 1821

The preceding evening Sultana and Ego extending best terms. This day when she entered biblioteca, Ego bowed as usual but no notice, probably was not seen before. Ego was sitting next to Cl——k——, and soon after Sultana had taken her seat she cast her eyes towards Ego, and the second Brownie Sorella next to him. It was a hostile sort of a look, and as she did not bow, Ego did not presume on the familiarity of bowing. During pranzo evidently in the highest displeasure at Ego, avoiding studiously looking towards that end of tavola. But on retiring and passing him condescended to give Ego a nod. After retiring to biblioteca from tavola, Ego sat on corner of canape talking to Brownie. Sultana in full flow of smutty talk about vigorous exertions of quindici volte of Piccolo Carrozze. All this time however eyeing every now and then Ego in the blackest way, and entering into a very animate confab with Piccolo Carrozze, doubtless by her glares, about Ego. And seemingly in a very violent rage, abusing someone who, from her expressions, she represented as ill-tempered and disagreeable. Soon after a tondo guico [a card game] was made al commercio, and there being some difficulty in completing it, Mach asked Ego, who accordingly went and filled up vacant sedia between the two old legitimate knights [Judges]. On taking his seat, Sultana who was within one of Ego, with an asperity of manners and language and an evident wish to bring Ego forward as an object of ridicule to the party and all subs. beside the K. [knights] lot, said: 'What, is Mr. Gorrequer deigning to play cards with us. This is really a very high honour, and unusual favour.' Ego merely replied drily that he certainly had not been in the habit of playing pony, as it was a game he had a great dislike to. In an instant after, and before she replied, Sotto Medico 66th [Dr. Walter Henry] came in; and the tables being full Ego immediately rose and offered him his seat, saying that he merely came in to fill up a vacuum and that he was very happy to have an opportunity of resigning it to him; which the Sotto Medico, after some excuses, occupied. Sultana at the same time merely saying: 'There was room enough both for Dr. Henry[1] and Major Gorrequer,' which the latter, however, did not notice.

22nd January [1821]

£3000 [illegible] O'Meara

22nd about Nincumpoop at the Perkins [?]

Governor spoke to Cole 3rd November, reminding him of his promise of opening the letters. He made no hesitation.

23 January 1821

Sultana, great caressing and petting of Yam, looking quite languishingly at him even whilst speaking to Ego.

25 January 1821

Sultana said that the Cadetta [Susanna] had this evening, on meeting Signora Cerceuil [Pine-Coffin], passed her without even looking at her, but galloped past. Her remarks about gothish [? goatish] and bearish manners, but said in that style rather to encourage than break her of it, for she was present.

Cadetta this very day looking at me without even making any inclination of head or taking any notice.

One of the Old Constipation's [Col. Charles Nicol] greater faults was not having altogether cut his Sotto Commandante [Lt. Col. Edmund Lascelles], when he returned to join after his disgrace.[2]

When Neighbour changed some of his palafrenieri [footmen], Mach immediately cried out about an intrigue for the purpose of letting them loose on the government that they might spread about reports of his cattiva salute [bad health].

Sultana telling Young Polisson how Pop Gun [Artillery] had put his nose out of joint, and again working up Cadetta to love. Yam now out of humour at being less petted than usual. How she had to work him back into good humour.

31 January 1821

Her vile attack against Lord Brougham's £700.

January 1821

Mach's detention of a parcel sent by *sbaglio* in his sacco for Cavalieri F. H. Kay, Isole Io., from 20th December to 18th January 1821. Anxious to open it, his fingers itching, all the time he was pawing it, to do so, and even observing to Ego, 'Why should it not be opened, it can be nothing but journaux.' And though at any opportunity asked by Ego to send it back, he always objected to it saying 'Oh next time. It is time enough.'

Sultana's coaxing ways to Yam when he made his appearance, however abused behind his back.

2nd [February 1821]

Governor mentioned about Mr. Boys [Rev. Richard Boys].

3rd [February 1821]

Governor said Mr. Balcombe had not followed his advice and suggestion. Mach said he had never observed anything of this sort before, though he had seen something on some former occasion but he had thought nothing of it; as he saw things would come right again.

Sultana never seeing me, but avoided, in slightest way, to thank Ego for all his trouble with her company.

[February] 1821

Tiffin at Alarm House, 6 February 1821. Had not asked Yam. Tiffin 29th January there also, not asked but taken into [? town].

[1821]

[Papers] necessary to be forwarded to the Adjutant General; never said a word about the half yearly return. It was only by accident it was found out to be necessary, having discovered a blank form by chance. Ninny neglected to forward that last half yearly return for the whole of 1820 and Ego had to make it out. The only thing he said to Ego about returns was that Brigade Major knew what was to be sent, and would send them to me neatly made out, and that I should have no trouble whatever with the returns; that they had been thus made out for him hitherto. The first was made out as he said after having been delayed 10 or 12 days. It was full of errors. I then took the matter into my own hands.

On going in to Fountain's [John de Fountain] House in town to look at Ninny's memorandum about his pay, I observed the lamp (no doubt one from the Longwood House) which used to hang up in Ninny's dining room, which he had bought from him.

He scarcely even would tell you if a ship was to sail or not. Though after having been told in the morning she was to sail, if he afterwards found out she did not, even so early in the day, and even though there was nothing pressing after all to be done, yet he would keep you quite desolate [?] for hours in expectation of every moment beginning dispatches. Therefore not wishing to take any thing at length but evidently in order that you should not have an opportunity of taking exercise, he came every ¼ hour, and walking into the office to see you.

Ninny said to Baxter: since he chooses to associate or walk with such fellows, they should give him up entirely and the whole of that set and confine themselves to some respectable house. I observed that I did not think it would be easy to make them do so. Was it to be expected they would give up people devoted to them and who were seconding their views in Europe; in fact all linked in the same plans and working hand in hand in the same pursuit. But a few months more might show (if the publication of clandestine matter was kept up) that there were others most probably who professed the same sort of feelings and assisted in their clandestine communications besides First Magnesia [Dr. O'Meara] and Second Naval ditto [Dr. Stokoe]. He answered nothing, but the meaning of his manner, the colour of his rage and his appearance altogether showed the struggle he was undergoing to check his resentment at what I said.

Saturday 4 February 1821

Returning with Mach from Our Neighbour's residence, we met Sultana and he went back. Ego proceeded on, having a ronzino [horse] subject to ritardare [slowness]. At pranzo when Sultana came into biblioteca she scarcely acknowledged Ego's low bow. Went in to dinner enquiring, 'Where is Yam?' in a soft tone. Took no notice of Ego any further than yea or nay to his invitation to help Sultana, but the moment Yam came in simpered so prettily and kindly in his face, asking him what he would have, which was repeated several times. Addressed confab to him immediately after he seated himself, and tho' Ego asked her to hobnob she made no attempt to join with him in confab, but purposely excluded him from it. For 15 or 20 minutes not a word or a look to Ego; then for the first time told him the Long family[3] had established themselves in their new mansion that day. Which Ego answered by saying he understood they were to come that day, if they could, but the last

time he spoke to him they did not appear certain. Sultana then
turned again to Yam engaging him with much attention about
sorella and his family parish; and again some time after, asked Ego
if Shrug's moglie [wife] was not ill.[4] This he answered that he understood she was, from the O.O. Not another word passed between
them, Sultana insinuating that people seemed to have nothing else
to do in this Island. For a long time Mach had not noticed anything
that happened, but 10 or 15 minutes after the second observation
from Sultana, he seemed to take notice of it and joined in confab.
All this time, and from the very commencement, Sultana looked
much out of humour whenever Ego had had the occasion to address
himself to her; but smiling and smirking at Yam [Den Taafe].
When she left though, she went into a sulk without one word, and
Mach followed. Ego preserved profound silence and gravity, but
placidity.

5 February 1821

Returning from my ride this evening Mach met me, as I came up
to the front door, and said there was something that occurred last
night extremely unpleasant, at the pranzo, with regard to Sultana
and Ego. It was perfectly unacceptable to him, it was a thing he
had never witnessed before, and it had caused him to leave the
tavola with Sultana. There was something in Ego's manner more
than in what he said, which he could not understand. That Ego
appeared determined to preserve an inflexible silence. Ego replied
that he kept silence because he had been excluded entirely from
confab by Sultana yesterday evening, in the same manner she was
in the habit of frequently doing, without his giving her any cause
whatever for it. That on her entering the biblioteca, before pranzo,
he rose from his seat and gave her, as he always did, a respectful
bow. That she scarcely, though her eyes were fixed upon him, took
any notice of him. It did not amount to anything like an acknowledgement of it. That she had all the appearance of being very much displeased with him. That on sitting down at mensa [dinner], he offered
her everything near him and asked her to do him the favour of taking
wine with him; and that during the whole time he obtained no further
notice from her than yes or no. But when Yam, who was late, sat down
she immediately began addressing him in the most friendly way, and
from that moment never gave him an opportunity of entering into
conversation. The only remark addressed to him being that the
Longs [Dr Shortt] had taken possession of their mansion that day,

and that Mrs. Shrug, she understood, was very ill; both of which he answered. Then she turned immediately to Yam. That the only reason he could assign for this was that she might perhaps have been displeased with him for not returning with her when they met her in the carriage, and that he, Mach, had turned back and proceeded on with her. That he did not do so on account of the ritardare [slowness] of the ronzino [horse], which he feared would have annoyed her, as had been complained of before. Mach said that it had made no impression on her. Ego's name had not even been mentioned during the ride. That he had particularly observed her and Ego during the whole time (bugia) at dinner and that she, as usual, in her affable, cheerful, polite manner, which she evinced on the occasion to everybody, had repeatedly addressed herself to Ego, and endeavoured to get him into confab. And that it was only after she had been repelled and repulsed in so peevish a manner by Ego, that she addressed herself to Yam. That Yam was not a person of conversation, and it was ridiculous to suppose she had selected him in preference. He was very well disposed, and did what he was desired, but he would not take a part in a conversation. That had I been in the habit of silence and reserve, it would have been a different thing, but I always entered into the conversation going on. But here there was a determined intention of avoiding it. I again repeated what had occurred, saying it had made the impression in my mind that she was offended; and urged how could I then attempt to force myself, which I would not otherwise have done, into a conversation addressed to Yam, almost entirely about his friends and personal commis. Sultana would have probably thought it very presuming and improper in me to have done so. That as I had done or said nothing whatever which could draw me on Sultana's displeasure or exclude me from her confab, I naturally felt hurt. He again insisted in an unpleasant high tone and manner and in a most contradictory way that she had done every thing to engage me in the confab. That the fault was entirely on Ego's side and in the most upstart vulgar way exclaimed: 'I like that, indeed, a good idea upon my honour, you feel hurt, indeed, the best thing I ever heard'. That it was she who had a right to be hurt at the treatment she received. I again went over putting nearly what I said before, that I met her with the greatest cheerfulness, anxious to pay her every attention and would have been highly delighted if she had condescended and addressed me. But as of course she gave the lead and impulse to the conversation, it was impossible to share in it except she gave me some opportunity of doing so. And when the whole of it was addressed to one person on whom her eyes were fixed the whole time, and it was a confab of such a nature that it was impossible to break into, it would have been improper and would have been disagreeable to her if I had done so; and it was a thing I never could do. That besides I would candidly say that Yam was on all occasions taken much more notice of, paid more attention to than Ego.

He said that what I had just said about Yam was what he did not at all understand, he really did not know what to say about that, it was quite beyond his understanding. He then went on 'A very good idea, ha, ha, Mr. Yam had more attention than yourself'. He repeated that and making similar remarks for some time in a tone of derision and triumph. A man expecting attention from a Donna, who ever heard of such a thing? 'Why I never in my life expected that a lady was to be attentive to me'.

Ego said that he did not expect attention from Sultana, but thought he ought to receive his share of notice in a party of 4 persons; that besides himself, Mach, and his lady there was only one man present and himself (Ego). If she chose to exclusively speak to that other person, and cut Ego completely out of the discourse, there was nothing left for him but to preserve silence. So it had happened the preceding evening when he had maintained silence, in consequence of his neither being looked at or spoken to.

Mach declaimed a long time upon the inattention shown to Sultana here, that she had to put up with a great deal and that nothing but her strength of mind and her good nature could have enabled her to put up with that. She was the first Sultana here, and that not only from her rank as the Capo's Moglie here; her birth or her rank in life (something to that effect) entitled her to every kind of attention.

7 February 1821

Sultana having been the day before visiting Neighbour's mansion [New Longwood House], at dinner this day exclaimed with all self-sufficiency and affectation, how superb, how elegant, the suite of rooms was. Plantation House was a mere hovel to it. She never could be reconciled to it again—she was quite out of patience with it— everything so mean and dirty about it! [She remarked on] how the former looked with the new furniture. (This was nothing but a few chairs, tables and sofas of the commonest sort and not the fourth part enough! and several of the draperies of the windows very mean and not half so good as any of the rooms at Plantation House).

She made the same sort of exclamation, when visiting the New House, to the Orderly Officer, and saying what beautiful trees there were. Oh! if they had such at Plantation House; but there were nothing of the kind!

7 February 1821

Sultana said that in her visit the preceding day to Neighbour's mansion the Orderly Officer had been studiously abusing Shrug's wife [Countess Bertrand], calling her the most violent woman in the world—that was all the cause of her illness—her ungovernable rage. She added that she supposed it was to make her say something in the same way—to sound her—that he must have thought she would have been pleased at it. But she had always spoken of her in the most friendly terms, sympathizing with and pitying her, and paid her all the attention possible—all but sneaking (the word used).

9 February 1821

Mach's rage about Medico Primo [Dr Shortt] having told Frog that his compliment was the same as that of Sultana. Sultana now patronizing subs. only, Young Polisson, Pop Gun any of those; making her change at pleasure; an apparently fixed determination about spectacle, balls etc., first by a little flattering: everybody expecting her; what a disappointment if she did not go etc.; what efforts for popularity even amongst the lower ranks.

10 February 1821

Mach strutting up and down in Neighbour's [Napoleon] mansion, and with all upstart pride and affectation, self-complacency and jack in office style—exclaiming what a magnificent house, what beautiful suite, how elegant etc. This was the burden of the song now, constantly.

February 1821

The favoured medico was appointed Quarantine Chirurgo with 10/- per diem plus one guinea for boarding each vessel, upwards of 300 coming yearly. All in consequence of Ninny's friendship. This

medico had, till arrival of Bob Long [Dr Shortt], £600 addition to
paga [pay].

February 1821

Mach's brutal behaviour about ronzino's ritardamente [horse's
slowness] and desiring Ego to keep off as he made the Sultana's
cavallieras [horses] uneasy. Tho' it was his own that began it,
and kept it up until he was obliged to get off when Ego's could
wait.

February 1821

Her forced civility to Ego, and her assiduous attention to Yam,
when constantly urging Cadetta to sit with pagas [?] by saying she
was never in spirits but when he was present.

11 February 1821

Cadetta complained of the rudeness and familiarity of Cannonino,
and of Ninny's sub., the boarder of 20th. Sultana professed to be
highly offended at it saying that the latter was a very impertinent
fellow, putting *his braccio al intorno of il busto* of Cadetta and holding
her in that position during cena [supper]—though she had, for
so many months before, been constantly encouraging the fanciulla
to fall in love with both them and several others. Sultana said
that Cadetta had told her that Cannonino had said that altho'
Sultana was getting tanta grassa [rather fat], she however did not
get so coarse as la troia [sow] di Davidi. [David was probably a
gardener].

12 February 1821

At spectacle when Sultana was laughing, and often turning to
Ego with observations and laughing at it; and the latter, of course,
obliged to join in to a certain degree in return. Mach reproved her,
and she retorted: 'Do you mean to prevent me from laughing too. That
is very good of you'. He then answered 'No, but there is Mr. G. who
is laughing'.

Leaving no wine to be got at when Ego was left behind, sometimes.

Her tenderness for Ego's commis [clerk], 20th Regiment. He really should not have much work given him—he was of a delicate constitution—required time to take exercise—should be allowed to ride on horseback—Mach ought to have a horse fixed up for him—could not stand much sedentary work—she had been told of his delicate constitution by Dr. Arnott—he was such an excellent man—wrote her such feeling grateful letters whenever she did anything for him or his family—what a contrast with her treatment of want of feelings for his predecessor, and only a few months before so angry that he and his family had been brought to the house, occupying a hut she had intended for a privati—and besides would be making it uncomfortable for the giovani prete's wife.

Her starting some fresh matter of complaint against the poor paga governante. The Bearess had written, and Bear also; as if, by their manner of writing, something very bad had been going on in the ship that brought her out. But Bearess had said they only used to get up in the afternoon, lying in bed till 3 o'clock.

12th February 1821

He desired me to write a plico to Polyphemes in answer to one from him. Dictating every word to Ego to write from memory and after preparing it objecting to a passage. Neglect of Capitano del Porto, which of all others was the part Ego best ricordiva, and could have sworn to, tho' Mach asserted it was not what he had desired. But he had been looking and pondering over the plico of only a few lines to try and find out something against it, and avoid confessing it was his own expression, and after 10 minutes, or $\frac{1}{4}$ hour, finding that out; which had it been contrary to what he had desired he would have immediately perceived. In his plico against Old Nick to Cercueil, he stated that Nincumpoop's (D.A.G.) [Deputy Adjutant General] 'observation had been frequently drawn to the same point as his, about irregularity [in the way] working parties had been conducted, and were dressed.'

Sultana affected so to admire Old Brick and Mortar because at the 2 or 3 last spectacles and Balli he said civil things to her, and had recently mentioned that she had by her attention to Old Frog so soon restored him, and made him look better than ever; that he had a great mind to be ill too to be invited there. Mach immediately said 'then he speaks better than he writes'. She continued that he was a most gentlemanly and agreeable person, extremely clever, highly accomplished.

Plantation House. The Governor's Residence.

Napoleon in 1820. By Captain Dodgin.

Dr Francesco Antommarchi.

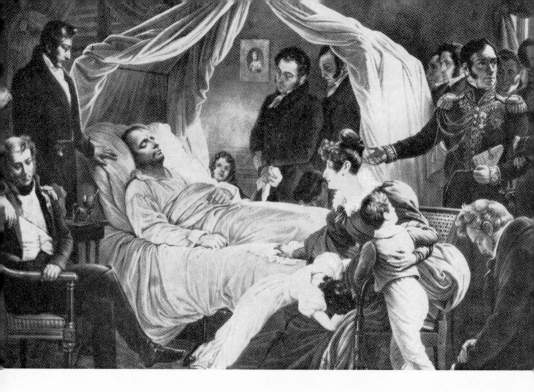

Napoleon on his death bed. By Steuben. Around him are, L. to R., Montholon, Antommarchi, Bertrand's little daughter, Marchand and another valet, Countess Bertrand and two of her children, Grand Marshal Bertrand (in foreground), Dr Arnott and Captain Crokat, and others.

Death Mask of Napoleon.

21st February 1821

His saying he put 2 books of Magnesia Primo [Dr. O'Meara] in his cupboard and now could only find one. Turning to Ego: 'Damned extraordinary that, very extraordinary thing, do you know anything about the other one?' In his suspicious manner evidently, he said of course I had taken it.

21st February [? 1821]

Donna's [Lady Lowe] conduct to Ego.
Her never calling on the Cerceuils [Pine-Coffins] or Longs [Shortts]. Calling on Mr. Guy [?] Leech five years after arrival.

22 February [? 1821]

Donna's astonishing attention to Obins. He [Captain Hamlet Obins] must dine, so long as he stayed. Came back after dinner to the company as she said to them it was the last day she could see them. Ninny never gave Ego a single return of the day; took books [?] to the 2 Inf. Dpt. Nothing was known of that Department until Denzil Periwinkle [Ibbetson] made an inspection. He never told me what the returns were. His explanation with Wynyard about visiting B———d [Bertrand] when he told me of the subject.

26 February 1821

Mach and Ninny's mystery about a letter sent down to latter by Sultana about some one to be appointed overseer or clerk. On Ninny returning the letter to Mach the latter said: 'There are few men on this island capable of writing such a letter as that.' (Note: I believe a private St. Helenian who had been once officer in 20th by the name of Foster.)

His moroseness and angry scolding and taunting way at Neighbour's House to Young Brick and Mortar [Wortham], about red stone walk, repeatedly saying: 'Ah that is exactly what I foresaw. The whole must be done after once commencing.' Though it was evident the walks never would have answered without that.

Sultana's affectation of greatness in sending an open memorandum to Mach from upstairs to the office, addressed by her to His Excellency the Governor, and inside 'wanted for the Castle before the Ball His Excellency the Governor means to give on St. George's Day!!'

26 February 1821

Mach's rage about Medico Livingstone [?] for not insisting on seeing Boney and going into Shrug's quarters, saying to Ego: 'Do you see how the fellow is shoving himself in again?' Meaning Shrug.

1821 [? February]

Mach's rage with Darky for sending Neighbour's servi by a ship touching at this [port]. And his rage against Polyphemes Secondo for sending them direct to Europe.

4 March 1821

Sultana holding up to ridicule Medico Primo's [Dr. Shortt] bons to Giovane Cappellano [young Chaplain Rev. Vernon] and moglie [wife] about his regulations for medicine being issued on bons only of Ninny. Mach himself and Sultana were in the habit of so doing for a good while at her parties.

She said to Ego: 'Well your friends the Cercueils have quite cut me now. They won't speak to me.' That the moglie had scarcely returned her obeisance, and she supposed after that, they never would pranzare [dine] at Great Man's again.

8 March 1821

Mach's insinuation that now nobody would believe anything said by those people (Neighbour's folks). They had got such a reputation for lying that anything they might say about his health would never be believed.

His jealousy of Orang Outang and Rib [Mr. Pauer and his Wife] and the other pair for calling on Shrug's wife viz. Russel and French Rib, Pondichery [Mr. Russel and his wife].[5]

8 March 1821

Mentioning at pranzo to Sultana that Medico Primo [Dr. Shortt] had ordered Old Frog champagne, and her reply: 'Ah, but we won't take the hint.' Finding out next day from Teutonic Scribe [William Janisch] that she had written to Old Frog a few days before a most kind invitation to spare nothing on account of expense, but to call for all he wanted and never think of the trouble.

Her tirade at his appropriating as a matter of right, because

ordered by Medico, the padovanella [phaeton], and his sending to
ask 'would she go with him, as he was going out in it?' Not, 'would
she allow him to go with her if she was going out in it.' Bearess said
they did not care what expense they put the Govt. to. Destruction,
wanton abuse of furniture, and every article lavished upon them.
His constant mean hits at Mr. Fne, about Naples. Ego mentioned
to Sultana in presence of Mach, at pranzo, the champagne recommended by Medico Long [Shortt] to Frog [Montchenu]. She said:
'Ah, but we won't take the hint.' Sultana is beginning to get tired
of Old Frog. Now he required the phaeton every day. It was now
'would she go with him?' and not: 'might he go with her?'

9 March 1821

Mach's meanness in saying he had torn a piece of sopha cover to
bring to Sultana to show the beastly dirt allowed. Mme Shrug
stated she had never been so disgraced. Still forcing in Ninny's
name every where and keeping Ego's as much out as possible.

10 March 1821

His attack having made Commis write in book (in the first
instance) a confab in order to avoid mistakes. His flying out because
he had given it himself. He said 'Copy off immediately', as it was
wanted. There was, notwithstanding this assertion, all this day to
prepare it. It was known at this time for certain that the ship did
not sail till afternoon or following day, tho' he never said a word to
me about it, nor did I know there was any vessel about to sail. He
cavilled for ¼ hour about Teutonic [Janisch] being employed
copying Old Frog's correspondence. That he did not attach any
importance to it. He attached much more importance to the
duplicates. Still he himself acknowledged he had desired Teutonic
to set the Commis about the confab, never thinking it proper to
desire Teutonic to prepare anything, or me either, though he saw
Teutonic writing the whole time and wanted to see what it was,
and gave him the directions about it; and had he given Ego confab,
he could have given it immediately to Teutonic to prepare, and take
it off the Commis [clerk] and so gain time. The former would have
done it sooner knowing French. And all the time he was thus
going on, he was preaching not to pay the Commis too much. Any
consideration he never felt or expressed for Ego or the former
Commis. Only pity lately learned from Sultana. Ego had induced

him to allow him more of his time, which he put off; stopping him
shortly, saying he did not desire Ego to do it himself.

28th March 1821

The dinner party at Plantation House consisted in Admiral
[Lambert], Dodgin's clerk, and Morris of 66th and Power of the
Artillery.[6] I came down with a severe rheumatic headache and had
intended at one time not to come down to dinner. But in hopes it
would go off I did. It increased a good deal and was very violent
when we broke up and I went into the Library. I took my tea and
no liquor, and when a party was made up for cards I told Den Taafe
how much my head ached. And as it was a whist party and several
of the guests were fond of it, I did not go near the card table—but
kept listening to some of them speaking to Mr. Clarke to whom I
mentioned several times the severe headache I had. Finding it
growing worse at 20 minutes before midnight I left the room, saying
to Mr. Clarke I felt too great a headache, to go to bed; perfectly
unconscious that I was leaving myself open to attack by so doing.
As I left Mr. D. T. was sitting in the Library and not playing all
this time. From the time we came into the Library till I left it, the
chief was absent, no doubt sleeping according to custom on one of
the sofas.

29 March 1821

Mach Chief asked me, 'Gorrequer what made you go away last
night?' Not recollecting immediately what was alluded to, I asked,
'When, Sir?' 'Why, last night, before the company broke up.' I
answered calmly and without the least warmth of feeling: 'Because
I felt so severe a headache that I could not remain any longer
below and was obliged to go to bed.' He replied in a rough tone and
angry look: 'I had a headache too but that did not prevent me from
staying.'

'There was only Mr. Den Taafe and myself left to see that the
company stayed up no longer. One of my eyes swelled and half
closed.'

Hurt at this reflection, as if what I had said was not believed, I
replied that I had a violent headache, which made me more fit for
my bed than for society. And that I conceived that when I felt
myself ill I had a right to go to bed. Here he flew out in a violent
gust of passion, rising from his seat and breaking out: 'I don't

understand you, Sir; I will not be spoken to in this sort of way.
I will not submit to this. I will not allow you to make use of such
expressions to me, Sir, as that you had a right to go to bed. I insist
upon you recalling those words, Sir, and that formally, although
there was nobody present to hear what you said.'

29 March 1821

Sultana and Capo di Vascello: what an impertinent fellow, and
the dressing Sultana gave him.

30 March 1821

Mach on arriving immediately attacked the O.O. [Captain
Lutyens] for not being more decisive, and not answering Veritas
[Montholon] when he was insulting in his answer; to be then
insulted by that great scoundrel to whom he had shown so much
deliberate consideration and forbearance and now guilty of giving
him so much trouble.[7]

1st April 1821

Soon after this day Medico 20th [Dr. Arnott] began addressing
all his reports to Mach, instead of Ego, about Neighbour [Napoleon],
in order to conceal them from him. Most likely to turn it to some
advantage on his side when necessary.[8]

1st April 1821

Mach's tortuous proceedings, surrounding every proposition of
Medico 20th [Dr. Archibald Arnott], as well as the fair ones from
Veritas [Montholon], with all sorts of captious, peevish objections
and difficulties, and agreeing to nothing; evidently wishing, if he
could, to prevent him being called in, if he could forge any deceitful
or plausible (to Big Wigs at Home) pretext. His repeatedly saying
that he should not see him in presence of suite, except Ninny was
present, or Ninny and Cercueil. Laying great stress upon making
Ninny a part.

6 April 1821

Sultana said Commandant of Artillery St Helena [Major
Kinnaird][9] was never intended by nature for a gentleman. That it

was a great mistake he ever was placed in a situation for which he was never fit, or meant to be placed in. Yam Ajutante [Lieut. David K. Pritchard], a sub. in his corps, was then present and Majordomo, sergeant in ditto, then also present, and all the rest of servitu. And on the 4th having said also loud at pranzo to Ego that Medico 20th [Dr. Archibald Arnott] would take care to make out the case of our Neighbour [Napoleon] as much better than it really was. Represent him in much better health than he really was because he knew it would please, and he was too much of a Scotsman not to be regulated by what he knew was desired or expected.

Her turn against Commandant of Great Gun Royal Artillery [Major James Power].

6 April 1821

Sultana again beginning her old trick with Ego and speaking of Yam Ajutante as a lover for Cadetta, and his perhaps waiting for her being old enough to marry. Her attack of Den, that he was so addicted to fibbing he could not now even open his lips without doing so.

7th April 1821

Polyphemes 4 told Ego that Cameriere Piccolo Vigo [Small, the Steward of H.M.S. *Vigo*] had told Capo di Vascello that Sultana had called Polyphemes 'a shabby, mean, dirty fellow', and had said the same of Capo. That they were a couple of . . . (as above), and Ego thinks 'nasty' was also one of the words.

7th April 1821

Mach's talking to Medico 20th [Dr. Arnott] respecting our Neighbour's [Napoleon] complaint, laying it down that it was a disease of the mind, and not of the body. Medico had for some time past (probably to give Mach satisfaction) declared it to be hypochondriasis; having often been told by Mach it was the state of his mind. [And that it was] the reflection of his impolite conduct here, and his behaviour to him, (and how differently he would play his game now, if he had to play it over again) that he was now suffering from. And he added with a furious satisfaction and the grin of a tyrant: 'If a person was to go in there (his apartments) and make a great clamour, it would be the most likely thing to revive him.

Depend upon it'. This was the cure he prescribed for rousing him from the state of despondency and hypochondriasis Medico represented him in.

Medico 20th waited on Shrug [Bertrand] at his house on his first visit to our Neighbour without any authority for so doing from Mach, and stated his state to him. Did the Conqueror Medico [Dr. Stokoe] do worse? Still no notice taken of it.

12 April 1821

In the second course a fillet of veal of a much larger size than any I had (during the 5 years) ever before seen was put before me at the head of the table where I sat. When I cut it to help Gen. W. . . . d who had asked me for some, I found it extremely coarse in the grain, brown, and all the centre very much underdone. After helping the Gen., Lady L. [Lowe] asked me: 'Pray, Mr. G. is that veal before you?' As it was only a party of about 12 or 14, she, the fifth from me, could see as well as I could that it was. But as she was always in the habit of doing whenever there was veal opposite to me, and I offered to help her, or she asked me for some, [she said] 'if it is that sort or kind of meat which is more beef than veal, or neither one thing or the other, don't send me any.' On another occasion she said 'if it is not veal, or that sort of half calf meat, I won't have any; for I cannot bear it.' Or if she asked me 'what is that opposite you?' and I answered 'veal,' she would say: 'that is not veal, it's too old for veal, and not old enough for beef, and I can't eat that'. All these and many more observations she had used. Indeed not perhaps more than 3 or 4 times in the last year had it occurred of veal being on the table, without [her saying so]. Therefore not wishing to send her what I knew she would not like, or that would draw some remarks, I answered (without looking or speaking in any manner that would possibly be construed with anything slighting or reflecting, but in the most natural way, without at the moment or afterwards thinking of what I had said or that there was the least impropriety): 'It looks more like beef'. When she replied, without apparently attaching the least consequence to what I had said by look or mean: 'For you know it is often pork instead of veal'. This could not have been suspected of being pork, from its size, for the fillets of pork were very small. Not one of the strangers at the table, I am certain, ever considered or suspected any impropriety or reflection on my part.

Sending in plants with plantation trees not in existence.

13 April 1821

Sultana went on again with abuse of povera pazza [the poor mad woman] to General and Mrs. Leghorn and party. She said that Capo of the Bastimento [ship], somebody had told her, would have been dismissed by the H.E.I.C., had he known that he had allowed pazza to permit Madame Bear [Balmain] to dance, with her, almost every night on deck with offiziale of bastimento, and till midnight, then going down to the officers' cabins or room to drink wine or negus.[10] She told Madame Bear there was no harm in her using a boucle de Cappelli [hat buckle] to pick turkey [?], and encouraging her to do it. Speaking in such terms of the Capo di Bastimento in fact, that all the convives [guests] united in strong terms of reprobation. Though he himself assured me of the falsehood of the attacks. Had they occurred, no doubt the business would have been heard of from the officers of the ship or young surgeon St Helena Regiment, who was a passenger.

17th April 1821

When pointing out to Mach that the words had brought on an irritating feeling against Capo 20th [Major Edward Jackson],[11] he said that it was attributing to them more than the note of O.O. bore out; for there was nothing said by Veritas [Montholon] to warrant that. (In fact he only expressed astonishment and shed tears). He broke out that if it was expected he should be so delicate, because Neighbour [Napoleon] was said to be dying, it was what he himself had no idea of. [He said] that Neighbour knew very well what his opinion had always been of him, and it would never be on account of his being in a dying state that he would alter his line of proceeding. That he'd be damned, or some such expression, if he'd pursue any other. He cared very little about it.

His flying out when I endeavoured to modify some of the harsh expressions to O.O. [Captain Lutyens], 'Major Gorrequer, after Captain Lutyens had always done every thing to try to please them at his [Lowe] expense, he cared very little about him [Lutyens].' (This was his complaint against all the O.O.s). He had no idea of managing or sparing his feelings. (And this letter was to be written too in my own name). He had behaved extremely ill to him; if he had followed the advices that he and Ninny had given him, instead of listening to the advisers who guided him, it would have been an easy line of duty. He was not the author of these letters, they were written by the advice of others. He had received wrong impressions from others; (as if this was intended as a hit at Ego) whose advices he had been more ready to follow than his own or Ninny's. He then spoke, in the most contemptuous way, of O.O.'s intellect and sense, and proceeded with a bitter tirade against him, in that strain, for his favourable leaning and inclination towards Neighbour and his folks; saying that he would be delighted, and vain at being employed as a medium between Neighbour and the 20th Regiment, and puffed up with his pride and vanity.[12] Then Mach imitated his, as he called it, conceit and ostentatious way, and then again broke out that he would attack him till he found out his advisers, those by whose suggestions he acted; that was the only way to deal with him; not to stand on delicacy with him, but work it out on him by bearing roughly upon him. Was not, he said, Tenente Croad [Lieutenent Frederick Croad] tampered with in the same way, by his own acknowledgement? After vapouring and storming for some time, he conceded to alter some of the harsh and offensive expressions in the epistle, though not altogether to cancel them, as I wanted. But he substituted some still very indelicate [words]. And after my having written out that fair, he again made a little alteration and added at the foot that he had allowed Ego to write that to O.O., and made him write another still with the word 'unbecoming,' which he himself had substituted for 'indecorous' and 'disgraceful'.

He sent the draft of epistle to Ego about 1.p.m. and a paper purporting to be a draft of a letter to be sent by Ego to O.O.

18th April 1821

Old Frog [Montchenu] told me of Sultana's [Lady Lowe] being annoyed that the Autrichien's [Stürmer] Donna had said so much more about Ego than any of her family or herself. "Dîtes mille choses aimables de notre part au Major Gorrequer' and had not even mentioned Cadetta [Susanna]; and that she was equally annoyed at the Bearess [Countess Balmain][13] being called by Autrichien's Donna 'Bear's femme' and not 'countess'; which, she said, she ought to have been called. She complained of the use of the term.

18th April 1821

A provoke [invitation] to tiffin was sent to Mach by officers of 20th for 23rd April (St. George's Day) and for 3 days of the races,

inviting him, Donna of the House and il suo Stato Maggiore—
which he answered for himself and Donna, but never had the
civility to show or mention the provoke to Ego. Nor did Ego know
anything of it, but by accident some days after, (3, I believe) when
Yam [Den Taafe] A.D.C. said Mach had desired him to answer the
provoke for himself and Donna. And the way he [Yam] became
aware that Stato Maggiore had been invited was that he gave him
the note to answer.

Notwithstanding the Sultana's constant abuse of Old Frog, how
she delighted in all his fulsome compliments, and how pleased
when he was attentive to her, and accompanied her in her rides in
the vehicle.

The curious circumstance mentioned to me by Grazzioso Thomaso
[Col. Lyster] when old Frog was at Plantation House, about his
coming to him in the Bureau, and requesting if he would translate
a plico just received from Sultana, which he found was to beg that
he would excuse any seeming want of attention on her part, because
she had so many causes of unhappiness at home. She was bewailing
her situation, and her being subject to so many causes for disquietude
and ennui, as if she was actually ill-treated by Mach. Any stranger
reading the note would think so.

19th April 1821

Fierce attack of Sultana on Polyphemes: 'he is a mean, dirty
fellow, I despise him.' He governed himself in the rudeness of his
conduct towards her by what he observed Mach do; he was rude
and inattentive to her when Mach neglected her.

20 April 1821

Notwithstanding the brutal letter about the vitale [food] Sultana
cried down the meat (horribly bad certainly), beef and veal, and
said that the two last times Capo of 66th [Col. Nicol] had pranzo he
had complained of it to her. No notice was taken of this, yet how
much more heinous than Ego's crime. And she continued about how
shamefully bad it was now at their table. She never could eat anything the contractor Baker had grown, such a good-for-nothing,
conceited fellow with all the money he had made, and was making.

21st April 1821

Sultana's old behaviour again today to Ego. On his rising and
bowing to her coming into biblioteca and enquiring about the

two piccolini [children], she answered in the most indifferent manner that she could hardly say. 'They were not ill, they were not well. They could not be called the one or the other'. She believed they were very well, in the most affected and nonchalant way possible. At table she began to abuse as usual the servitu, and treated Ego with marked slight. She received Yam [Den Taafe] with all the simpering smiling ways possible, who came in when soup was almost over, a thing which he not infrequently did, and which would have been high treason with Ego. Sultana continued her proceedings towards Ego for some time, noticing merely Yam, and then all at once in middle of pranzo changed her manner and became civil again. Her constant rating of servants at pranzo quite annoying, with her cross noisy manner of going on for hours at a time.

Her brat Cadetta's airs of grandeur and affectation.

All the Medici called in the moment any of her brats or herself had any idea of complaint. The fuss and bustle made, and Ego when known to be ill was supposed to be shamming. Her abuse of all the Medici.

22 April 1821

Her contemptuous slight to Ego and high favour to Yam.

24 April 1821

Bitter invectives at Yam: proud, conceited, useless, disagreeable fellow, who did nothing in the world but now and then look at roads, and ride with Cadetta. Just one of those sorts of idle people who contrived to give satisfaction to Sir Hudson. His rudeness and stupidity; being too proud about doing anything, because it was not expected of him. Would not himself go to the pantry to speak to the servitu, nor take his cup out of the room, but rang the bell without stirring himself. Lasted 20 minutes of a most bitter philippic.

Her ostentatious way of relating how Capo Vascello had been knocked under and promised never to quarrel again; and the vanity when repeating that Old Frog's A.D.C. and Capitano of Caveton [?] had shown them their fingers, all cut by breaking the bicchierini [glasses], drinking her brindisi [toast] at the Ball.

25 April 1821

Going to seek popularity at races, in spite of the terrible weather and meandering with Cadetta alone with 50 men. Polisson then there still.

26th April 1821

His rage when he became informed of the civil message delivered
by Veritas [Montholon] in Neighbour's [Napoleon's] name to O.O.,
upon his returning from office in disgrace, and his suspicious
insinuations that he was implicated in some nefarious transactions.[14]

27 April 1821[15]

Sultana now professing great respect and affection for Mrs.
Shrug [Countess Bertrand]. Sending her present of osprey's feathers,
and visiting her, and expressing herself highly pleased with her,
and this after all the abuse.

A considerable time after Neighbour [Napoleon] had been confined from his last illness, Ninny wrote to Mach characterizing it as
a 'scene of acting'.

Now Ninny [Reade] was sneaking after Shrug [Bertrand] when
the business was made up until their embarkation; and immediately
on seeing Mach's bitterness returning towards them, he resumed
the old strain of railing soon before their departure, and persevered
in it. He remarked one day at pranzo after they sailed, speaking of
Shrug: 'I am sure I did not like him.'—'No,' said Sultana, 'I am sure
you never did.' He was however a great patron and visitor to them
on first arriving, and till he saw Mach getting bitter.

27th April 1821

Mach's furious rage at the epistles of the two Bricks and Mortars
—if they choose to begin a correspondence they shall have enough
of it. I'll lash them. I'll settle them.

29 April 1821

Ninny [Reade] wrote to Mach: 'My opinion is still that he
[Napoleon] will get better.' Though Medico 20th [Dr. Arnott],
the great oracle, had the preceding day reported him dangerously
ill. His opinion, indeed!

30 April 1821[16]

Sultana's anger that at the races Capo (Maggiore) 20th was so
abstracted, and himself and all the officers so inattentive and rude
to her; and this was, she said, because they were disappointed at
Madame Shrug not coming to merendare [lunch]. The affection

and admiration of that corps for our Neighbour [Napoleon] was very unaccountable and, after his death, if he had lived longer and if 20th had remained where they were, God knows what would have been the consequences in time.

The business about the books was thrown entirely on Capo 20th, in order to get it off his own shoulders; and that any unpleasant consequences with regard to the prigionieri [prisoners] under charge might be made to fall upon him. The refusal of the reception and return of them [i.e. the books], as they had certain titles and inscriptions, should have been all done by himself.[12]

1st May 1821

Sultana renewed her attacks on officers 20th for not paying more attention to her, commenting bitterly on their attention to Mrs. Shrug [Countess Bertrand] and their attachment to the captives. They were all out of spirits because Mme Shrug was not there. This was at pranzo, Ninny present. Soon afterwards Mach handed a letter (from Mme Shrug to him), to Sultana. And on her returning it to him, he handed it to Ninny, who read it and gave it back to him. He then put it by on the corner of the desk, himself and Ninny ridiculing the subject; when Sultana, struck apparently with his brutality towards Ego, snatched the letter and handed it to me.

Sultana constantly talking of elegance and beauty of nuova casa [New House].

3rd May 1821

Now Sultana [Lady Lowe] was praising the beauty and accomplishment of Bear's [Balmain] wife, and turning to Old Frog's [Montchenu] A.D.C. [Captain de Gors] asked him: 'If ADCs to Sovereigns were not obliged to have pretty wives for their master?'

Mach launched out in praises of Bear, and said he had never met a man who wrote so well. Though when he was formerly out of favour, and when Ego ventured sometimes and remarked on some of his letters that they were well written, he ridiculed them saying 'that they were like himself, vain, frivolous, with not a single argument worth a pin or a damn.'

Sultana's constant admiration of Cadetta's beauty in her presence and to herself, after having several times also expressed, in her hearing, her dissatisfaction at her being so much praised, and her being spoiled by so many admirers.

This morning returning home he said to me: 'It is my intention to send Captain C. [Crokat] home with the dispatches.' He [Crokat][18] certainly had seen him since his death (which he [Lowe] had not done before). It would appear that the proposal or intention had been made to Captain C. [Crokat]. For the next morning early, even before we went in to see the corpse, Shortt spoke to me about it and of Ninny [Reade] (who had got spooney the evening before) blabbing out all the arrangements about the troops, artillery, 66th Regiment, re going home immediately. And a few minutes after seeing the corpse, the Brigadier and the Brigade Major spoke to me about Captain C. [Crokat] going home and they seemed a good deal surprised at it. The latter particularly, after so short an attendance at Longwood (he having been only from the evening of the 26th April doing O.O.'s duty). I found that the report of his taking home the dispatches was quite current at Longwood, where at this time a great number of persons were assembled.

On the morning of the 7th he began dictating to me a preparation for the dispatches and I was occupied, from a little before till breakfast time in the business, and afterwards resumed it. Ninny, who arrived to breakfast, and Mach walked together for sometime when they entered the office to answer a letter from the Admiral, after being sometime cogitating and whispering and talking low to each other and planning an answer. He desired Janisch to leave the room, and soon afterwards handed me over the letter from the Admiral saying 'Read that'. I found it was informing him of sending home a Naval Officer with his own dispatches (Captain Hudson) and enquiring whether he himself intending doing the same. Not knowing why he wished me to read the letter, I was at a loss as to what part of it to fix my attention on particularly. This was at a little past 10 o'clock and I had written the evening before, by his desire, to Captain Crokat, to inform Count Montholon that the letter he had for Europe should be at Plantation House between 4 and 5 as he had told me the vessel would sail at 5 in the afternoon. After I had read the letter and he told me about recommencing the perusal, he said: 'Do you wish to go? Do you think it will be of any advantage to you?' This was said with perfect indifference, in a very dry, cold manner, with an air of displeasure, his face colouring up as he asked me the question. As he, or Ninny, had already spoken to Captain C. [Crokat] on the subject, and as it was rumoured publicly he was the person going, and after what he had said to me the evening of the 5th of his intention to send that officer, the proceedings and manner were too gross and unfeeling altogether to hesitate in declining it. I was immediately struck that it was all a trick at the suggestion of Ninny; (to cover the proceeding that it should be offered to me at so late a period and after exposing that Captain C. [Crokat] was going and notifying it to C. [Crokat] himself). Very naturally supposing after such conduct I would not accept it. And by that means it would give him the advantage of saying: 'I offered it to him and he did not think proper to accept.' Not wishing however to take them at their word, and thinking that by turning the table against them by accepting so late I should be descending too much by so doing as I conceived, I answered that I had no particular desire to go, nor did I look forward to any advantage from it, if I did. I observed a glow of pleasure when he saw I felt indifferent about it. But as if to give a mask of candour to his manifest hypocrisy he adopted a more conciliatory manner and tone and said: 'Perhaps you wish to consider it?' I replied I did not feel it required any consideration, that I did not desire to go. He added: 'You better think of it however for half an hour' and he proceeded to finish an answer to the Admiral. The only thought I gave to the proposition was that it might be as well to say I thought my sending home a memorial ought to be of use. And in a few minutes, when I saw him disengaged I said I thought it would be well for me to send a memorial on this occasion, if he were good enough to transmit it for me. He suddenly resumed his angry looks and frowns and said: 'If you ask me to send a memorial home for you, why, I'll forward it.' And then rising from his seat, began in a harsh, angry tone and passionate manner saying: What could he do more for me than what he had already done; if he was to rack his brain for ever he could not add another word to what he had before said in my favour; that 'I had already sent a memorial and what more could I urge than what I had stated there'; that when he had forwarded it, he had also sent a private letter recommending me in the strongest terms; that he could not have said more for his own brother; he had also requested Sir George Bingham to support his application, which Sir George Bingham had done.[19]

I said I was perfectly sensible of Sir G.B. [George Bingham's] kindness on the occasion. He continued that again on the occasion of Colonel W's [Wynyard's] going home,[19] he once more recommended me, and that notwithstanding, when the answer came it appeared I was not satisfied and did not think he had done enough for me.

Why did not Colonel W. [Wynyard] exert himself for me; he,

who was so well known at the Horse Guards and had so much interest there, and was one of my friends?

I replied that Colonel W. [Wynyard] had not an opportunity of seeing Sir H. Mor. [Morton] or Sir H. Tay. [Taylor], but for a very short time; but he had done what he could. But I had no right to expect he would go and plead for me there; it was what I could not ask him to do when he went away. He said: 'Why not? He might have done it.' I said I never would have thought of taking the liberty of asking Colonel W. [Wynyard], nor would I have wished him to go and interfere with his (Sir Hudson Lowe's) recommendation of me without his previous consent. 'Ah well,' he replied. He reverted to my proposal to send a memorial, beating about over the same grounds again of 'could he say, or I say, more if I was to send a hundred memorials'; I had no right to expect promotion for being Military Secretary; he really could not see what claim I would urge for my services here; I estimated them most probably at a much higher rate than he himself did; he did not attach any importance to them. I answered I never had presumed upon them whether they were important or unimportant, or attempted to bring them forward in that light, or attached importance in my memorial. I had simply stated the length of my services and touched very slightly on their nature. I had left my duties here to be mentioned in whatever manner he himself thought proper, and transmitted documents from several general officers under whom I had served which spoke of my services before he was pleased to appoint me to his staff. He said again he did not see what claims I had on account of my services here but: 'I'll tell you when I think you have not been sufficiently considered, and that is for your former services;' that it was for that reason he had brought that point in so prominent a manner in his recommendation: that he should never forget the dissatisfaction I had shown on the receipt of the answer to his last application in my favour; he never could, nor would forget it. He again asked what could I say new in my memorial, or what could be added to what he had already stated. I said that however my services were rated I could at all events claim consideration for the laborious work I had done here. He said that was no plea; it would never be considered; that pecuniary compensation was all that ever was thought of for labour; that I had received my pay which was an equivalent to it. I said my pay bore no proportion to my labour compared with other officers here; for upwards of 4 years it was £1. 18–. a day only, whilst that of a Lieutenant of Engineers was £1. 18. 10.; that my whole day and more, was taken up in the performance of my duties; that I could frequently take only an hour's ride, or even mount my horse only once in 3 weeks: that in addition to my many other duties I had for 2 years the accounts of Longwood to attend to, which took a great deal of my time and caused me much trouble for which I never had received any compensation, though it was granted to the officer who superintended them before me; that since Colonel W. [Wynyard] left this [island], in June last, my pay was certainly increased and I had not complained on that score. He answered that as for Mr. W. [Wortham] he belonged to the Engineers and he had nothing to do with them (though he had himself fixed that unusual high rate, contrary to the idea of every one who heard it); that with regard to the Longwood accounts that certainly was a subject which was entitled to consideration, there was something in that; that altogether I did not receive the pay of Aide de Camp and Military Secretary. [He said that] before Wynyard's departure I received that of the latter appointment, and he really did not know when I ever did the duty of his A.D.C. (If I did not do it, then it was not done at all, for certainly W. [Wynyard] never did more nor so much as an A.D.C. should have done. But this is as correct a statement as all the rest, for I did, not only my own A.D.C.'s duty, but a good deal of the Island A.D.C. [duty] for a great while, and whatever Wynyard was short of tending, and also that of Commissary of accounts. I frequently wrote on the Commissary's service and prepared masses of letters which were signed by Sir Thomas Reade; besides all the conferences at Longwood, with Commissaires etc.)

I said that the duties I perform took up the whole of my time completely; that in consequence of Colonel Wynyard being appointed to act as Deputy Quarter Master General it withdrew him from a great deal of the business, which otherwise would have been done in the office, and which would have much relieved me. [He said] 'And he got no pay for that particular duty.' I said 'No, he did not, but it took him away from a great deal of other works.' He said he had often offered me assistance by employing more people in the office. (I most positively assert that instead of showing an inclination to offer me assistance he positively did the contrary.) I frequently told him I felt unable to continue such constant labour, that it injured my health and repeatedly asked him for assistance, naming the young Kay, Ensign Dodd (Half Pay), Mr. Haynes; and showed samples of their writing as well as of several non-commissioned officers, and a purser's clerk of the *Conqueror*;

and he never would consent to my employing any of them. Mr. Oakley was mentioned by Sir Thomas Reade for the same purpose and I suggested Mr. Darroch[20]; but he shuffled any attempt I made, absolutely refusing, but there was always some obstruction where to put them; he would take no other officer in the house; where could a NCO be put—though there were places in abundance for the latter. I spoke of Rock Cottage, unoccupied for 2 years, for an officer, and suggested other accommodations. He refused the man from the *Conqueror* pretending his writing did not please him, tho' he wrote very well and was highly recommended.

He certainly often did say that he intended to have 5 or 6 clerks and had listed, he pretended, an officer for this increase of number; but whilst he mentioned it I evidently perceived he never meant it, and said so to Wynyard. His wife even told Mrs. Wynyard showing this new office with ostentation, saying that Sir Hudson Lowe meant to have a great many clerks there, 6 or 7.

He said they would not even listen at home to any claim on account of labour; it would only make them say: 'Why did not Sir Hudson Lowe make him a proper allowance and pay him according to his labour and not come upon us for compensation by promotion?'

There were only two instances, he said that had occurred, of undue promotion since his appointment to this command. That was Captain Poppleton's and Major Emmett's; that the first was claimed for former services, and he had been taking care not to recommend him for any service here. How unlike the facts this is. That as for the latter, though he would be always willing to speak of his talents or abilities as an Engineering Officer, and to express his satisfaction with his services here, he never would recommend him; though he had, about 3 weeks before, thought proper to apply to him for recommendation. That he attributed to him many of the unpleasant circumstances that had occurred, and that he had been the man who had thrown many difficulties in the way of his duties here. That it was not what people actually did, it was from appearance he actually judged. It was the mind and inclination; and persons who showed a disposition to assist him, evincing at the same time a feeling of humanity and kindness for the persons under his charge, who were the persons whom he considered as having claims upon him and for whom he was ready, at all time, to do all in his power. What hypocrisy, what deceit!! Did Ninny ever show any other disposition than that of hostility and abuse of those persons; and were not all his favourites chosen for the abuse and enmity they showed towards those very persons? He then talked about the previous letter he had written in my favour, which I might ask Sir H.T. [Taylor] to show me if I chose, on my arrival in England; [and said] that he had even sent to him the recommendation I wrote out; that as for the official letters they were entered in books and I might take copies of them, if I chose, and make use of them as I pleased; that I might show them to whoever I liked; that I might also try, if I liked, to get promotion through any other channel besides his, as I chose. He thought little or no good would be gained by saying anything on the subject. It might do more harm; and that if I was to be influenced by any opinion he might give, or were I to ask him his advice and be guided by it, he would recommend me to do nothing at present but leave things to take their natural course. That he thought the proper method was to wait until my return to England; that things would soon be wound up here, and he did not intend to remain the Company's governor of St Helena, but return home as soon as the burial arrangements were made. I might go home too, with him, and then apply to him for his assistance and support in forwarding my claims. This, he thought, would be the most proper way.

I told him, as I had repeatedly done during the conversation, that the idea of forwarding a memorial had just struck me at the instant, and was thrown out by me as a mere idea for his consideration, and had said 'if he would'.

6th May 1821

After having written out dispatch fair, respecting defunct Neighbour [Napoleon], Mach [Lowe] made Ego write it over again for the purpose of leaving out that part where he said he went in accompanied by his staff.[21] Because Capo di Vascello Bruno [Captain Thomas Brown], as he said, might be annoyed or take offence at it; though Bruno and two Capi di Vascelli were mentioned in it. It was because he thought most probably his staff being named would not convey the understanding that Ninny was one, and that it might be understood he was. The affectation of poking in Ninny's name about being referred to, respecting the cuore [heart] at the dissection [the post-mortem].[22]

He frequently said he did not consider our Neighbour [Napoleon] as a man of superior mind or talent, or a man of judgement. He pretended to hold him quite cheap.

7 May 1821

Mach worried Dr. Shortt and Dr. Arnott to make them alter the report of the dissection [post-mortem], and the whole of the doctors concerned, who after much noise and much rage on his part, did alter it. By dint of persevering in worrying the two above named, he obtained letters from them, to annex to reports subsequently sent, saying that Napoleon would not have lived so long had it not been for the adhesion of liver. Ninny told Dr. Arnott that he had expected Napoleon would have given him 1000 instead of 600 Napoleons. Madame Shrug told Ego, 6th May, that it was well for Mach, Neighbour did not die of fegato [liver].[23]

[8 May 1821][24]

Medico Vigo [Dr. Charles Mitchell][25] dined 8th May with the Shrug family before reconciliation. Old Frog [Montchenu] and his Ajutante [Captain de Gors] visited there also, the very next day after his [Napoleon's] demise, and were constantly commiserating. Nothing said about it. Medico 20th [Dr. Arnott] and Fat a-se Moll dined with Veritas [Montholon], receiving presents from Followers. No notice. The centrepiece for the table with Eagles, Crowns and 'N' sent to Medico 20th [Dr. Arnott] for his kindness by Madame Shrug. Nothing said to Medico himself about it. The advice and support he gave to O.O. not noticed to him by Mach, though the Bricks and Mortars were nearly annihilated by it. Medico 20th had the allowance forced upon him to the funeral day inclusive; at a time too when he was constantly associating with the O.O.s dining with them and they with him, walking arm in arm about the town under the very nose of Mach and nothing done to Medico. And yet Young Smithy deprived of boarding situation, allowance and forage, and sent in exile merely for being seen frequently in the same society, and walking arm in arm with them. Young Conqueror Rocket also exiled to Sandy Bay with Smithy for having had the circumstance of the books mentioned to him; the impression against them being more a suspicion than anything else.

9th May 1821

Sultana's conduct to Ego on day of sepoltura [Burial of Napoleon][26], averting her eyes purposely from him (when passing her in procession, she in her carriage looking towards him) the moment she perceived him, and at the grave also; scarcely even answering him when addressing her at Alarm House; the same at pranzo at Plantation House. Yam [Den Taafe] told me afterwards that, the evening Medico Shortt was sent for, when he stood speaking to Yam and I in the library, she came down in a furious manner to rate the servitu in the anteroom; and that she told him it was me making the noise, though I had only spoken a few words in answer to some questions from Medico.

10 May 1821

Sultana's rudeness to Ego again this day. Particularly at cards. Saying Ego had better not play it if was against his inclination. 'We shall be enough to make up a party, it is not really necessary; I can lay my cards on Yam Stock, ADC.'

10th May 1821

The Old Fool Frog [Montchenu], after all the abuse and ill treatment, wrote to Mach a blarney letter which Mach called 'amende honorable'. The old fellow could always re-establish himself in the good graces of Mach or Sultana by a little flattery.

11 May 1821

Polyphemes [Admiral Lambert] showing letter from Povilero calling Sultana affable, entertaining and beautiful, and her delight at it.

11 May 1821

Sultana at pranzo where besides famiglia there was only Polyphemes present, was giving an account of all the curiosities she had been seeing at our Neighbour's [Napoleon's], which had been exhibited that day. Ego enquired whether she had not seen a tabatière [snuff box] forsaked by our Neighbour to Lady Holland, as she had not mentioned it. This gave rise to her description of it immediately, as she had seen it. On this Polyphemes observed he had not yet seen it.[27]

12th May 1821

Mach said to Ninny [Sir Thomas Reade] and Ego immediately after the examination of Shrug's [Bertrand's] papers, that from the accounts of the establishment, which were then laid before him by Shrug, he did not think that any unknown money transaction to any amount had taken place besides the £3000 given to Providatore [Balcombe] (of this last after all there was no other proof whatever but what Veritas [Montholon] had mentioned and no doubt it was the very same deposited with Holmes[28] and given to Providatore for the purpose of his lodging it).

Ego having maintained to Mach that the Troad wished to go home with the Shrugs and Veritas and that set, he eagerly replied, and with a grin of oppression: 'If he will give the name of the person who advised him, he shall go'.

12 May 1821

His evident suspicion that, when Veritas [Montholon] called Ego back after examination of papers, and when accompanying Mach [Lowe] to Shrug's [Bertrand] (to speak about the way the sum intended to be left by Marchand[29] for his fils was to be disposed of), some treasonable business had been in agitation between Veritas and Ego. He repeatedly asked Ego what he had stopped him for. When told, he questioned whether it was for nothing else. There appears something very artful, he said, in his thus stopping you about that money. It was hardly justifiable to stop about such matters; it was extraordinary; there must have been something else, apparently endeavouring to entrap Ego in some unguarded observation, which he might have twisted so as to make it appear there was something mysterious, or sinister, to extract from me that seemed to have some meaning in it. He said he probably had called me back to give me a gold snuff box or money or something by way of a quitto [parting gift].

12 May 1821

Immediately after breakfast, being in the office with Mach, he asked Ego how he came to mention at dinner yesterday the tabatière [snuff box]; that he thought it very extraordinary that a thing which he had not mentioned to any person whatever and which he had kept concealed, should have been mentioned by an officer of his staff, at his own table after his forbidding anybody to mention it either; he had not told him a single word about it being offered, and having too taken the precaution to desire Sultana not to mention it to anybody. He would hardly have expected to have first heard it mentioned at his own table and that by Ego, before Polyphemes to whom he had not even said a word about it, and who knew nothing of the matter till then. What must he think of him? What would he say of his want of candour towards him in concealing it? He should however take great care to make it known at home that if the knowledge of it became public he was not to be blamed for it; that it should be known how it had been made known. Ego replied he was sorry; he had not known the circumstance was intended to be kept secret; but as there were only present, when Ego mentioned it, Polyphemes (who, he was under the impression, had seen it, he being in the room at the time that Mach and Ego were looking at it), Sultana and the persons who were with her (Yam ADC and Cadetta) I conceived I was only mentioning the circumstance before persons who were all as much acquainted with it as myself. I had always made it a rule never to mention anything about Longwood and I was not now, or had ever been, in the habit of repeating what I heard or became acquainted with. He replied he knew I was not, in a placated tone, having till then spoken in the usual boisterous, rude manner.

The very day at the staff mess Young Brick and Mortar told all the party (a large one) that this box was shown to all those present and described the cameo to Old Pick Axe and me.

12 May 1821

Mach and Ego having proceeded to inspect the papers and boxes (sealed up) of our Neighbour [Napoleon], on arrival found Young Brick and Mortar there. Mach on seeing him asked the Troad [Lieut. Frederick Croad] how he came there, and with whom he had been. Troad said he came in without a pass to see the things exhibited and had been with Veritas [Count Montholon]. He then became furious, attacked Brick and Mortar tooth and nail. How dare he presume to venture within the grounds? He highly disapproved of his having any communication whatever with the persons there, and he knew these were his sentiments. The other excused himself by saying he understood any officer wishing to see the house would be admitted. Mach asked him whether he had seen the orders. He answered no. It was his business to see them, as he would then have known how he was to come. How dare he take the liberty to make his way there without permission, and hold communication with the persons there contrary to the Regulations? He never heard of such presumption. After treating him 'de haut en bas' for some time longer, he at last said he was surprised that he should have the presumption to remain a moment longer after his expressing his dissatisfaction of his conduct, and ordered him immediately to quit the grounds.

14 May 1821

Mach said that Shrug [Bertrand] and Veritas [Montholon] were both more attached to Louis XVIII than Frog [Montchenu]—in consequence merely of their having made some observations on Young Neighbour [Napoleon's son][30] about his face being in great resemblance to the Austrian countenance.

Mach wrote home to say Neighbour was very unwilling to die; that Signora Shrug had said so.

14 May 1821

Mach after having had before him the confab of the 12th May, all the 13th and part of this morning's, approved of it and even desired it might be commenced to be written out fair (on the preceding evening), without having before objected to one single part, but having expressed himself highly satisfied. This day, after it was pretty well written out fair, on reading what had been already prepared, he began to cavil and object. He repeated that he had expressed to Veritas a desire that the property he had left might be appropriated as he had bequeathed it. He disputed the expression 'in toto'. And after a long scene of cavilling and shuffling, he at last only required a little alteration, which he himself made on the notes. Tho' Ego was positive in his own mind that he had put it down accurately, and that Mach had so expressed himself.

He also disputed what Ego was most certain of on the first day of seeing the property (viz. that Veritas had mentioned that the seals of four other persons had been annexed to Neighbour's own so that the boxes might not be opened without the consent of all; and that to consent to it 'il faudrait violer notre promesse à ses dernières volontés). Notwithstanding the cavilling he stated pretty clearly the same thing afterwards in his letter home on the subject. Mach, on Veritas saying that the principal part of the papers had been sent home by private hands, enquired eagerly of him who the persons were. Then Veritas answered: 'Vous me pardonnerez de ne pas les nommer. Ce serait les compromettre et les trahir. Et c'est ce que je ne puis faire'.

14 May 1821

Sultana adverted to all the changes and vacancies, to bring in Polyphemes' brother as Capo Commandante, and said Polyphemes [Admiral Lambert] was 'a sort of fellow who does any job, any dirty job'. And Mach followed it up by ridiculing Poly for his want of success in mediating a reconciliation with Shrug [General Bertrand]; and Mach said how soon Ninny [Sir Thomas Reade] did it. Sultana joined in and said it was she who advised him about sending Ninny, for she knew that Polyphemes would rather prevent it, if he could do so, than adjust it.[31]

15 May 1821

Ninny told Ego that Old Brick and Mortar and Dandy Goldeye [Capt. Goldie] were trying to get the 20th and O.O. and ordonnance to dine together before departure, and that it was the intention to exclude from it the Etats-Majors. But that Capo of Great Guns had prevented it. Great Tiffin at Plantation House to celebrate the reconciliation between Sir Hudson and Bertrand. The extraordinary care with which the matter was patched up—notwithstanding the proscription announced against any one speaking to Bertrand, before held out as an infamous character, unworthy of being associated with—all at once white-washed merely by a call. Sir Hudson Lowe being Chief here never had demanded anything more than merely, that it was not etiquette for him to call first; but if Shrug [Bertrand] called he would return it. It however so happened that on the 12th, Mach did go to Shrug's house, to look at his papers, and therefore became the first visitor. Shrug's papers[32] might have been examined at the Old or New House. Until Mach's going on that day, Shrug had resisted making the first call. But waited on him the following day along with Veritas [Montholon] (13th May).

21st May 1821

Yam told me that Sultana had said (most shamefully false) that it was himself (Yam) [Den Taafe] and I made the noise the night she came down about the Brats, and that I made most, in fact that it was Ego. Here false. Yam was standing at the door of the Library, and it was he who was talking all the time, and if anyone was heard it was him. Ego was sitting at the other side of the table reading and did not speak more than 5 or 6 words, and those in a low tone.

Yam told Ego of Ninny's abuse of Vidal[33] and Marryat, and in consequence of what he said to Sultana she saying she would not again sit down at table with them.

Both Mach and Ninny's delight that [name blotted out] and Morsely were absent when Neighbour [Napoleon] died. They would be so damned mad; making out in fact that they had not proper feelings and were Neighbour's adherents.

22 May 1821

Mach's rage at some idea (which next day appeared to have been repeated through Cadetta, who heard Coxwell say Madame Shrug had said to him 'I wish you would take me home with you'). [He said] that Madame Shrug [Countess Bertrand] was intriguing to go on board as Chinaman, and was dissatisfied with going on H.M.S. *Camel*. The angry letter he immediately wrote to Shrug, which on my advising not, the rage he got into. He'd be damned if he would not, he was determined upon it, abusing both and saying I don't care a damn if I quarrel with that fellow again. All evidently because they had tried him constantly under the reconciliation. He again repeated before Sultana that he dared say he'd have another quarrel with them yet before they went; and she answered: 'Of course you will, if you are determined upon it.' Sultana's constant attack on Mrs. Shrug ever since 2 or 3 days after funeral, for not returning the things she had lent her as patterns, telling every body of it, and saying she had no doubt it was Madame Shrug's intention never to return them but take them away with her.

Even the day before 66th dined at Plantation House, anger with Old Nick [Capt. George Nicholls] at sending for his fantesco [man servant] to go and attend sick officer's wife; and Mach's tirade against him, saying that it was exactly like him; that was the way he liked to show his authority, and what he can do. The next day however 22nd May, the fulsome manner in which both [Lowe and Lady Lowe] made their court to 66th; he by his speech after pranzo, she all the evening, declaring, when the officers went away, 'after all I think they are all a better set than 20th'. Such constant efforts for popularity now by both to the other side.

Note: required from the stores a pair of soldiers' shoes for officer of administration's shoes.

26 May 1821

Sultana boasted that Veritas [Montholon] had told her that our Neighbour [Napoleon] was once prepared and dressed on purpose to go out and meet her, when she went up in consequence of Veritas having promised her at the races to show her the grounds. But that he, Veritas, declared he knew nothing of her being there (for which neglect of his not being informed, she abused the O.O.). Sultana said that on this occasion she had gone to visit the Shrugs [Bertrands] and that both assured her Veritas was not home. That they pretended 2 or 3 times to send for him, and then said he was gone out to try a horse. That Shrug went out himself, and returning said he could not find him. One of the servants was also sent out who brought back the same answer.

That Veritas said that had he known she was there, he would have gone immediately to receive her and procure her a sight of Neighbour. That he added had she seen and conversed with him, she would easily have brought about everything and restored a good understanding between Mach and him. In fact her meeting Neighbour was all that was wanted. Veritas told her also that Neighbour had been looking at Cadetta [Lady Lowe's daughter] through the window, and admired her much, saying she was very pretty (all this was said before Cadetta). She believed, she said, that Madame Shrug prevented her meeting Neighbour for fear she might supplant her. She was jealous of her being introduced to him, and feared he would be making a present to herself and figli, which would be depriving Madame Shrug and her figli of them. It was in fact her apprehension that Sultana would put her (Mme Shrug) nose out of joint. Veritas had begged her permission to send her presents from Paris, bonnets etc., and pressed her to pay them a visit at Paris, and to consider him entirely at her commands for any commission she might desire to have executed there. That he said he understood Mach was to go out as Governor General to India, and that he thought it very likely etc. This made Mach cock up his ears, and a suffusion of self complacency and consciousness of meriting it spread over his countenance, and he appeared quite delighted at the prospect. Sultana was quite in rapture at Veritas' politeness, he was so pleasant, so amiable, so clever and gentlemanly, after all the abuse she had so frequently lavished on him!!

29 May 1821

Sultana's hit at Medico Longo [Dr. Shortt]—she understood he was living very economically.

Grazzioso Tomaso [Thomas Lyster] on the 27th told me of the astonishment of every one at her talking to Old Brick and Mortar

in the way she did at the races; saying that she had not a friend in
the world—so loud as to be heard a great distance. That he himself,
Grazzioso, heard a party of Naval officers walking in the streets
one evening, talking about her, and one saying that he would not
suffer his moglie or sorella—I forget which he said—to visit her.

30 May 1821

Sultana's anger at Medico Longo and moglie [wife] not coming to
dinner. She would leave her card the first time she knew Madame
Longo was out, and have done with her altogether. Mach, she said,
deserved such treatment for forcing invitations upon people in the
way he did. It was against her own desire, and he himself had
agreed with her as to their rudeness in often refusing to come;
and they ought not to be asked for a long time.

May 1821

Ninny told Ego that all the unpleasant circumstances of O.O.
20th, the Bricks and Mortars, etc. had occurred in consequence
of Mach's mildness and forbearance. Had it been Roaring Bob or
the Dutch Lord how soon they would have been settled; that he had
always thought it was owing to his too great forbearance and ease,
and told him so!!! That he ought to have crushed them at once, as he
saw Lord W. did with officers of 21st in Sicily.

Mach called to see papers at Shrug's, 12th May; and Shrug and
Veritas came next day to Plantation House and stayed to Tiffin.

Polyphemes, calling Neighbour 'L'Empereur', his wife 'L'Imper-
atrice' and 'les princes et princesses de sa famille' to Shrug, the first
day we saw the property left behind, 10th May. One of the charges
against Medico Conqueror [Dr. John Stokoe] was for calling him
'Napoleon'.[34]

The objection made by Mach to a plate being put on his grave
with his christian name alone, he insisting upon surname following,
which they refused and the plate was consequently not put on.[35]

The small figures of plaster of Paris purchased for busto [death
mask of Napoleon] cost £22–10–0, and were broken up to form
it with. Notwithstanding, Medico 66th [Dr. Francis Burton],[36]
insisted upon getting the mask as his property, in which he was
instigated by Mach, who told him he ought not to give it up, but
persevere till he got it; advised him to keep up the correspondence,
and to threaten to have recourse to the interference of Mach to
compel Madame Shrug to give it up.

May or June 1821

On Ego's speaking to Mach about De Bofrets' book, and remarking that Sir Jo. Campbell had written some lines of great praise and recommendation of him, he answered it was no wonder, for Sir J. was just such another fellow as D.B.

Sultana complained that Mach was too easy, that he allowed any body under his command to do as they liked, that he was far too much so and overlooked everything.

Forcing pay on Medico 20th [Dr. Archibald Arnott] up to the date of interment inclusive, and desiring at first to give it him from the date of his being ordered to be in readiness to attend. But Ego represented that it would look very extraordinary to give it to him before he was admitted even to see him [Dr. Arnott first attended Napoleon on 1 April 1821] as well as after he was defunct; and that besides, several others who received the same order had equal rights. He said 'Very well, then, from the 1st day he saw him; but let him have it to the interment inclusive, as he assisted at the opening [autopsy].' How many others were there who equally assisted, and even slept there whilst the other [Arnott] was sleeping at his own quarters![37]

Forcing ditto on sub medico 20th (Dr. George Henry Rutledge) for merely putting cuore and stomacho [heart and stomach][38] in cases and soldering them. Was not this a scheme for remuneration to Medico 20th for attending on his own famiglia. Why all the Provost gang kept in pay after demise also commis of commissary Jones, one upholsterer and one paper hanger!

May and June 1821

The continued efforts to gain popularity of Mach and Sultana. Mach and Ninny for some time past doing all in their power to regain the affection of Maggiore of St Helena Great Guns, both frequently joining and walking with him, asking him to dinner, conversing with him, and Ninny making fishing parties with him. Mach once or twice hinting to me the prospect of his being replaced at the head of Telegraphs as he took a dislike to the then incumbent (Thorne) and threatened if he did not mend to dismiss him.[39]

Medico 20th [Arnott] notwithstanding that he frequently got the bastimenti [ships] boarded by his deputy, pocketed the guinea; whilst he was at the same time receiving a pound daily for attending Neighbour [Napoleon] and 10 shillings for health medico. Notwithstanding his activity in the conspiracy, always a guest of

Mach, and enjoying every mark of favour; no remonstrance with him, evidently however to have him in reserve, by this attention and kindness, in any case of future need or emergency in explaining matters respecting Neighbour's health satisfactorily. Ninny however highly indignant and exasperated against him, though he had interfered so that he should not be sent home with dispatches as he would be so great a loser by it, particularly if his Corps went out to India.

Mach's vociferations and anger when Ego asked him his decision on the application made for passage money for officers 66th, and my showing him a memo in writing from the Pagatore [Paymaster] specifying various instances and mentioning names of individuals to whom it had been granted, as precedents. He flew out saying it was damned hard that because he might wish in some instances to do a thing out of consideration to certain individuals and be inclined to do a favour to one person, that it should be adopted immediately as a precedent and as such thrown in his teeth. He never intended it as a general thing and he would not give it. It was damned officious of Pagatore to make out this statement. After a long battle however he said at last he would give them a modified allowance of 2/3, but ended after all in granting the full allowance. But it was the result of a long and angry contest on his part. The Secretary of War, he said, had no authority here; he was independent of him and could act as he thought proper. He had nothing to do except with Ministers.

End of May 1821

Sultana always complaining since Neighbour's death of poverty. As for them they were going home worse than they came here. They had saved nothing though others might. Others in their situation were able to save big amounts but not Mach. He neglected all that was for the good of his family. He spent everything. How she exclaimed against the Duke of Manchester. 'Was it intended that people should profit by what the government allowed; was it not subject to be spent?'

3 June 1821

Her burst at the Medico Longo [Dr. Shortt] family just after he left the room. Their gross rudeness to Mach and her. They dined with every body but them. All Ego's intimate friends behaved rudely

to them. She wondered I did not tell the Longos of their rudeness.
They had given no reason for not dining, in their refusal. Ego said
he had mentioned that to Medico. It was very odd, she again
repeated, that my intimate friends were the rudest to them. It ought
to be painful to Ego to see Mach so insulted. The Vignobles
[Wynyards] behaved in the same manner and they were my friends.
In fact there was only Lady Swell [Bingham] who had good sense
enough to be above all that, who always behaved like a lady. But
she was a gentlewoman, born of a respectable family, her father
was a man of behaviour. How often, until Lady Swell became such a
constant correspondent of hers, has she complained of her rudeness
to her and her vulgarity. Sultana then attacked [the] man for
wanting her to dine with Polyphemes. How could he ask her to go
to a house to be insulted by that impertiment fellow E.E. Vidal
[Naval Secretary] and the Capo di Vascello [Captain Thomas
Brown]? She spoke of the meanness of the Polyphemes, a dirty
fellow etc. But she would soon be out of the way of them all. It was
distressing to call in Medico Longo's attendance, a person on whom
one is not on terms and, except he was paid, he would not think
himself well treated. Mach said it was his duty; there was no com-
punction to call him. The enmity to her proceeded because she was
the first lady here, and had a better house and more servants. But
Lady Swell had consideration for her, and did not expect her to
return visit for visit; she knew she had children to look after, and she
called without all that ceremony. Old Mach joined in the chorus
that Lady Swell was the only one who behaved properly to Sultana.

8 June 1821

Sultana's telling Mach Old Grazzioso Tomaso had now no sort of
business here, or excuse for remaining. He ought to go immediately.
But he was so fond of money that he would stay till he died, before
he went away. He (Mach) ought to give him a hint to go; it was a
shame his staying here any longer. Mach said he would give him a
hint to that effect.

Saturday 9 June 1821

Sultana's abuse of Secretario Navale [Vidal]: 'I can't bear that
nasty, disagreeable fellow. I detest him. Is that fellow coming to
dinner here on Monday? How could Mach continue asking people
to his table so disagreeable to him?' She did not think she ever

would dine at the same table again with those two impertinent, disagreeable fellows who had behaved with so much rudeness, who took pleasure in irritating her (viz. Secretario and Capo di Vascello).

June 1821

How tone was altered about Tenante Troad on his denying having used the word 'spy' on the day after confab; or, if he had, that he did not mean to say the term had been used. He said that he was a complete blackguard and he ought to have brought him to a Court Martial and broken him, as well as every one of his advisers, or any body who had anything to say to him; and every one of them would have been broken that had been brought forward. Troad, notwithstanding his suspicion of him and having scarcely done anything for him, was thanked and obligations expressed to him; and he received, for between 3 or 4 years, 7/6 per diem for assisting in superintending workmen, and had £1 per diem for staying in an empty house after departure of O.O. 20th [Captain Crokat] until the very day of his departure, viz. from 8th May till 12th June. He forced £1 per diem on Medico 20th [Arnott who attended Napoleon] for going twice, sometime once a day, only 3/4 mile on a horse, sent for him, and staying a short time, in fact nothing but a pleasant walk, from 1st April to day of funeral inclusive; whilst at the same time he received 10/- per diem and 1 guinea for every ship arriving, though that duty was done by his deputy, and though for some months scarcely any ship arrived, and all were in perfect health. Forcing also the allowance of £1 per diem on sub Medico Great Guns [Dr. Verling] after his leaving our Neighbour's house, from [there is a blank space here] to [blank space here] merely because Madame Shrug begged he might now and then call on her. Forcing the allowance of ——— on sub medico 20th [Dr. Rutledge] merely for soldering up the vases containing heart and stomach, an hour or two hours' work.

The difficulty in getting him to allow officers of the troops of the navy the pano they were entitled to. How Povilardo buttered up Mach in a letter to Capo di Vascello Brown, saying he had done the same at the Cape. How he was adored by the lower classes and slaves; the charming, amiable manners of Sultana, and such stuff. After the ridicule and abuse she had bestowed upon him behind his back. Old Polyphemes [Admiral Lambert] showed the letter to Mach who was delighted and quoted him afterwards as a sensible clever fellow. When Polyphemes told Sultana at pranzo of this letter, and was going to show it to her (without first taking the precaution of saying how she was lauded and extolled in it) she began immediately attacking Povi, saying that he was such a stupid, insipid sort of fellow. Polyphemes put it back in his pocket without showing it to her.

His urging Post Office Master [Joseph Cole], also the newly arrived colleague from London, to prosecute and persecute Shrug. His eagerness to crush him again, if he could, and how he excited them against him.

Great dislike manifested by Sultana in the autumn of 1821 to Capo of Royal Great Guns [Major James Power]. How ill tempered, cross and disagreeable he had grown; how angry and morose he now often looked.

11 June 1821

His brutal way of going on again this morning about Pagatore's accounts of 66th, and his rage; but he would be damned if they would not draw for the broken period; he did not care a damn about the difficulties and trouble it caused.

15 June 1821

Praising Cadetta sky high for her various beauties and charms; that everything about her was pretty; telling her of all the praises she heard of her.

16 June 1821

Ninny said at pranzo to Grazzioso Tomaso that Capo Medico Primo [Dr. Shortt] only wanted to be asked to remain here; that he applied to go under an idea; and would be prepared to remain. But was disappointed. That he might depend upon it, he had ever since and would always reject [? regret] it. He would have given anything to stay. There was nothing the matter with his liver.[23] Grazzioso said he could not conceive what could have induced him to say that to him, if it was not the case; that he assured him it was, and he was always under the impression that that alone had been his motive. Then, said Ninny, he had told (Capo of Great Guns) Old Poderoso [Major James Power] a very different story.

17 June 1821

Ninny said at pranzo to Sultana that Mme. Shrug [Madame Bertrand] had told him that she did not care for any of her children, except the little one [Arthur, born at St Helena]. She did not care what became of the others so long as he was well ! ! ! This was merely an invention to please Sultana, showing so much more affection for the puisne [youngest] and so little for the figlia.

He cutting up Medico Longo [Dr Shortt]. He could not bear him, detested him; 'think of his having told me he was sorry I had taken up such a ridiculous idea as the belief that the debility produced by taking medicine was prejudicial'. How he harped on the observation of the 'ridiculous idea' used by Medico.

19 June 1821

When at Dinner, at Sir William Doveton's,[40] Giovane Cappellano mentioned an anecdote evidently meaning it to the prejudice of Mach. He said that, happening once to be at Longwood with Las Cases, and the conversation turning on their want of a clergyman and their desire to obtain one, he made him promise on his honour he would mention to Mach what he had stated on this point; which he accordingly did on his return from there. Some months after this however, whilst spending a few days at Plantation House where there was only the family party, and whilst drinking some wine after dinner, Mach with a severe frown fixed his eyes upon him and asked him: 'Pray, Mr. Vernon, did Count Las Cases charge you with such a message (viz the above)?' When he answered 'Yes, he did so'. 'Why did you not immediately inform me of it?' rejoined the other. To which he replied he had informed him of it immediately after his return from Longwood, mentioning the fact and other circumstances whereupon the other dropped the subject.

20 June 1821

Sultana cutting up the Cercueils [Pine-Coffins] and Longo [Shortt] again today; turning into ridicule the mode of treatment of Medico Longo, and her anger at his ordering her child such strong doses of argento vivo [quick-silver—mercury] as likely to establish a disease by that means, to which he was now a stranger.

Ninny showed her a note he had received from Cercueil, and she read it, and soon after made known its contents (generally) to the whole of her guests: 6 penny twist and 9 penny roll.

20th June 1821 (or thereabout)

Nincumpoop's delight when he found Cochon of 20th [Mayor John Hogg] had committed himself. Major Jackson ought to bring

him to a general Court Martial; he hoped to God he would do so
and break him; he must be broken if he did it, and he was a damned
fool if he did not, now that he had him in his power. He had £20,000
and he could well afford it. I should be damned if he did. About this
day Ninny told me Mach wanted for some time to make an allowance
of 10/- per diem to H-d-n [Major C. R. G. Hodson] as Deputy
Judge Advocate. The moment Sultana went down to Town all
work within the hearing of children was immediately ordered to be
discontinued until after she was up—about 12 or half past 12. Bells
ceased ringing at those hours also. No music or drums allowed to play
at the relief of main guard, though it was the constant practice;
and even then [she was] dissatisfied; saying that there was still some
trifling bustle or noise before she was up. The rudeness of Cadetta
still continuing towards Ego. Her appropriation of [? gift] though
never handed over to her as a present.

22 June 1821

Sultana's incivility to Ego at Weeping Willy's pranzo and her
assiduous attention there, and from some time before, to Ninny,
always having him at her side and giggling.[41]

23 June 1821

Madame Buller said to me, speaking of our Neighbour's demise,
'that it was too much the endeavour of those at St Helena to impress
the belief, and establish it as the general opinion, that he was not ill,
but merely feigning to be so'.

23 June 1821

I left this morning after collecting the list (given me by Ninny)
of Courts of Inquiry and Court Martials made out by il Longo
Yamstock as D.J.A. [Major C. R. G. Hodson, Deputy Judge
Advocate] in the book of War Office Regulations, at the page where
the Secretary of War's letter is entered. On my return to the office
soon afterwards I had received a list of Court Martials; and opening
the book at the same time to show it to him, he interrupted me by
saying: 'Yes, I know; wait a moment'. He then looked at some papers
and soon afterwards said to me: 'Oh, let a warrant be made out for
Hodson for those Court Martials'. I said that I observed besides

the Court Martials there were also Courts of Inquiry charged. He answered: 'Yes certainly this took up his time as well as the Court Martials'.

26 June 1821

When Sultana got out of the vehicle at Polyphemes she bowed, smiled and spoke to Ego, who was waiting to bow to her in a kind manner; going upstairs the same [occurred]. But Ego sitting himself between Signora Cercueil [Pine-Coffin] and Signora Corto [Shortt], before and at pranzo, and paying as much attention as he could, soon perceived her rage. She eyed him, and his neighbours viciously. And when he asked her to bibere [drink], to see how she would behave, she scarcely deigned to open her lips and gave the most stiff bend of the head.

Capo of Vansittart (Dalrymple) accompanied Signora Corto [Madame Shortt], cantando in Toscana favella [singing in Tuscan language]. I heard Sultana enquiring of Ninny [Reade], with whom she was flirting and had been all day, 'What language were they singing in?' Ninny said 'Chinese'.[42] Whereat she got in a furious gust, and said he had been tutored at H. Knoll [High Knoll][43]; that she could not suppose he could of himself behave to her in that way. And then attacked both Cortos [Shortt] and Cercueils [Pine-Coffins] who, she said, had behaved with the greatest incivility and rudeness to her as well, and insulted the Swells [Binghams] who were her friends; that they all set themselves up against her.[44] She said that the Cortos refused provocations [invitations] without giving any reason for doing it, though at the same time they were dining with anybody else who asked them, and even borrowed her carriage to go and dine out the day after refusing her. She had not seen anything but that was proper in Madame Corto, but it was the Dottore who instigated her; that whenever anybody behaved ill to her, or turned against her, Ego made it always a point to make those persons his most intimate friends. She also said that she would have the bastimento [ship] to herself going home; for she was sure there was nobody on the Island who would go on the same ship with her. She had none but enemies here, and even since she had been known to be going home, any one needing to go should not. She kept eyeing in a hostile way the two ladies and, on entering drawing room, scarcely made an inclination of the head, sailing on to a corner to be with the men. And on going away took no notice of any of the ladies whatsoever.

27 June 1821

Mach told Ego he had better remain in Town, when the famiglia went back to Plantation House, not leaving it optional; therefore most probably Sultana was at the bottom of it.

27 June 1821

Capo of Vansittart [Dalrymple] told me again today, after pranzo, that the Sultana had been again cavilling at the Longos [Shortts], the Cercueils [Pine-Coffins] and Ego, worse than the preceding day. Had also abused the Vignobles [Wynyards] but praised the Swells [Binghams]. Sultana thought proper to give Ego an inclination of head, which Ego drily returned.

27 June 1821

Capo di Vascello told me today that Ninny had done everything in his power to excite him against Saul Sapiens [Saul Solomon, shopkeeper] (who had been strongly recommended by his predecessor Capo di Vascello *Phaeton*). He had told him how ill he had behaved to him; and that he allowed his fantesco [man servant] to run up a conto [bill] against him for £500 without his knowledge. He said that believing these statements, of course, he [Capo di Vascello] spoke to Sapiens about it, expressing his surprise at his acting in such a way; and that Sapiens assured him he would show him in black and white the proof of what he was going to state to him, which was a faithful relation of the occurrence, viz. that when Ninny [Reade] was anxious to get the lease of his villa, near Stercoraceous's [Thomas Brooke], it was necessary to advance a sum of money in order to get possession of it and get out the then tenant; and that for this purpose Ninny was obliged to borrow £300, which Sapiens advanced for that purpose to him. (Or else pay it himself on his account). He said that he [Sapiens] besides lent him [Sir Thomas Reade] £30 to £40 so that, out of the Bill which amounted to £608 (Ego thinks), about 350 was actually money. But that he never would have asked him for it; but being about to make a purchase he was obliged to do so. That Ninny flew out into a terrible rage on receiving it; but after all could only object to a bottle of mustard overcharged, which was 8/– and was deducted, Sapiens not being aware that it had been put down to him. He said that he [Reade] was for a long period constantly at Sapiens' house, and used to live for some time almost entirely upon what he got from Sapiens; the articles thus furnished him for consumption being a portion of the Bill. That Sapiens saw then that it was expected by Ninny that he should charge nothing for what he had got from him; and that he would not have asked him if he had not been pressed for cash; that he only got the Bill paid through the interference of Capo di Vascello *Phaeton* [Captain Stanfell], who expostulated with him about it and insisted on his paying it.

The Cercueils had also told him (Capo Vigo) [Captain Brown] he had found Sapiens a very different man from what he had been represented to him on his first arrival. And that the Deputy Judge Advocate also gave him a very good account of him, and represented him in a quite different light; but that Ninny was doing every thing which malignity could suggest against him to injure him. That Ninny had done all he could to prevent the officers of the troops of the Navy getting pano for uniforms, and had taken the greatest hatred to their Maggiore. He then mentioned to Ego that Colonel Caldwell (India Artillery), having brought with him here a box full of casts of Neighbour's [Napoleon's] medals, gave it to Sapiens to dispose of for him; and that Hodson looking at it, whilst Sapiens was showing it, observed how pleased Ninny would be if he had it; and that Sapiens said: 'Well, then, he shall have it.' He said that he paid upwards of £13 for it, and immediately sent it as a present to Ninny. And as Capo [Captain Brown] said to me, he afterwards gave it to Sultana, saying it had been brought out from England for him; but that he would take some opportunity, if he could, of telling Sultana how it happened. Ego recollects being present at Ninny's villa, coming from races, when he gave it to Sultana, after showing it to her saying at the same time it had been sent out to him from England. Colonel Caldwell was here about February 1821.

28 June 1821

Poderoso XX [Capt. Robert Power], and his rib [wife], now getting into high favour with Sultana; invited by her to make use of the grounds of Plantation House for themselves, nurse and child. What a fuss was often made about the Vignoble's maid presuming to do so. Now she began to speak in praise of Poderoso XX; how pleasant again he had become. After all the abuse.

Her saying Dandy Captain of Vansittart [Dalrymple] had told her Medico Longo was jealous of his wife.

How she again attacked Polyphemes [Admiral Lambert]; saying
that she detested him; could not bear the sight of him; he was the
most abominable hypocrite she had ever met with; there was always
some low intrigue about anything he did; her anger that she had
lent her calèche when she found he had been riding in it, as well as
the Donna Buller. Il Maggiore di Brigatta [Captain Charles
Harrison] and Capo of Great Guns [Power], Ninny's constant
associates; took every opportunity for Maggiore di Brigatta to get
his house and his horses off his hands.

Il servo Dobbins told Yam A.D.C. [Den Taafe] that Cadetta
[Susanna] was in the sulks and had not confabulated with her
Madre for four days.

28 June 1821

Mach desired that Ego should stay in Town whilst he and Sultana
were in the country; not leaving it to his own choice by saying:
'had you not better, or would you like or prefer?'

29 June 1821

Medico Navale told Ego that Sultana gave as a reason for Medico
Capo Longo not having bowed to her at the dinner at Polyphemes,
when the grand fracas took place,[44] his being offended and jealous
at Medico Navale being consulted; that however Mach on speaking
to him about it had said there was some misunderstanding beside s.

Besides the £100 a year allowed Ninny for Deputy Adjutant
General's office, which he never had and which was not required,
he had another allowance of £100 a year for the office as Deputy
and Brigade Major, the latter of which had nothing to do.

1821

The extraordinary indent of dictionaries that arrived this year;
Chinese, German, Portuguese, Spanish.

June 1821

Pick Axe mentioned to Ego that Mach had said that he did not
think any one here was entitled to promotion or would get it,
except Ego, and that he thought they must do it for him.

June 1821

The Deputy Advocate General [Major Hodson] told Ego, on speaking to him about the 2 guinea allowance and explaining to him the Regulations on that head, that he had kept no memorandum of the days, except what he had collected from the proceedings of the General Court Martials and Courts of Inquiry, not having expected any extra allowance whatever. He said that he had been desired by Ninny to make such a list, which he had given him; but it was returned to him by Ninny, who said that Mach had desired to tell him to charge also Courts of Inquiry to Ninny and him, and settled that he was to charge 3 days. That he was not aware of any regulation about it and certainly did not look for any allowance on that head, being already Deputy Judge Advocate to the Island. I told him he had better again look over the minutes, from which he could easily ascertain the dates of the adjournments, and that I would give him an extract of the regulations stating the manner in which to have it made up; which I accordingly did the day after, expecting he would adhere to the regulation. But after waiting some time and finding he did not, I laid it before Mach for his sentiments on this (Vide note of what passed).

Mach informed Big Wig Secretaries Downing Street, 5th June 1821, of the cadeau of a centre piece from Madame Shrug [Madame Bertrand] to Capo Medico 20th [Dr. Arnott] for the mensa 20th [Mess of 20th Regiment], saying it was indicative 'of much impertinent pretention even to the very last of the Shrug family'.

Medico Longo [Dr. Shortt] telling Ego that Sultana had said, 'that from the moment the thing was up (Neighbour's demise) Medico Longo had turned against her or become her enemy'.

In the first days of July 1821

Ninny [Reade] told Ego that his furniture (his horses and carriage not mentioned) was valued at upwards of £2,000; I think £2,300. This was after asking me how much Vignoble's [Wynyard] came to, and as a comparison. Mach must have assisted him in housekeeping, or given or got him money through some other channel than his regular allowances.

Monday 2 July 1821

Mach and Sultana cried out against Cappellano Primo's [the First Chaplain's][45] sermon preached in Country Church the preceding day. Ninny said Mach had a right to call for a copy of it, which he in consequence did in union with the council. Sultana's cutting up the junior Cappellano [junior Chaplain, Rev. Vernon] and mogli for their uncourteous reception of her when visiting them a few days before; and next day, notwithstanding, so kind and civil to him, leaning on his arm in the Town.

Yam ADC told Ego that Giovane Cappellano had called the two figli of Sultana 'liars'.

Poderoso Capo and Great Guns [Major James Power] told Ego that La Signora Obins said Sultana treated her with the greatest rudeness.

5 July 1821

Ninny told Ego that our Neighbour was brindisied [toasted] at mensa [mess] of 20th [regiment].[46]

8 July 1821

Ninny showed Ego the scraps of carte [cards][47] picked up near Veritas' [Montholon] quarters, where it was said that the writer had received his letters which would be sent to England; and about Stokoe desiring to know if the pittura had been received at our Neighbour's, and about sending messages through him. Pearls spoken of. Next day Ninny, and Deputy Judge Advocate examined Saul Sapiens. In the scraps it was also said that Mach had the papers with the Antigallican ciphers, but could not make them out without a key.

14 July 1821

Mach's abuse of Cortoculo [Lieut. Shortis],[48] flying out at him in a furious manner, and denying having said what Shortis asserted on his honour he had said; denying giving authority for many things equally asserted by the other, who even quoted the place where given; but which, being verbal, Ninny swore positively he had never mentioned. Cortoculo laid his hand emphatically on his breast, declaring with great earnestness that he positively, on his honour, had done so. And Ninny, after having begun to put his signature, apparently annoyed at the other's delaration, furiously rose, dashing the pay list and pen from him, swearing he would not sign it and that he could make him pay what he disputed; his having given orders about which was approbation money for Maggio

H.N.E.—9*

il falegname [May, the carpenter] who, there is no doubt, he had then ordered to be paid when in favour, 7/– or 7/6 per day in addition to his pay.

16th July 1821

Sultana's great attention to Madame Major Great Guns (Island) [Major David Kinnaird of St Helena Regiment], holding out her hand to her, and shaking hands with her when they meet; her eulogies of her and of his cleverness.

16 July 1821

Ninny's horrible blow up of the clerk of ordnance (Webb), and the furious manner in which he attacked him and afterwards Old Brick and Mortar, when he sent for them to make the former complete his estimate of the house.

Sultana's admiration of Medico Vigo [Dr. Charles Mitchell]; what a delightful man, how well he understood children's diseases. It was intended I should repeat it to Medico Longo.

Pretty Thomas [Col. Lyster] told Ego that Royal Great Guns Capo [Major James Power] had repeated to Ninny that the 20th had brindisied [toasted] Neighbour [Napoleon]; that he had it from Obins[49]; that Great Guns Capo was trying to get himself into favour by carrying him tales; that this was the way he and Ninny had got so thick.

18 July 1821

No tiffin except for Mach and Sultana, and Ego waiting in the office at the Castle. My asking Yam A.D.C. if he knew the reason, and the latter, on enquiring found the servants had been told not to mention that tiffin was getting ready for them. An inferior one was served up, and Ego, annoyed, did not go. The same thing exactly occurred a day or two afterwards, when Ego acted again in the same way.

Ninny and Sultana's fulsome and loathsome flattery of Mandarine, even giving him as a toast at the public pranzo of Sir William Doveton, as having rendered such services; after his so much disliking him whilst here.

Mach's anger with Old Nick Capo of 66th [Captain George Nicholls] for ordering payment to Thorne, of 66th, Overseer of water course to Ladder Hill, to attend some Regimental business for a few hours (Court Martial Ego thinks); and saying it was damned impertinent of him to do so.

26 July 1821

Again about confab of the 16 February. His harsh scolding manner, his cavilling and his strongly asserting that it had not been said; altering some words of the minutes, and in a certain degree affecting or wanting to make me suppose by his remark that he did not wish for many changes in it. He said that 9 o'clock had never even been spoken of. Ego would not be able to find it in the conversation, letters or any document whatsoever. It was in fact putting down the very words they would then hardly have wished; it was in their own view; to their advantage alone. See the captious suspicions and evil designed insinuation, as if Ego was their instrument. But was it not themselves that said it? Was it not the repetition of the words of one of them, and therefore natural for him to have urged it in their favour. His assertion that Veritas said it was a thing which they now gave up, and then neither had been returned to England. It was a [?] and another note again, and returned it to its posting place.

[July] 1821

Sultana's still inveighing bitterly against Young Brick and Mortar for wishing her figlia, the year before, to speak to Young Polisson. And notwithstanding this, soon afterwards taking the latter into the greatest favour, though his being noticed by the former was one of his greatest crimes. He was allowed to go through the Plantation and all over the grounds with Cadetta[50] and ride themselves alone, after it had been asserted some months before, in presence of Cadetta, that the latter had complained to her of Polisson's indelicate proceedings towards her when walking together. Her affected interest in every thing that related to Yam ADC, and continually talking to him about what concerned him and his friends.

Mach's reflecting on O.O. for bringing in, in a post-scriptum, a remark on Neighbour's [Napoleon's] appearance, saying he had looked deadly pale; on which he observed in a bitter and vengeful manner: 'who knows what may be his object in inserting that in his post-scriptum?'

July 1821

At a pranzo at the Castello Old Mach abused Old Frog [Mont-
chenu] for not entertaining, saying he had not given more than
6 pranzos; in which abuse Sultana joined most heartily. Great
Gun Capo of Royal Artillery inadvertently observed he had
certainly given more than that, for he himself had dined there full
as many times as that.

August 1821[51]

Maggiore di Brigatta [Capt. Charles Harrison] told Ego that
Mach had given a lease of 21 years of Hardings' Spring to the
Judge Advocate for £40 per annum, a mere trifle as he observed,
for such a valuable acquisition. He was so suspicious, when he first
heard of it, that he would not believe it, nor did he till the Deputy
himself told him so. The Brigadier here remarked that it was just
as much as if he had actually put £5000 in his pocket. It since
appeared that the Deputy got besides another lease of a considerable
extent of grounds, adjoining Harding, for a trifle of rent.

Cappellano Primo [had arrived] soon after Mach's departure
from pranzo with officers of 20th Regiment.

1 or 2nd August 1821

Medico Corto [Shortt] told Ego that whilst in Old Saul Sapiens'
bottega [shop] he was told by Saul that Ninny had left the island
without returning him a bed, a couch, different articles of plate,
spoons, knives and forks which he had lent him, although he sent
repeatedly to him 5 or 6 days before his departure. He said then he
would send them back. Then Saul appealed and sent shop boy to
ask him whether it was so or not, and he confirmed what he said.
He said that he stated he had sent home an account of Ninny's
conduct towards him, which would be published in the Times
Newspaper and other papers, and a copy of the paragraph would be
delivered to Ninny on his arrival at home. Medico Corto had also
been informed of the business of the medals, with the different
form that he had given Colonel Caldwell some Chinese articles, in
value of exchange, and not money.

4 August 1821

Madame Cercueil told Ego that Giovane Cappellano [Rev.
Vernon] had called a few days back on Signora Corto [Shortt] and

that she observed he appeared not to have much sense; he spoke so foolishly; that he was justifying Cappellano Primo for his conduct towards Mach, saying the latter would rue the day he had behaved ill (or misbehaved or to that effect) towards him; that the Cappellano Vecchio [Rev. Richard Boys] had a great deal of interest at the India House.

15 August 1821

Medico Longo [Dr. Shortt] also told Ego that Old O.P. archy medico [Dr. Archibald Arnott] had abused both Mach and Sultana, through thick and thin, when dining at his house the preceding week. And that Yam ADC [Den Taafe] had also abused them both one evening after dinner some days before, when he got a little mellow with wine; tho' he spoke in their favour before company so as to keep up appearances he supposed.

Lieutenant Taylor Blossun was highly annoyed with Ninny for not noticing him here, though friendly with him when in the Mediterranean.

18 August 1821

Medico Primo Longo told Ego that the account sent home by Saul Sapiens about Ninny was a detail of the transactions about the bill of £500, and a statement of Ninny's having, as he said, stolen the things from him, viz. that he had borrowed and did not return but even refused it when sent for by Sapiens; that he had even taken on board a sofa which he, Saul, had amongst other things claimed from Mach.

The meanness and fulsome adulation of La Fontaine [John de Fountain][52] respecting Mach, praising his justice, goodness and impartiality!! after what Mach and Ninny had done to ruin him. But his getting into the Council was brought about by gross cringing and mean flattering.

August 1821

Medico Longo [Dr. Shortt] told Ego that Ninny was indebted £30 to Medico Livingstone and had got a nuovo cappello [new hat] from him besides. Neither article was ever paid for and he went away £15 in his debt.

1 September 1821

Medico Longo mentioned to Ego that Jenny Jumps [Jenkins][53] had this day told him Ninny did not pay his domestic soldier; that to those he had from 20th he paid nothing.

5 September 1821[54]

Medico Corto [Dr. Shortt] told me of the same thing, adding that he said he would triumph over Mach; that he had so much interest with the Court of Directors that he would entirely upset all that Mach had done against him, and that he would make Old Stercoraceous tremble in his shoes.

Madame Corta [Shortt] explained that he had said that so long as Mach lived he would rue the day he had behaved in that manner to Old Cappellano. Both expressed their wonder at Giovane Cappellano speaking so foolishly.

6 September 1821

Medico Longo again told Ego that Mach had taken in Old Medico 20th [Arnott], and left orders that only 10/6 should be given to the boarding officers, whoever they might be, of ship's arriving, and the other half to form a fund to repay the company for the allowance of 10/– a day granted to the Quarantine Surgeon (Old Medico 20th).

Sultana and Ninny endeavoured to make the public believe the followers were delighted at Bony's death, affecting to say they were delighted.

September 1821 (about 26th)

Capo Medico Corto [Shortt] told Ego that Sampson had told him (Cercueil and Moglie present) that Ninny had sent a message or word to him and to others, that Medico Corto's carriage was an old, worn out one; that he had it in Sicily with him, and that it was all knocked about. Ninny had (as Medico also before told me) on a former occasion informed Saul Sapiens that Cercueil's carriage had broken down one day coming up from town, or going to Plantation House or to Church. Ninny told about the same.

October 1821

Saul Sapiens told Ego, in presence of Cercueil and Brigade Major of Hutt's Gate, that Captain Graham of *William Pitt* had said last year on his way home, at his ship's table, before a large party, that Ninny had never paid him for the phaeton, though he had bought it of him in 1819, for which he was to pay him £180 or £184. And that, notwithstanding, he had sold it since to the people of Longwood; at which he, Graham, was greatly incensed.

Doctor Longo told Ego that Ninny had also set about a report that Cercueil's vehicle had broken down on the way to Plantation House one day going to dinner there, and this was with a view to preventing Saul Sapiens from buying the vehicle which he was in treaty for. And Saul on the above occasion said that he had been so injured; but did not say if Ninny gave him the information or not.

[October]

He said that my requests might be easily past if they thought proper to refute them. That the rank of Major was of much less value or importance than that of Lieut. Col., and besides, I had been holding a staff situation for six months. Lord B. [Bathurst] wrote to him to say he had supported his claim as O.O. in consideration of his recommendation. He was so far from recommending him on that ground that he never acknowledged Lord B's letter. That with regard to the persons I had consulted, he said in a reproachful manner that [?] men often argued coincidentally, and very improperly on precedent, and made further applications when they ought not to be brought forward. He replied by admitting to my having certain friends and acting by their advice. I explained to him I had consulted no person whatever; that I had merely written to some on supposing I had good prospects of success in obtaining the antedate. And that though it failed I had been told I was not to give up the idea of obtaining it for the period so far. He said that Capt. Nicholls had not thought of that.

End of 1821

Mach's endeavour to awe, by the severity of his tone and the strangeness of his aspect and his black frown, ragged and brutal manners. He wished to be surrounded by mean slaves,[55] like a cruel Eastern tyrant. Gloomy, unsocial and ferocious. He was both unreasonable and unjust. That self complacency; the undefinable adjunct of an honourable man; self reverence; a determination of mind which rejects whatever might stain integrity of spirit and compel to part with the approbation of one's own heart. The independent and honourable mind, and the proud heart revolt when the caprice of him who has authority shows itself, and when the wand of command is exhibited in abrupt nakedness. The neck which had never bowed to the condition of a slave revolts at such usurpation. Give sorrow words: whatever sentiment finds its way to the lips and vents its energies through the medium of language, by that means finds relief. His countenance, his gesture, his tone of voice were all subjects of aversion. Darting glances of reproach; breaking out in sharp rebukes and overhelming you with angry, bitter, wanton taunts.

Curtness, despotic disposal, insolence and petulance, malice and deliberate cruelty.

Frank and easy and communicative and sensitive and sympathetic.

Invariably reserved and suspicious and for ever disposed to regard x x x with thoughts of hostility and ferocity. . . . A cruel man who watches with abject spirit the eyes of another waiting timidly till he should have told him.

Brabazon [William Brabazon, Master-Attendant of the Harbour], I am pretty sure, was the person who mentioned to me the day before Ego embarked, that mad Prit. [Pritchard][56] on his being appointed to the works, used to quiz Fat A—se Moll when he came down to Town.

By your quarrelling with Mach you got yourself turned out of a good berth. Whilst I, by the same means fished myself into a snug situation, that's all the difference between us, you see.

Brabazon assured Ego that the persecution he experienced from both the Cavaliers was the chief cause of his going home; he inveighed most bitterly against the scoundrels. Tresorier of ship coming home told Ego that he never heard a man so abused as he heard Ninny [Sir Thomas Reade]; he seemed to have made an immense number of enemies; he had been at a party of 8 or 9 persons, every one of whom had some heavy complaint against him, and who seemed to be exasperated against him; so bad indeed that he at last took Ninny's part. Mr. Mayne was very violent against purser (I think he said) of the *Atlas*, and had mentioned the circumstance of a surgeon of the Company (I believe of the *Atlas*) having been aggravated and roughly spoken to by Ninny on account of his giving, or writing a note to send up with some small presents to Longwood.

Chapter Six
1822-1823 Post-Mortem

11 March 1822

Saul Sapiens told Cercueil and Ego that when Ninny found out he had got the medals, he sent Dutton to him to enquire whom he got them from. He desired to know how they were brought on to the Island and by whom, and [asked him to] send him their names. After which Saul Sapiens told him he had them as a present from Colonel Caldwell; and that he sent word to Ninny that he made him a present of them also. He said that the next day Dutton [Thomas Dutton, Register Master] came back thanking Saul Sapiens in the name of Ninny, and saying how much obliged he was to him for them. Saul Sapiens said that Colonel Caldwell did not actually make a present of them to him; but had told him that, though he did not wish to have it said that he sold them, he would exchange them for some thing else; and he [Sapiens] gave him 5 ivory fans in exchange. He said that Ninny owed Mr. O'Connor £380 and gave him his carriage for which he charged £200, saying he would give harness for 4 horses for which he wished to pay off the Longwood House and told him he might get the £180 from [?] and not to be that particular of the date.[1]

24 March 1822

Young [?] boarding officer 20th told Ego that Ninny had reproached him one day with saying he would not go home in the same ship with Sultana; and with having said on another occasion 'that man [Lowe] has lost £12,000 a year soon after Neighbour's [Napoleon's] demise'. That it was for some expressions reflecting on his professional character that Jenkins J. [also called Jenny Jumps][2] had quarrelled with Ninny; and had called him out at St. Helena. But the other had pleaded his official situation there. And that Jenkins had declared to Ninny that whenever he (Ninny) left St Helena, if he (Jenkins) was employed in the E.I.C. [East India Company], he would immediately leave his ship when in port to follow him, to bring him to account for what he had said.

Denzil told me he thought the quarrel was still about what occurred in Sobury's shop; that he knew that Jenkins, who was then staying at Rock Cottage, had refused dining at Plantation House; and that on Mach's enquiring into the business he was told by Wallis it was because he would not meet Ninny.

Wednesday 27th Nov. 1822

Called on [Mach]. He told me in an ungracious manner (having stood a long time after he had taken a seat, he had at last asked if I would not sit down), with his back turned to me as he was looking over some papers: 'I have not yet sent your memorandum. In fact I have not had time.' I observed I had not wished to press him. He then began saying that he must again tell me what he had several times done before, that he did not at all agree with me as to the grounds on which I made my claim. And as to the promotion of Captain Poppleton, that it was no precedent. If it was, it was a bad one, which he would not admit as being applicable to my case. They (meaning Secretary of State) did not like to have it urged to them. He would not give up his opinion and judgement to mine. It was one he could not relinquish, and he would not appear before the Duke of York or Lord Bathurst as giving his countenance to, or acknowledging, such a precedent. His recommendation of Captain Poppleton was not on account of his being O.O., but for anterior services. This period he did not even know before being at St Helena and Sir G.B. [George Bingham] and Colonel M. [John Mansel, in command of 53rd Regiment in 1816] first refused to support his recommendation. And although [he approved] Captain P's [Poppleton's] promotion, it was only on seeing that Captain Crokat got it, that they made this application (this is not at all applicable to me). I said I was obliged to urge them to strengthen my claim on renewing it. He said I must not expect he would express it. That all he could do was to recommend my anterior services. (He never has given me his support scarcely for my services with him, though it was only that which I wanted from him. I had testimony from others for previous services.) That, he said, he would do, and then let any application otherwise rest upon its own merits. He thought I should not at all quote precedents, or mention the O.O. [Orderly Officer Poppleton], but leave it all to former services. He said that I had dwelt too much on the precedent of O.O. He would however forward the letter, as I had thought proper to dwell so much upon that point. Did I wish him to forward the memorial also, as it was very long, and it had already been sent before. I said that the memorial was not from the same date as the last, but from the day on which Earl Bathurst had originally recommended me; and that in case he did not wish to recommend me from December 1817 but decided to do so from the 5th August 1819, that one might be substituted. I said that perhaps his Lordship might not read it, but if he should agree to it, it would be necessary for the agreement to the memorial being for another date.[3]

23 January 1823

On leaving Mach's house[4] in company with him this afternoon I said to him that I hoped he would take an opportunity of mentioning to Mr. W . . l . . tt [Wilmot, the lawyer of Lowe] how much mortified and depressed I was at finding the manner in which Earl Bathurst had brought my name under the consideration of the Commander in Chief, without even the word 'recommendation' in it; after the manner too in which he had recommended me in August 1819; and after a personal application and letter from Lord William B. [? Beckwith] and Sir H. Morton urging my claim to promotion, had been addressed to him in June 1821, a letter which had been written without my knowledge or any solicitation on my part. They had first waited together on Sir H. Taylor, who recommended them to apply to Earl Bathurst, who had himself suggested their writing him such a letter.

N.B. On the 24th he desired me to bring him the copy of Sir H. Morton's letter of August, and of that of Earl Bathurst to him of 20th August. These I took to him the following day; but found him out and left them with Dutton [Thomas Dutton, Register Master] with a note to him.

He said he could not conceive what was the cause of it; that he himself had never had any verbal communication with Lord Bathurst on the subject; it was all in writing. He thought it was very odd after Earl Bathurst had recommended me once before; that perhaps, though it was only an idea of his own, it might not be thought proper to urge any such matter at the present moment, whilst the question of a prosecution was pending [probably Lowe *v.* O'Meara].[4] He however had always been of opinion I ought not to have brought forward as a precedent the promotion of Poppleton.

And he also thought that if I had confined myself to the period of Earl Bathurst's recommendation for an antedate, Big Lords would not have objected to recommend me; but that my asking for a period so far back had staggered him and had defeated the object. Though that was his opinion at the time, he did not think it right to discourage my application for it; that it was a difficult thing to interfere when people's own interests were operating in their minds.

I proceeded in making some more observations as to why there was greater mark of favour conferred on others, when he peevishly and tremblingly said, 'I will take an opportunity of speaking to Mr. Wilmot about it. You know how occupied I am at this moment, but if you think your own affair one of greater importance than the prosecution, I will give yours the precedence, and speak to Mr. Wilmot about it this very day instead of the other subject.' I said, certainly not, I only had begged him to take an opportunity of doing so. He replied: 'I have told you I will do so, are you satisfied?' I bowed in answer. But the rapidity with which we were walking, and the cold wind we faced, prevented me answering for some seconds whilst I was getting breath. Then he, in a most hasty rating tone, began to say that he had expected I should have replied 'certainly' and expressed my satisfaction with what he had said he would do; but that my hesitation showed I was not satisfied. I told him he had put a construction on it which my character did not warrant; I was satisfied and not attempting to push the thing upon him at all.

About 1 February 1823

Mach speaking about the letter he had read a day or two before from Great Gun Magnesia [Dr. Verling], said it was a mean, low, vulgar piece of cunning to elude giving him a direct answer to that from himself to him; that he had only answered 3 points though he had put 6 or 7 distinct questions to him; that he had himself behaved with the greatest candour and openly with him, and that was the return he received; but he would yet make him answer the whole; he had not done with him. He was extremely angry and spoke for some time in the same strain.

The 4th he told me in calling at my lodgings that he believed I should get the antedate. It was in a proper claim, and he believed it would yet take place. He had given Mr. Wilmot a copy of notes and letters from Earl Bathurst to him, respecting me, besides the copy of that of 20th August (from the same); and Mr. Wilmot was taking such steps about them with Sir H. Taylor as he, Sir

Hudson, thought would effect the object. A few days before he had also told me he had given the letters, which he had me copy for that purpose, to Mr. Wilmot; who did not say much on the subject, but who was fully aware of all the arguments; and would, he did not doubt, do something about it.

21st December 1823

Dr. Alexander Backstairs [Dr. Baxter] told Ego that he came up to Mach and Medico Primo of Longwood [Dr. O'Meara] as stated in his book, and heard him apply the words there mentioned viz. the anfani [chatter] used between Ali Pasha [Napoleon's valet][5] and N.B. [Napoleon]. He said that Mach wrote to him at Paris,[6] to ask him what he recollected of it, prefacing his inquiry by a denial on his part, and saying that it was not likely that he should have observed Ali Pasha, who had been so civil to him. Dr. A.B. [Baxter] also told me he recollected his applying the term of black-hearted villain to N.B., and asked me whether I did not recollect it.

He told me also that Mach had got up an affidavit for him to make out, but that he erased nearly the whole of it; and that he would have written it out himself, mentioning things as requested, rather than have come over as a witness to the trial, and would willingly have sacrificed £400.

August [? 1823 or later]

Mach is but a machine—he is just what his nature and circumstances have made him. He slogs the machine which he cannot control. If he is corrupt, it is because he has been corrupted. If he is unamiable it is because he has been marked and spitefully treated. Give him a different education, place him in other circumstances, and treat him with as much gratefulness and generosity as he has experienced of harshness, and he would be altogether a different nature. A man who would be anxious to be loved rather than feared; and instead of having the accusation of being a man who was satisfied to spread around him anguish and despair, one who has an instinct for kindness. To some his meaning was [? open] to ambiguity. It is dangerous particularly when you have to do with an anxious and inexperienced mind and do nothing to improve a fault; and live in a great [? illusion] in the opinion of others, especially those we respect. While thought incapable of an error, it is difficult [if you] fall into one; but if warned, particularly in a case which gives one doubt of your capacity [?], you have already a means of escape.

Notes and Explanations

CHAPTER ONE

1 3 June 1817
Sir Hudson Lowe. *See* Biographical Note.

2 3 June 1817
The Cottage. The gardener lived in this small house in the grounds of Plantation House. Major Gorrequer also lived there for a time.

3 3 June 1817
Plantation House. Official residence of the Governor.

4 11 June 1817
Lady Lowe. Married Sir Hudson Lowe on December 31, 1815. She was the widow of Colonel Johnson. Her two daughters, Charlotte and Susanna Johnson were with her in St Helena. She was 35 years of age when she arrived in St Helena.

5 11 June 1817
Captain Henry Meynell (1789–1865) was commander of H. M. S. *Newcastle*. When Admiral Malcolm paid visits to Napoleon, Meynell often accompanied him and recorded the conversations.

6 11 June 1817
George Boorman was a plumber and repairer and did work at Longwood. His wife, a seamstress, prepared the interior of Napoleon's coffin.

7 July 1817
The Foreign Commissioners called on Sir Hudson Lowe about their visit to Longwood. They asked if they could go as private persons as Napoleon would not receive them in their official capacities. But Lowe would not agree to this.

8 July 1817
The Earl of Bathurst was the then Secretary of War

9 July 1817
Baron Barthelemy von Stürmer (1787–1853) was the Austrian Commissioner in St Helena. He came on June 18, 1816, and left in July 1818 and went to Rio de Janeiro.

10 23 July 1817
Orderly Officers by rota were appointed by the Governor to Napoleon's residence at Longwood. The sequence of orderly officers was as follows:
Captain T. W. Poppleton, 10th December 1815 to 24th July 1817
Captain Henry P. Blakeney, 25th July 1817 to 16th July 1818 and again 25th July 1818 to 5th September 1818.
Lt.-Colonel Thomas Lyster, 17th July 1818 to 24th July 1818 during Blakeney's absence.

Captain George Nicholls, 5th September 1818 to 9th February 1820.
Captain Engelbert Lutyens, 10th February 1820 to 26th April 1821.
Captain William Crokat, 26th April 1821 to 6th May 1821.

11 25 July 1817
Lt.-Colonel Christopher Fagan, who had been a Judge in Bengal. Napoleon received him on 19th June 1817 and this lead to Lowe's disapprobation.

12 26 July 1817
Lady Bingham was the wife of General Sir George Bingham, who was in command of the troops in St Helena.

13 27 July 1817
Thomas Henry Brooke (1774–1849) was Secretary to the St Helena Council, and also a local magistrate. He had considerable influence in the Island. After Lowe's departure he was for a time Acting Governor.

14 16 August 1817
Dr Barry O'Meara (1782–1836) was surgeon in the *Bellerophon* when Napoleon surrendered to Captain Maitland. Napoleon asked if he could come as his personal physician to St Helena. He attended in this capacity until 25th July 1818 when he was dismissed by Sir Hudson Lowe. He returned to England on 2nd August and published his book, *Napoleon in Exile, or A Voice from St Helena* much of which contains his condemnation of Lowe.

15 8 September 1817
Count Alexander Antonovitch Balmain (1779–1848) was the Russian Commissioner. He arrived in June 1816. He was a rather controversial character so far as the authorities were concerned. In 1820 he married Charlotte Johnson, Lady Lowe's elder daughter, and the following week on 3rd May 1820 in the *General Harris* he left with his wife for St Petersburg upon his recall.

16 8 September 1817
Colonel Edward Buckley Wynyard (1780–1865) was officially Military Secretary to Lowe, but almost all the work of this office was carried out by Gorrequer. He came on 6th May 1816 and left in June 1820.

17 September 1817
Dr Alexander Baxter (1777–1841) was Deputy Inspector of Hospitals. He arrived in the *Phaeton* on 14th April 1816. Lowe wanted Baxter to be in medical attendance on Napoleon but Napoleon would not accept him as such. Baxter made medical reports to Lowe from statements obtained from Dr O'Meara. He left St Helena in 1819.

18 2 December 1817
The apostille was a marginal note made by Napoleon on a letter from Lowe about this time. Napoleon said he did not want to receive any more letters from the Governor, whom he strongly criticised for his treatment.

19 2 December 1817
General Count Henri Gratien Bertrand (1773–1844) was Napoleon's Grand Marshal and senior member of his staff at Longwood. He had his own house at Hutt's Gate. He was a most devoted servant of the Emperor. His Memoirs of St Helena days were published in 1949.

20 2 December 1817
Sir Thomas Reade (1785–1849) was Deputy Adjutant General in St Helena. He came out with Lowe in April 1816. Lady Lowe remarked that he was the real governor of St Helena. He did not leave St Helena until July 1821, after Napoleon's death.

21 2 December 1817
Colonel Wynyard was living some distance away at this time at Rock Rose Cottage, near Sandy Bay. He also lived at Alarm House.

22 2 December 1817
Lieutenant Basil Jackson (1795–1889) was a lieutenant in the Staff Corps. He came out with Lowe. He was quite an artist and made some water colour paintings of Napoleon and of scenes in the Island, and assisted in drawing the plans for New Longwood House. Left 8 July 1819. Returned later it seems.

23 2 December 1817
Colonel Wynyard's work as Military Secretary was mostly done by Gorrequer.

24 8 December 1817
Taylor was the under-gardener at Longwood.

25 23 December 1817
See Diary entry of 11 June 1817.

26 December 1817
Lowe had summoned O'Meara to Plantation House for a discussion with Dr Baxter. There occurred a heated quarrel concerning the reports which the Governor required regarding Napoleon's state of health. O'Meara was refusing to comply with all the Governor's wishes and they were getting more and more at loggerheads. *See* O'Meara's *Napoleon in Exile* 20th January 1818.

CHAPTER TWO

1 First days of January 1818
Hudson Lowe was sending home his reports about O'Meara and the differences that were occurring.

2 4 January 1818
Two portraits of Napoleon's son by Marie Louise had been brought to St Helena, and confiscated by Lowe, so that Napoleon should not get them. *See* O'Meara *Napoleon in Exile* 16th February 1818.

3 6 or 7 January 1818
Colonel Fitz-Gerald, who was Governor of Mauritius at the time, visited St Helena on his way home, but Napoleon would not receive him.

4 10 January 1818
General Sir George Ridout Bingham (1776–1833) arrived on 15th October 1815 in H.M.S. *Northumberland* with Napoleon on board. He was in command of the troops at St Helena up till 24th May 1820 when he left. He had frequent interviews with Napoleon.

5 20 January 1818
Dr O'Meara was able to correspond with various friends in London including John Finlaison, the Keeper of the Records at the Admiralty. Lord Liverpool was then Prime Minister.

6 26 January 1818
Joseph Lusan was an Agent in Cape Town of the East India Company.

7 27 January 1818
There were considerable numbers of Chinese workers in the Island engaged in various employments including some at Longwood.

8 27 January 1818
Lieutenant John Edward Shortis of the St Helena Regiment and Superintendent of Public Works. The reference is to an argument concerning the charges in the accounts regarding Napoleon's establishment at Longwood.

9 27 January 1818
John Paine (Popie) was a painter and decorator who was sent out with
Andrew Darling to do repairs at Longwood.

10 27 January 1818
Napoleon Bertrand, the son of General Bertrand.

11 28 January 1818
Franceschi Cipriani, Maître d'hôtel to Napoleon. He was a Corsican, and
came out with the Emperor. He died on 26th February 1818 after a sudden
illness, probably acute appendicitis or perforated peptic ulcer.

12 28 January 1818
See Note 8 of Chapter 1.

13 5 February 1818
William Janisch, referred to as the German. He was a good writer and was
employed by Lowe as a clerk.

14 5 February 1818
Napoleon had a molar tooth extracted by Dr O'Meara on 16th November
1817 and another tooth extracted on 26th January 1818. These would no
doubt have been the cause of Napoleon's swollen face. *See Napoleon Immortal*
by James Kemble.

15 7 February 1818
See Note 18 of Chapter 1.

16 11 February 1818.
Rear-Admiral Sir Pulteney Malcolm (1768–1838) was in command of the
St Helena station succeeding Sir George Cockburn on 17th June 1816. He
got on very well with Napoleon, and he and his wife often visited Longwood.
It is obvious from the Diary that Lowe did not like him. His command
terminated in June 1817.

17 12 February 1818.
General Baron Gaspard Gourgaud (1783–1852) of Napoleon's staff, left
Longwood on 13th February 1818. Prior to departing from St Helena he
stayed with Lieutenant Basil Jackson at Bayle Cottage. On 12th–14th February
Major Gorrequer inspected Gourgaud's papers. Gourgaud's Diary was first
published in 1899. Did he take his diary notes away with him secretly when
he left on 14th March?

18 13 February 1818
New Longwood House was to be built as Napoleon's residence. He however
never lived to occupy the house.

19 17 February 1818
Dr O'Meara was summoned to Plantation House this day, and there was a
fierce altercation between him and Lowe. Lowe said O'Meara repeatedly
insulted him in his answers. *See* O'Meara's *Napoleon in Exile* of this date.

20 26 February 1818
Rear-Admiral Sir Robert Plampin was in command of the St Helena station
after Sir Pulteney Malcolm left, from July 1817 to July 1820.

21 5 March 1818
William Balcombe (1779–1829) came with his family to St Helena in 1807
to an appointment with the East India Company. Napoleon lived in the
Pavilion at The Briars, Balcombe's home, for the first seven weeks after his
arrival until Longwood was ready, and became very friendly with the family
particularly young Betsy, then fourteen. Balcombe became Purveyor to Longwood. Lowe was suspicious of his friendship with Napoleon, and Balcombe

left in March 1818. He subsequently became Colonial Treasurer of New South Wales.

22 5 March 1818
Joseph Cole was Postmaster and a partner of Balcombe.

23 9 March 1818
Lady Lowe (1781–1832) was a sister of Sir William de Lancy. Two daughters of her previous marriage, Charlotte and Susanna Johnson, were in St Helena a part of the time.

24 14 March 1818
Ross Cottage belonged to William Balcombe.

25 16 March 1818
Count Charles Tristan de Montholon (1783–1853) came out with Napoleon, next senior on his staff to Count Bertrand. His wife came with him, but she left in 1819. Montholon stayed to the end.

26 16 March 1818
Denzil Ibbetson (1788–1857) came out in the *Northumberland* with Napoleon on board. He was a Commissary in the army. He was Purveyor to Longwood succeeding Balcombe.

27 18 March 1818
From time to time Napoleon sold some of his silver.

28 21 March 1818
Andrew Darling was sent out by a furniture firm in London and did repairs at Longwood. He was undertaker at the funeral of Napoleon.

29 21 March 1818
Alarm House was at various times the residence of Colonel Wynyard and of Sir Thomas Reade.

30 21 March 1818
Saul Solomon with his brothers Lewis and Joseph were merchants. He was undertaker at Cipriani's funeral. The Rev. Richard Boys officiated and was given a snuff box by Napoleon.

31 22 March 1818
Gourgaud left on 14th March. Lowe sought a statement from him regarding the papers he was taking. *See* Note 17 of Chapter 2.

32 24 March 1818
Major James Powet in command of the Royal Artillery.

33 Beginning of April 1818
J. W. Cairns was senior lieutenant in H.M.S. *Conqueror*.

34 14 April 1818
Dr O'Meara left St Helena on 2nd August 1818.

35 25 April 1818.
Naturally Balmain, the Russian Commissioner, would wish to go on board a Russian ship visiting the Island.

36 April 1818
Lt.-Colonel John Mansel commanded the 53rd Regiment in St Helena. He was brother-in-law of Sir George Bingham. Major Oliver Fehrzen commanded in Mansel's absence.

37 1 May 1818
The date of this entry is definitely 1st May but no year is given. 'Physician' must mean Physician to Napoleon. So Dr Verling it seems was being already at this date mentioned as successor to Dr O'Meara, though O'Meara was not dismissed until 25th July 1818.

38 12 May 1818
One of the Governor's proclamations concerning limitations upon Napoleon and those at Longwood.

39 12 May 1818
Egg Island just off the coast of St Helena.

40 24 May 1818
Marquis Claude Marin Henri de Montchenu (1757–1831) the French Commissioner.

41 10 June 1818
La Roche did not come out with Napoleon, but was taken on as cook at Longwood after Le Page. Montholon had some difficulty in getting Lowe to agree to this.

42 10 June 1818
This refers to the letter Napoleon had written to the Prince Regent at the time of his surrendering himself to Captain Maitland in the *Bellerophon*.

43 30 June 1818
Montholon had complained to Wynyard about the conditions at Longwood.

44 14 July 1818
The Hollands in England had great sympathy with Napoleon and his entourage in exile in St Helena.

45 14 July 1818
'Buggiardo' (Liar) here seems to be the pseudonym for Count Montholon. Gorrequer throughout much of the Diary refers to him as 'Veritas'. Anything for a change! The reference is to Montholon's letters about engaging La Roche as cook at Longwood.

46 20 July 1818
By Big Wigs, Gorrequer refers to Lowe's dispatches to the Government in London.

47 23 July 1818
At this time Lt.-Colonel Thomas Lyster was Orderly Officer at Longwood. Dr O'Meara was ordered by Lowe to report to Lyster. Lowe goes on to discuss his decision to dismiss O'Meara and send him home from St Helena. It was this violent antagonism between Lowe and O'Meara which had its repercussions in England.

48 24 July 1818
Later Count Balmain, the Russian Commissioner, married Lady Lowe's daughter Charlotte.

49 25 July 1818
Lowe had dismissed O'Meara, and prior to his leaving restrictions were imposed upon him.

50 25 July 1818
J. R. Glover, Secretary to the Admiral Sir George Cockburn.

51 30 July 1818
O'Meara had objected to the manner of his dismissal. He also said some of his belongings had been removed during the inspection of his trunks.

52 2 August 1818
On this date Dr O'Meara left St Helena for England.

53 3 August 1818
Stürmer, the Austrian Commissioner, left St Helena on 11th July 1818. *See* Note 9 of Chapter 1.

54 16 August 1818
Previous to going to St Helena, Lowe and Gorrequer had been at Marseilles.

55 22 August 1818
Major Gorrequer himself was a bachelor.

56 6 September 1818
Captain Den Taafe (Dentaafe) was an A.D.C. to the Governor.

57 16 September 1818
Philippe Welle, a botanist, came on 18th June 1816. He is said to have brought with him a lock of the hair of Napoleon's son for the Emperor. Lowe had suspicions of him and he left the Island after a short stay.

58 9 October 1818
The New House intended for Napoleon near Longwood was completed in 1821, but Napoleon never lived in it.

59 9 October 1818
After O'Meara's dismissal, the Governor appointed Dr James Roche Verling in his place at Longwood. Verling looked after the Longwood staff but he never attended Napoleon.

60 26–27 October 1818
Henry Goulburn, an Under-Secretary of State for War.

61 26–27 October 1818
This refers to Admiral Pulteney Malcolm. *See* Note 16 of Chapter 2. There was talk of his going to a post at the Admiralty.

62 2 November 1818
Pierron (Piéron) was butler to Napoleon at Longwood.

63 9 November 1818
Scandals were circulating about Admiral Plampin's association with a certain lady and the Rev. Boys had decried him.

64 14 December 1818
Admiral Sir George Cockburn had brought Napoleon in H.M.S. *Northumberland* from England to St Helena. He was, in those first months before Lowe's arrival, responsible for the provision and for the custody of Napoleon.

CHAPTER THREE

1 19 January 1819
This probably refers to Sir Henry Bunbury, an Under-Secretary of State under Lord Bathurst, who was Secretary of State for War.

2 20 January 1819
Major Anthony Emmett was in command of the Engineers. He arrived with Lowe. At this period he was in charge of the building of New Longwood House for Napoleon's use.

3 22 January 1819
Dr John Stokoe (1775–1852) was surgeon in H.M.S. *Conqueror* and was then aged 44. He was called to attend Napoleon on the night of 16th–17th January 1819 when he was taken suddenly ill. Stokoe treated Napoleon for the next four days, including a bleeding. Lowe was very dissatisfied with Stokoe both because of his diagnosis of hepatitis and also because of his sympathy for Napoleon. The following week on January 30, Lowe dismissed Stokoe and sent him back to England. *See Napoleon Immortal* by James Kemble.

4 January 1819
For the year 1817, the expenses of the administration amounted to £243,675. The Governor's salary was £12,000.

5 3 February 1819
Sir Henry Bunbury, an Under-Secretary of State for War.

6 21 February 1819
Lord Cathcart, the British Ambassador to Russia.

7 4 March 1819
Dr Baxter who came out with Lowe in 1816 did in fact leave St Helena three years later in 1819.

8 13 March 1819
Lowe was disturbed because Captain James Gray had had an interview with Napoleon on 25th August 1816 without his prior consent.

9 2 April 1819
See Note 34 of Chapter 3.

10 4 April 1819
See Note 13 of Chapter 3.

11 4 April 1819
Charles Milner Ricketts, a relative of Lord Liverpool the Prime Minister, had an interview with Napoleon on 2nd April when he was given a letter to take to the Prime Minister.

12 7 April 1819
Lowe issued instructions that, provided he had reports that Napoleon was in Longwood House, he need not require detailed statements on his state of health.

13 7 April 1819
After Dr O'Meara was dismissed, Lowe had appointed Dr Verling as medical officer to Longwood. Napoleon would not accept him as his personal physician because he was appointed by the Governor, but Montholon had asked Verling if he was prepared to accept a position in the direct employ of Napoleon at a salary.

14 16 April 1819
This may refer to the 'confab' that Lieutenant R. H. Reardon had with the Bertrands about the time of O'Meara's dismissal. An inquiry was held and Reardon had to leave St Helena. *See Lowe Papers.*

15 17 April 1819
Montchenu, the French Commissioner, had received a letter from Paris asking him to supply certain further information, regarding conditions in the Island.

16 22 April 1819
Captain Henry Blakeney was Orderly Officer at Longwood from 25th July 1817 to 5th September 1818 with one brief break.

17 29 April 1819
Dr Alexander Baxter left St Helena in 1819.

18 1 May 1819
The ship *William Pitt* arrived at St Helena on 6th May 1819.

19 11 August 1819
This is about the case of Captain Shortis who shot some Chinese in 1819.

20 15 August 1819
New Longwood House was now being built for Napoleon. Incidentally this date, 15th August 1819, was Napoleon's fiftieth birthday.

21 21 August 1819

Dr John Stokoe, surgeon in H.M.S. *Conqueror*. *See* Note of 22nd January 1819. Stokoe was court-martialled and dismissed the Navy.

22 8 September 1819

Dr James Roche Verling had been appointed medical officer to Longwood by Lowe following Dr O'Meara's dismissal. Dr Francesco Antommarchi, a Corsican by birth, had now been chosen by Napoleon's family in Italy to go out to St Helena as the Emperor's personal physician. Antommarchi arrived on 18th September 1819. *See Napoleon Immortal* by James Kemble.

23 22 September 1819

Lewis Solomon, brother of Saul and Joseph, had a small store in Jamestown.

24 28 September 1819

Andrew Darling was the man who was sent out from England to repair the furniture at Longwood and Plantation House.

25 7 October 1819

Count Balmain, the Russian Commissioner, was to marry Lady Lowe's daughter early in 1820.

26 20 October 1819

Captain Jean Claude de Gors was A.D.C. to the French Commissioner Montchenu.

27 20 October 1819

Mrs Kingsmill (Signora Molino del Re) was the wife of Lieutenant W. Kingsmill of the 66th Foot Regiment.

28 30 October 1819

Napoleon through various intermediaries was able to keep up clandestine communications with Balcombe and O'Meara who were now in London.

29 1 November 1819

O'Meara after his dismissal was writing to newspapers condemning Lowe's conduct.

30 2 November 1819

This refers to Lowe's decrees regarding the limits permitted to Napoleon for excursions and exercise.

31 7 November 1819

Gorrequer writes definitely 'Povera Pazza', Italian for 'The poor mad woman'. *See also* 13th April 1821.

32 13 November 1819

Theodore Hook visited St Helena in 1818 on his way home from Mauritius. He wrote a book about the treatment of Napoleon, which supported Lowe. O'Meara wrote a reply in 1819.

33 25 December 1819

Susanna Johnson was Lady Lowe's younger daughter by her first husband. She came out in the ship *William Pitt* on 6th May 1819.

34 25 December 1819.

Captain Knox of the ship *William Pitt*, 'Kitty'.

35 27 December 1819

Gorrequer had requested promotion, and Lowe had written to London on his behalf.

36 End of 1819

Lieutenant J. W. Cairns and Lieutenant A. S. Pearson of H.M.S. *Conqueror* were on Madame Bertrand's visiting list.

37 End of 1819
  See Note 11 of Chapter 3.
38 End of 1819
  Count Balmain married Lady Lowe's daughter on 26th April 1820.

CHAPTER FOUR

1 19 January 1820
   Gentilini was *valet de pied* to Napoleon.
2 28 January 1820
   All visitors to St Helena, and there were many, wished to be received by
   Napoleon, but of course the Governor had no means of access to the privacy of
   Longwood.
3 12 February 1820
   Captain Engelbert Lutyens was Orderly Officer at Longwood from 10th
   February 1820 to 26th April 1821.
4 14 February 1820
   Colonel Henry Keating, Governor of the Ile de Bourbon was received by
   Napoleon on 27th July 1816.
5 17 February 1820
   See Note 32 of Chapter 3.
6 29 July 1820
   Dr Alexander Baxter. *See* Note 17 of Chapter 1. He left St Helena in 1819.
7 7 August 1820
   Dr Verling although he was medical officer at Longwood never attended
   Napoleon.
8 16 August 1820
   Lieutenant Frederick Croad, 66th Foot Regiment.
9 September 1820
   The wife of General John Pine-Coffin, in command of troops in St Helena
   from August 1820.
10 10 September 1820
   Matthew Livingstone, surgeon to the East India Company. He was present at
   the autopsy on Napoleon and was one of the five doctors who signed the report.
11 14 September 1820
   The Chief of Police from Madras was returning home, and with his family
   called at St Helena.
12 23 September 1820
   Sir William Webber Doveton, a local St Helenian. He was a Judge, a member
   of the Council, and for a time was Paymaster. His home was at Mount Pleasant,
   Sandy Bay.
13 28 September 1820
   The then Orderly Officer at Longwood was Captain Lutyens.
14 13 October 1820
   Admiral Robert Lambert with his wife had arrived on 14th July 1820 to be
   in command of the St Helena naval station. He remained until 11th September
   1821.
15 18 October 1820
   Major Anthony Emmett and Lieutenant Hale Wortham were in charge of the
   building of New Longwood House.

16 22 October 1820
Captain G. L. Goldie, 66th Regiment, arrived in 1818.

17 27 October 1820
Baron Stürmer had left St Helena on 11th July 1818 and went as Consul General to Rio de Janeiro.

18 3 November 1820
Sir William Doveton. *See* Note 12 of Chapter 4. 'Little Joey' was his baby son.

19 December 1820
At this time though suffering from severe constant dyspeptic symptoms, Napoleon was making efforts to take some exercise by going for drives in his carriage.

20 December 1820
Balmain had left St Helena on 3rd May 1820.

21 3 December 1820
Lord Liverpool was then Prime Minister.

22 3 December 1820
Count Balmain with his wife, Lady Lowe's daughter here referred to as 'Bearess', was now back at the Imperial Court at St Petersburg.

23 3 December 1820
In July Napoleon had developed severe and persistent gastric symptoms, which were becoming progressively more aggravated. His staff were very disturbed about his condition and Bertrand had written a letter to Lord Liverpool, sending it to Lowe for transmission. The Governor refused to accept it.

24 3 December 1820
When in 1815 Napoleon had escaped from Elba and returned to Paris, Hudson Lowe was on the staff of the Prince of Orange, who was then Commander in Chief of the Allied Armies prior to the arrival of Wellington. Lowe was despatched on a mission to Genoa just before Waterloo and was not present at the battle.

25 5 December 1820
Captain James Bennett of the St Helena Foot Regiment.

26 10 December 1820
The Governor had asked the Orderly Officer Captain Lutyens to peep into Napoleon's room to obtain a personal view of him and of his state of health. Lutyens wrote refusing to do this. He frequently relied upon the statements of the gardener in order to confirm his reports upon Napoleon.

27 14 December 1820
Francis Plain. From this camp the troops marched on parade to church.

28 14 December 1820
The 'Capo' of the 66th Regiment, 1st battalion, was Colonel Charles Nicol. They had been on service in India before coming to St Helena in 1817 and there seems to have arisen some discontent from their long service abroad, as evidenced by this entry of 14 December 1820.

29 16 December 1820
A small stone square building somewhat resembling a squat Chinese pagoda had been built in the gardens of Longwood, and here Napoleon used to sit in an armchair and could see the going-ons without himself being seen.

30 25 December 1820
Gorrequer was again seeking support for promotion, and had asked Lowe to recommend his application in letters to London.

31 30 December 1820
Napoleon's son by his second wife Marie Louise. He was King of Rome and also had been named by Napoleon as his successor to the Imperial throne of France. Marie Louise had taken the boy to Vienna at the time of Napoleon's exile. Young Napoleon (L'Aiglon—Napoleon II) died at the age of twenty-one on 22nd July 1832 probably from tuberculosis.

32 1820
Count Balmain had married Lady Lowe's daughter Charlotte and they had left St Helena on 3rd May 1820 upon his recall to St Petersburg. It seems the ship's departure had been delayed for their convenience. In the Diary the exact date of sailing of the ship *General Harris* is left blank.

CHAPTER FIVE

1 19 January 1821
Dr Walter Henry was Assistant Surgeon to the 66th Regiment. He was present at the autopsy of Napoleon and subsequently wrote his own account of the findings.

2 25 January 1821
Colonel Charles Nicol commanded the 66th Regiment, and Lt.-Colonel Edmund Lascelles was his 'Sub-Commander'. Lascelles was sent home by Lowe as a result of the Governor's disapproval of O'Meara's association with the Officers' Mess. He was however allowed to return and this is the matter referred to here.

3 4 February 1821
Dr Thomas Shortt, Principal Medical Officer after Dr Baxter left. He arrived in December 1820 and stayed till the end. He supervised the post-mortem examination of Napoleon.

4 4 February 1821
On this date Countess Bertrand was taken ill with a threatened miscarriage. She was attended by Drs Antommarchi, Livingstone and Arnott and next day, to Count Bertrand's great relief, 'Fanny was delivered of the foetus without further complications.'

5 8 March 1821
Mr Russel with his French wife called on the Bertrands on their way home from India.

6 28 March 1821
Lt.-Colonel Daniel Dodgin and Captain S. C. Morris were of the 66th Foot Regiment, Major Power of the Royal Artillery.

7 30 March 1821
Napoleon was now gravely ill and Antommarchi had himself consulted Dr Archibald Arnott about the symptoms. Lowe had instructed the Orderly Officer Lutyens to ask Montholon to let him personally see Napoleon. This Montholon refused.

8 1 April 1821
On this date Napoleon finally agreed to allow Dr Arnott to be called to see and treat him which he continued to do along with Dr Antommarchi until the end. Arnott was surgeon to the 20th Regiment. See *Napoleon Immortal* by James Kemble.

9 6 April 1821
Major David Kinnaird of the St Helena Artillery.

10 13 April 1821

'Povera Pazza' and the rest of the sentence is exactly as written by Gorrequer, though his meaning is obscure. *See* Note 31 of Chapter 3.

11 17 April 1821

Lt.-Colonel Samuel South was in command of the 20th Regiment up till 3rd September 1820. Then his second in command, Major Edward Jackson, came into command.

12 17 April 1821

Napoleon had presented a copy of *The Life of Marlborough* to the 20th Regiment and as it had on it the Imperial inscription, Lowe and also Major Jackson disapproved of Lutyens accepting it.

13 18 April 1821

Count Balmain's wife was Lady Lowe's daughter, Charlotte.

14 26 April 1821

Captain Lutyens resigned his post as Orderly Officer on this day as a consequence of the storm in a tea cup over Napoleon's presentation of a book to the 20th Regiment.

15 27 April 1821

This date, 27 April 1821, is quite clearly written in the Diary and yet the context here obviously indicates that the entry was made later, namely sometime 'after Bertrand had sailed away from St Helena' on 27th May 1821.

16 30 April 1821

This date is also clearly written, but the entry was evidently made *after* Napoleon's death on 5th May 1821.

17 5 May 1821

On this day 5th May 1821 at 11 minutes to 6 o'clock in the afternoon, Napoleon died. It is a little curious that Major Gorrequer, while making his entry this day, one of the longest entries in the whole Diary, makes no mention, except indirectly, of Napoleon's death. It must surely have been a day of great activity, even if Gorrequer himself was excluded from any presence at Longwood or direct contact with the persons and the events occurring in Napoleon's household.

18 5 May 1821

'He' means Captain Crokat. In the text 'who' was first written then crossed out. Crokat did in fact take the dispatches about Napoleon's death to England in H.M.S. *Heron*.

19 5 May 1821

Sir George Bingham had left St Helena on 24th May 1820. Colonel Wynyard left in June 1820.

20 5 May 1821

Lieutenant R. C. Oakley and Ensign Duncan Darroch were in the 20th Regiment.

21 6 May 1821

The morning after Napoleon's death, Sir Hudson Lowe went to Longwood to view the deceased, whom he had not visited in person for nearly five years. That afternoon the post-mortem was held. *See Napoleon Immortal* by James Kemble.

22 6 May 1821

Napoleon's heart was subsequently sealed up in a silver vase with spirits of wine as a preservative. The stomach showing a large cancerous growth was also sealed in a silver casket. Both were buried with the body in the coffin.

23 7 May 1821
Lowe had consistently and to the last refused to recognize the seriousness of Napoleon's illness. After Napoleon's death he was anxious that there should be no mention in the post-mortem report of any disease in the liver, as this might lend support to the accusations that it was the climate or the conditions of confinement that had contributed to the death. Lowe accordingly insisted on the doctors making alterations in their initial report. In fact it was found by the doctors that Napoleon had died from a cancer of the stomach. *See Napoleon Immortal* by James Kemble.

24 8 May 1821
Gorrequer does not date this entry. But it seems it should be 8th May 1821. Napoleon died on 5th May 1821.

25 8 May 1821
The surgeon of H.M.S. *Vigo* was Dr Charles Mitchell. He was one of the eight doctors present at the post-mortem upon Napoleon.

26 9 May 1821
On 9th May the coffin was carried in a long procession from Longwood and buried in a specially built sepulchre at Slane's Valley.

27 11 May 1821
This refers to a snuff-box left by Napoleon to his old friends Lord and Lady Holland in London.

28 12 May 1821
William Holmes acted as an agent for Napoleon in London.

29 12 May 1821
Louis Marchand, Napoleon's head valet, returned to France with the rest of the staff and in his advanced years was created a Count. He was one of Napoleon's executors. He had had a son by his mistress Esther Vesey a local St Helena girl, and before he left he deposited a sum of money in favour of the boy.

30 14 May 1821
See Note 31 of Chapter 4.

31 14 May 1821
After Napoleon's death, Sir Hudson Lowe through the intermediation of Admiral Lambert and Sir Thomas Reade endeavoured to effect a reconciliation with Count Bertrand and Count Montholon.

32 15 May 1821
Napoleon's papers and personal belongings had been packed up and sealed, but Lowe called to examine the papers of Bertrand and Montholon before they left.

33 21 May 1821
E. E. Vidal was in H.M.S. *Vigo*, secretary to Admiral Robert Lambert. Captain Frederick Marryat was in command of H.M.S. *Beaver*. He was the Captain Marryat, author of the many popular sea stories.

34 May 1821
The Governor always vehemently forbade the use of the title of 'Emperor' by anyone on the Island, and even of the name 'Napoleon'. He rigidly insisted on the reference always being to 'General Bonaparte'. This was a bitter bone of contention from Lowe's first interview with Napoleon.

35 May 1821
Bertrand had a plate put on the coffin engraved 'Napoleon'. Lowe insisted on 'Bonaparte' being added. As a consequence no name was inscribed on the coffin.

36 May 1821

The surgeon of the 66th Regiment, Dr Francis Burton who had arrived on 31st March 1821 made a plaster death mask of Napoleon on 7th May but this was appropriated by Count Bertrand and taken away with him.

37 May or June 1821

Seventeen persons were present at the post-mortem, including eight doctors.

38 May or June 1821

Dr George Henry Rutledge, Assistant Surgeon to the 20th Regiment sealed up the heart and the stomach in two silver vases. Napoleon had requested that his heart be sent to Marie Louise after his death. But Sir Thomas Reade objected to this and it was buried in the coffin. There it still remains in Les Invalides tomb in Paris.

39 May and June 1821

Lieutenant Thomas Thorne, Adjutant to Captain (Major) Henry Huff Pritchard.

40 19 June 1821

Sir William Webber Doveton, a St Helenian, Member of the Council of the Island, in the service of the East India Company.

41 22 June 1821

See Diary entry of 19 June 1821.

42 26 June 1821

This is one of the few humorous touches in the whole diary.

43 26 June 1821

High Knoll was the residence of Robert Leech, a Judge in the Island. The reference may be to the barracks nearby.

44 26 June 1821

There was no love lost between Lady Lowe and the Shortt family and with the impending departure from St Helena such scenes as these were becoming more frequent.

45 2 July 1821

According to Gorrequer the date of the sermon preached by the Rev. Richard Boys, to which the Governor took such objection, was 1st July 1821. Boys was Senior Chaplain of the East India Company in St Helena. He was most outspoken and fearless in his denunciation of anyone whom he thought to have acted wrongly. In this sermon the Rev. Boys denounced the morality, indeed the profligacy, of those in the island and in particular of those in the 'higher society'. When Lowe with the Council asked for a copy of the sermon he was rebuffed by Boys.

46 5 July 1821

Napoleon seems to have always been on very good terms with the 20th Regiment.

47 8 July 1821

A torn letter concerning earlier secret correspondence carried on between Napoleon's staff and those at home was found near Montholon's rooms.

48 14 July 1821

Lieutenant John Edward Shortis, St Helena Artillery and Superintendent of Public Works.

49 16 July 1821

Captain Hamlet Obins of the 20th Foot Regiment.

50 July 1821
Lady Lowe's younger daughter, in whom she was promoting the interest of the subalterns of the staff.

51 August 1821
On 25th July 1821 Sir Hudson Lowe with his family and many of his staff including Major Gorrequer left St Helena in the ship *Dunira* for England.

52 18 August 1821
John de Fountain had been in the service of the East India Company and had been dismissed.

53 1 September 1821
See Diary entry of 24 March 1822. Also Note.

54 5 September 1821
As Gorrequer had left St Helena on 25th July some of these entries must have been of the nature of post-scripts, perhaps from earlier notes.

55 End of 1821
Talking of slaves, it might be noted that Lowe during his period in St Helena abolished slavery there.

56 End of 1821
Major Henry Huff Pritchard, St Helena Regiment Artillery, sometime in charge of telegraphs.

CHAPTER SIX

1 11 March 1822
See Diary entry of 27 June, 1821.

2 24 March 1822
'Jenkins J.' also called 'Jenny Jumps' was George Blenkens, a Deputy Paymaster and storekeeper. He is said to have challenged Sir Thomas Reade to a duel, or perhaps a fight. (Amusing how Gorrequer chose some of his pseudonyms. This seems to come from the game 'Up Jenkins'). *See* Diary entry of 1 September 1821.

3 27 November 1822
Major Gorrequer did subsequently attain the rank of Lieutenant-Colonel.

4 23 January 1823
Lowe was then engaged in preparing an affidavit in order to prove in court the malignity of the accusations in the book of O'Meara *Napoleon in Exile, or A Voice from St Helena.*

5 21 December 1823
Ali, Louis Etienne Saint-Denis, *valet de chambre* to Napoleon.

6 21 December 1823
Sir Hudson Lowe was contacting and writing to many former associates collecting opinions and information for the purpose of his proposed law suit against Dr Barry O'Meara.

Index of Pseudonyms
and their Identification

ANGELBRIGHT: Captain Engelbert Lutyens, 20th Regiment. Orderly Officer at Longwood from 10th February 1820 to 26th April 1921.

ARCHBISHOP: The Rev. Richard Boys.

ARCHY MEDICO: Dr Archibald Arnott, Surgeon to 20th Regiment. Arrived at St Helena in 1819

AUTRICHIEN: Baron Stürmer. Austrian Commissioner from June 1816 to 11th July 1818.

BACKSTAIRS: Dr Alexander Baxter. Deputy Inspector of Hospitals. 14th April 1816 to 1819.

BARON, THE: Baron Stürmer.

BEAR: Count Alexandre de Balmain. Russian Commissioner, from June 1816 to 3rd May 1820.

BEAR CONSUL: The Russian Consul.

BELLA CATERINA: One of Lady Lowe's servants.

BELLO: Sir Thomas Reade. Deputy Adjutant General to Lowe.

BELLO TOMASO: Sir Thomas Reade.

BIG WIGS: Heads of Government in England.

BIRRO CAPO MADRAS: Chief of Police of Madras.

BLACK CAT: A servant at Plantation House.

BOB LONG: Dr Thomas Shortt. Principal Medical Officer from December 1820.

BRIGADE MAJOR: Captain Charles Harrison (Brigade Major).

BRUNO: Captain Thomas Brown, H.M.S. *Vigo* Flag Captain, 14th July 1820 to 21st September 1821.

BUGGIARDO: Count Montholon. *See also* 'Veritas' *and also* Note of 14th July 1818.

CADETTA: Lady Lowe's younger daughter, Susanna Johnson.

CAIRNS: Lieutenant J. W. Cairns, of H.M.S. *Conqueror*.

CANNONINO: A young artillery officer.

CAPPELLANO PRIMO: Rev. Richard Boys (*See also* Old Cappellano, Cappellano Vecchio).

CAPPELLANO SECONDO: Rev. Bowater Vernon (*See also* Young Cappellano, Giovane Cappellano).

CAPPELLANO VECCHIO: Rev. Richard Boys.

CAPO DI BANDIERI: Captain Thomas Brown of H.M.S. *Vigo*.

CAPO (MAGGIORE) 20TH: Major Edward Jackson. Second in command 20th Regiment. Colonel Samuel South in command to 3rd September 1820.

CAPO 20TH: Major Edward Jackson, after 3rd September 1820.

CAPO MEDICO PRIMO: Dr Thomas Shortt.

CAPO MEDICO 20TH: Dr Archibald Arnott.

CAPO PHAETON: Captain Francis Stanfell, of H.M.S. *Phaeton*. At St Helena April 1916 to January 1818.

CAPO ROYAL GREAT GUNS: Major James Power. In command of Royal Artillery Corps.

CAPO 66TH: Colonel Charles Nicol. In command of 66th Regiment. Arrived St Helena 1817. Left 1818. Returned 1820.

CAPO OF VANSITTART: Captain Dalrymple.

CAPO DI VASCELLO: Captain Thomas Brown.

CAPO DI VASCELLO PHAETON: Captain Francis Stanfell.

CAPO DI VASCELLO VIGO: Captain Thomas Brown.

CAPO VIGO: Captain Thomas Brown.

CAPTAIN OF VANSITTART: Captain Dalrymple.

CASTOR AND POLLUX:

CATHOLIC, MR: Lieutenant Charles McCarthy (probably). A cousin of Dr Walter Henry.

CATTIVA ARIA: William Fowler. One of the purveyors and a Superintendent of Public works.

CERCUEIL: Brigadier-General John Pine-Coffin. In command of Troops from 23rd August 1820, succeeding Brig.-General Sir George Bingham.

CHIEF, THE: Sir Hudson Lowe.

CHIRURGO PRIMO: Dr Alexander Baxter. He left in 1819.

CHIRURGO SECONDO OF 66TH: Dr Walter Henry. Assistant Surgeon to 66th Regiment. 5th July 1817 to the end.

CHIRURGO XX REGIMENT: Dr Archibald Arnott. He first attended Napoleon on 1st April 1821.

COCHON OF 20TH: Major John Hogg.

CONSTIPATION: Colonel Charles Nicol.

CORSE MAGNESIA: Dr Francesco Antommarchi. Napoleon's medical attendant, from 18th September 1819 to the end.

CORTO: Dr John Thomas Shortt.

CORTOCULO: Lieutenant John Edward Shortis, of St Helena Artillery Regiment, and Superintendent of Public Works.

COSTIVE OLD SCRATCH: Colonel Charles Nicol. He also served in India.

DANDY CAPTAIN VANSITTART: Captain Dalrymple.

DANDY GOLDIE: Captain G. L. Goldie, 66th Regiment. Arrived 26th June 1818.

DANDY IN CUT GLASS: Captain Goldie.

DANDY OCCHIO D'ORO: Captain Goldie.

DEAN TUFF: Captain George Andrew Den Taafe. A.D.C. to Lowe. St Helena Artillery Regiment.

DEAN TURF: Captain Den Taafe.

DENZIL PERIWINKLE: Denzil Ibbetson.

DEPUTY JUDGE ADVOCATE: Major Charles R. G. Hodson. St Helena Foot Regiment.

DOMINE: Sir William Doveton?

DOMINE PADRE WALES:

DONNA: Lady Hudson Lowe.

DONNA VERITAS: Countess Montholon.

DOTTORE CORTO: Dr Shortt.

DOTTORE GREAT GUNS: Dr James Roche Verling. Surgeon to the Artillery Regiment. Arrived July 1815. Left 25th April 1820. At Longwood August 1818 to 18th September 1819.

DRAGON: Smythe.

DRAGOON: Cornet J. W. Hoath. In command of Dragoons.

DUTCH LORD:

EGO: Major Gideon Gorrequer. A.D.C. and Acting Military Secretary to Sir Hudson Lowe. Arrived 14th April 1816.

E.I.C.: East India Company.

ESTABLISHMENT, THE: Longwood, Napoleon's Residence.

EURYDICE: Captain of H.M.S. *Eurydice*.

EXISTING STONE: Dr Matthew Livingstone. Surgeon to the Hon. East India Company. Was at St Helena from 1815 to the end.

FANTASTICO: An Orderly.

FANTESCO: A man-servant. Probably same as Fantastico.

FISICO LINGO: Dr Verling.

FISICO OF 53RD: Dr Robert Leaver?

FISICO OF 66th: Dr Francis Burton. Surgeon to 66th Regiment. Arrived 31st March 1821.

FISICO PRIMO: Dr Alexander Baxter. Left in 1819. Followed by Dr Shortt.

FOLLOWERS: Napoleon's staff at Longwood.

FOREIGN MAGNESIA: Dr Antommarchi.

FOREIGN MEDICAL PERSON: Dr Antommarchi.

FROG: Marquis de Montchenu. French Commissioner. June 1816 to 29th July 1821.

FROG's WIFE: Madame Montchenu.

FRIGHTENED RABBIT:

GEORGE: George Boorman, upholsterer, plumber.

GERMAN: William Janisch. Clerk to Lowe. Arrived with him 14th April 1816.

GIOVANE CAPPELLANO: Rev. Bowater Vernon.

GIOVANI CAVALIERI: Sir Thomas Reade. Deputy Adjutant General to Lowe.

GIOVANI ETAT-MAJOR: Captain George Nicholls.

GIOVANI PRETE: Rev. Bowater Vernon.

GIOVANI STAFF: An officer on Lowe's staff.

GORS: Captain Jean de Gors. Secretary and A.D.C. to Montchenu.

GOURGAUD: General Gaspard Gourgaud. Arrived with Napoleon. Left 14th March 1818.

GRAPE: Lt.-Colonel Edward Wynyard. Military Secretary to Lowe. Arrived 6th May 1816. Left June 1820.

GRAZZIOSO: Lt.-Colonel Thomas Lyster. Arrived 14th April 1816. Orderly Officer at Longwood for a short time July 1818.

GRAZZIOSO GIOVANI: Lt.-Col. Thomas Lyster.

GRAZZIOSO TOMASO: Lt.-Colonel Thomas Lyster.

GREAT GUN MAGNESIA: Dr Verling.

GREAT GUNS ROYAL ARTILLERY: Major James Power.

GROS COCHON: King Louis XVIII.

HEAD OF TELEGRAPHS: Major Henry Huff Pritchard, Artillery Regiment. For a time in charge of Telegraphs.

H.E.I.C.: Honourable East India Company.

HENRICO IL MEDICO: Dr Walter Henry.

HISTRION: Theodore Hook.

HOCUS POCUS COLONEL: Lt.-Colonel Sir Henry Keating. A Governor of Île de Bourbon, near Mauritius, who visited St Helena in July 1816 and had an interview with Napoleon.

HONORABLE JOHN: Honorable East India Company.

HUMBLE SPINE: Captain Henry Pierce Blakeney. 66th Regiment. Orderly Officer at Longwood, 25th July 1817 to 16th July 1818 and 25th July 1818 to 5th September 1818.

ILE MAURICE: Colonel Fitz-Gerald, Governor of Mauritius, who visited St Helena in January 1818.

IL GRAZZIOSO: Lt.-Colonel Thomas Lyster.

IMPERIAL BEAR: Czar of Russia.

ISPETTORE TELEGRAPHI: Major H. H. Pritchard.

JACK'S FIGLIO: Major Edward Jackson. Second in command 20th Regiment.

JENNY JUMPS (also called JENKINS): George Blenkens, Deputy Paymaster.

JESUIT: Count Las Cases.

JEUNE CAVALIER: Sir Thomas Reade.

JOE POP 'EM OFF: Captain T. W. Poppleton, 53 Regiment. Orderly Officer at Longwood 10th December 1815 to 24th July 1817.

JOLI: Sir Thomas Reade. Deputy Adjutant-General.

JOLLY TOMASO: Sir Thomas Reade.

JUDGE ADVOCATE: Major C. R. G. Hodson.

KING COLY COLY: Joseph Cole. Postmaster.

KITTY: The Ship *William Pitt* Captain Knox.

KNIGHT OF JOY MOUNT: Sir William Doveton.

LADY B.: Lady Bingham.

LADY SWELL: Lady Bingham.

LA FONTAINE: John de Fountain. A member of the Council.

LA MARCHESA: Madame Montchenu.

LAMB: George Lambe. Factor with East India Co.

LA ROCHE: Laroche. Cook at Longwood.

LEGITIMATE KNIGHTS: Judges. Sir William Doveton and others.

LINGO: Dr Verling.

LITTLE JOEY: Son of Sir William Doveton.

LITTLE POLYPHEMES: Admiral Robert Plampin.

LONG ADJUTANT: Captain de Gors.

LONG GUT: Captain de Gors. Adjutant to Montchenu.

LONGO: Dr Thomas Shortt.

LONGO YAM STOCK: Major C. R. G. Hodson.

LORD BEAR OF ETHIOPIAN COAST: Lord Charles Somerset.

LUNGI FAMILY: Dr Shortt's family.

MAC: Sir Hudson Lowe. The Governor arrived 14th April 1816. His residence was Plantation House.

MACH: Sir Hudson Lowe.

MACK: Sir Hudson Lowe.

MADAME SHRUG: Countess Bertrand.

MADAME VERITAS: Countess Montholon.

MAGGIORE DI BRIGATTA: Captain Charles Harrison.

MAGNESIA: Various doctors. Up to 1818, especially O'Meara.

MAGNESIA PRIMO: Dr Barry O'Meara. Came with Napoleon as his medical attendant. Lived at Longwood House. Left St Helena on 2nd August 1818.

MAJOR (MAGGIORE) GREAT GUNS: Major James Power. In command of Royal Artillery. Arrived with Lowe 1816.

MAJOR MIGHTY: Major James Power.

MAJOR ST HELENA GREAT GUNS: Major David Kinnaird. In charge of Artillery St Helena Regiment.

MARK ANTHONY: Major Anthony Emmett (Engineers).

MARQUIS: Marquis de Montchenu.

MEDICO CONQUEROR: Dr John Stokoe. Surgeon in H.M.S. *Conqueror*. He attended Napoleon 17th to 21st January 1819, and was then sent back to England.

MEDICO CORTO: Dr Thomas Shortt.

MEDICO GREAT GUNS: Dr James Roche Verling. Surgeon to Artillery Regiment.

MEDICO IN CAPITO: Dr Alexander Baxter (Up to 1819).

MEDICO LONG: Dr Shortt.

MEDICO LONGO: Dr Shortt.

MEDICO OLD ARCHY: Dr Archibald Arnott.

MEDICO PRIMO: Dr Alexander Baxter was Medico Primo up till 1819 when he left. Dr Thomas Shortt was Medico Primo from December 1820 when he arrived as Principal Medical Officer.

MEDICO 66TH: Dr Francis Burton from 31st March 1821.

MEDICO 20TH: Dr Archibald Arnott.

MEDICO VIGO: Dr Charles Mitchell. Surgeon in H.M.S. *Vigo*.

MRS MOLINODELRE: Mrs Kingsmill, wife of a lieutenant of 66th Regiment.

MOUNTJOY SQUIRE: Sir William Doveton. Member of the Council, Judge and for a time Paymaster. Lived at Mount Pleasant.

MOGGY:

NEGRA KATE: One of the servants at Plantation House.

NEIGHBOUR: Napoleon. Longwood was his residence.

NINCUMPOOP: Sir Thomas Reade. Deputy Adjutant-General to Lowe.

NINNY: Sir Thomas Reade.

NORTHERN BEAR: Count Balmain.

NOTO:

NYMPH, THE: Miss Mary Anne Robinson. Daughter of a local resident.

OBINS, MRS: Wife of Captain Hamlet Obins, of the 20th Regiment.

OCCHIO D'ORO: Captain G. L. Goldie.

OLD BRICK AND MORTAR: Major Anthony Emmett. In command of Engineers. In charge of building New Longwood House. Arrived 14th April 1816.

OLD CAPPELLANO: Rev. Richard Boys.

OLD CAVALIER: Thomas Henry Brooke. Secretary to the Council.

OLD COMMANDER: Sir Hudson Lowe.

OLD CONSTIPATION: Colonel Charles Nicol (*See also* Capo 66th).

OLD COSTIVE: Colonel Charles Nicol.

OLD FROG: Marquis de Montchenu.

OLD KENT: Lieutenant Mark Kent, of H.M.S. *Conqueror*.

OLD LORD BEAR OF THE ETHIOPIAN COAST: Lord Charles Somerset.

OLD MACH: Hudson Lowe.

OLD MEXICO: Father Buonavita.

OLD NEPTUNE: Rear-Admiral Sir Pulteney Malcolm. In command of Navy at St Helena, 17th June 1816 to 14th July 1817.

OLD NICK: Captain George Nicholls, 66th Regiment. Arrived 26th June 1818. Left 12th September 1820. Orderly Officer at Longwood, 5th September 1818 to 9th February 1820.

OLD NOTO:

OLD PODEROSO: Major James Power.

OLD POLYPHEMES: Rear-Admiral Robert Plampin. In command of Navy at St Helena, July 1817 to July 1820. Also called Polyphemes Secondo.

OLD SCRATCH: Colonel Charles Nicol.

OLD STICK: Dr Stokoe.

OLD YAM KNIGHT: Sir William Doveton.

OLD YORKSHIRE:

O.O.: Orderly Officer. *See* Note of 23rd July 1817.

O.O. 20TH: Orderly Officer Captain William Crokat of 20th Regiment. At Longwood 26th April to 6th May 1821.

ORANG OUTANG AND RIB: Mr Pauer and his wife.

ORDONNANZA (ORDINANZA): Captain Engelbert Lutyens (Orderly Officer).

OSTRICH: Baron Stürmer. The Austrian Commissioner.

PAGATORE: Sir William Doveton. The Paymaster. Resigned 1817. Deputy Paymaster was George Blenkens. Assistant Paymaster was Anthony Beale.

PARADOX:

PERIWINKLE: Denzil Ibbetson, one of the Purveyors.

PERROQUETS:

PICCOLO CARROZZE: A young coachman.

PICK AXE: Lt.-Colonel Thomas Lyster (*See also* Grazzioso).

PIETRA EXISTENZIA: Dr Livingstone, Surgeon to the East India Company. From 1815 to the end.

PIOVANO: The priest. Rev. Richard Boys or Rev. Bowater Vernon.

PLATONIAN:

PODARGUS: H.M.S. *Podargus*, in the command of Captain James Wallis.

PODEROSO: Major James Power.

PODEROSO XX: Captain Robert Power 20th Regiment.

POLISSON: Lieutenant Basil Jackson of the Staff Corps.

POLYPHEMES: The various Admirals, according to period of command.

POLYPHEMES PRIMO: Sir Pulteney Malcolm. In command of the navy at St Helena 17th June 1816 to 4th July 1817. Sometimes Admiral Sir George Cockburn.

POLYPHEMES SECONDO: Sometimes Sir Pulteney Malcolm, and sometimes Sir Robert Plampin.

POLYPHEMES TERTIO: Rear-Admiral Sir Robert Plampin. In command July 1817 to July 1820.

POLYPHEMES QUARTO, OR 4: Rear Admiral Robert Lambert. In command 14th July 1820 to 11th September 1821.

POP GUN: A Sub-Lieutenant in St Helena Artillery Regiment.

POPIE: John Paine, painter and decorator.

POSSO:

POSTMASTER: Joseph Cole.

POVI: One of the purveyors.

POVILARDO (POVILERO): One of the purveyors.

PRETTY THOMAS: Lt.-Colonel Thomas Lyster.

PRIMATE: Rev. Richard Boys

PRIMO BOMBARDIERO: Major James Power.

PRIMO FISICO: Dr Alexander Baxter, left in 1819. Dr Thomas Shortt, arrived December 1820.

PRIMOGENITA: Lady Lowe's elder daughter, Charlotte Johnson.

PROFESSOR: Dr Antommarchi.

PROVIDATORE: Sometimes William Balcombe, sometimes Denzil Ibbetson. Both were Purveyors at different times.

RACOON: H.M.S. *Racoon*.

RAGAZZA: Lady Lowe's daughter, Charlotte Johnson.

REGIMENTAL ENGINEER: Major Emmett.

REVERENDISSIMO: Father Buonavita.

ROARING BOB:

ROBINSON CRUSOE: John Robinson (Père).

ROMAN CANDLESTICK: Lieutenant Charles McCarthy.

RUSSEL AND FRENCH RIB: Mr Russel and his wife.

SAPIENT KING OF HEBREWS: Saul Solomon, a shopkeeper.

SAUL SAPIENS: Saul Solomon.

SCOTTO CHIRURGO: Dr Livingstone.

SCOTYESE: Dr Baxter.

SECOND FISICO MARINARO: Dr John Stokoe.

SECOND MAGNESIA NAVALE: Dr John Stokoe.

SECRETARIO NAVALE: E. E. Vidal, secretary to Admiral Lambert in H.M.S. *Vigo*.

SHRUG: General Count Bertrand, Grand Marshal to Napoleon.

SIGNORA MOLINODELRE: Mrs Mulino del Re. Mrs Kingsmill.

SIGNORA SHRUG: Countess Bertrand.

SIR P. M.: Sir Pulteney Malcolm.

SOTTO MEDICO 66th: Dr Walter Henry.

STERCORACEOUS: Thomas Henry Brooke. Secretary to the Council. Also a magistrate.

STICK: Dr Stokoe.

SUB-MEDICO 20TH: Dr George Henry Rutledge. Assistant Surgeon to the 20th Foot Regiment. At St Helena from 1819 to the end.

SULTANA: Lady Hudson Lowe (*See also* Donna).

SWELL: Sir George Bingham. Brig.-General in command of the troops. Arrived on 15th October 1815 in H.M.S. *Northumberland*. Left on 24th May 1820. Succeeded by Brig. General Pine-Coffin.

TENANTE TROAD: Lieutenant Frederick Croad, 66th Regiment.

TEUTONIC: William Janisch. Clerk to Lowe.

THORNE: Head of Telegraphs for a time.

TOMASO: Sir Thomas Reade. Deputy Adjutant-General.

TOWN MAJOR: Captain Thomas J. B. Cole.

TROAD: Lieutenant Frederick Croad.

TUFF: Captain Den Taafe.

TULIP: Count Balmain ?

TWILIGHT: Captain James Wallis.

VECCHIO: Sir Hudson Lowe.

VECCHIO CAVALIERE: Thomas Henry Brooke.

VECCHIO PRETE: Rev. Richard Boys.

VERITAS: General Count Charles Tristan de Montholon. Came to St Helena with Napoleon and remained to the end.

VICINO: Napoleon (Neighbour).

VIGNOBLE: Lt.-Colonel Edward Buckley Wynyard. Military Secretary to Sir Hudson Lowe 6th May 1816 to June 1820.

VINCITORE: H.M.S. *Conqueror*.

WALSHWIG:

WEEPING WILLIE: Sir William Webber Doveton (*See* 19th and 22nd June 1821).

YAM: A Yam was a local St Helenian.

YAM: Captain Den Taafe (*See also* Dean Tuff).

YAM AJUTANTE: Lieutenant David K. Pritchard. An A.D.C. to Governor Lowe. A Sub-Lieutenant in the St Helena Artillery Regiment.

YAM MAGGIORE LONG SHANKS: Major C. R. G. Hodson.

YAM STOCK. Captain Den Taafe. Also acted as an A.D.C. to Lowe.

YOUNG BRICK AND MORTAR: Lieutenant Hale Young Wortham. Of the Engineers. Subordinate to Major Emmett in the building of New Longwood. Arrived 14th April 1816.

YOUNG CAPPELLANO: Rev. Bowater Vernon.

YOUNG CAVALIER: Sir Thomas Reade. Also given several other pseudonyms.

YOUNG GRAZZIOSO: Lt.-Colonel Thomas Lyster.

YOUNG POLICE: (*See* Young Sbirro).

YOUNG POLISSON: Lieutenant Basil Jackson (*See also* Polisson).

YOUNG RT. STAFF (REGIMENTAL): One of the officers of the Staff Corps.

YOUNG SBIRRO: Young Police.

Index

Index of Ships